Queering Black Churches

Queering Black Churches

Dismantling Heteronormativity in African American Congregations

BRANDON THOMAS CROWLEY

OXFORD
UNIVERSITY PRESS

Oxford University Press is a department of the University of Oxford. It furthers
the University's objective of excellence in research, scholarship, and education
by publishing worldwide. Oxford is a registered trade mark of Oxford University
Press in the UK and certain other countries.

Published in the United States of America by Oxford University Press
198 Madison Avenue, New York, NY 10016, United States of America.

© Oxford University Press 2024

All rights reserved. No part of this publication may be reproduced, stored in
a retrieval system, or transmitted, in any form or by any means, without the
prior permission in writing of Oxford University Press, or as expressly permitted
by law, by license, or under terms agreed with the appropriate reproduction
rights organization. Inquiries concerning reproduction outside the scope of the
above should be sent to the Rights Department, Oxford University Press, at the
address above.

You must not circulate this work in any other form
and you must impose this same condition on any acquirer.

Library of Congress Control Number: 2023936357

ISBN 978–0–19–766262–5 (pbk.)
ISBN 978–0–19–766261–8 (hbk.)

DOI: 10.1093/oso/9780197662618.001.0001

"With courage and conviction, *Queering Black Churches* affirms the inherent sacred worth of Black Queer folx against the toxicity of human suppression and denial that defines most Black ecclesiastical spaces. Crowley inaugurates a new wave of queer theological studies that helps Black churches speak to the specificity of context and the rich diversity of congregants. This is an essential resource for all church leaders who desire to move beyond performative allyship to sincere inclusion."
—Jonathan Lee Walton, President, Princeton Theological Seminary

"*Queering Black Churches* is a brilliant account of LGBTQ+ persons as active, supportive, and needed members of local Black churches. Crowley provides compelling historical evidence regarding ancient African same-sex expressions and contemporary case studies to craft his strategies for creating LGBTQ+ affirming and inclusive worship spaces. Clergy, scholars, and students will find *Queering Black Churches* a particularly insightful and relevant book that should be considered vital for understanding the depth of Black ecclesiology."
—Pamela Lightsey, Vice President for Academic and Student Affairs and Associate Professor of Constructive Theology, Meadville Lombard Theological Seminary

"Brandon Crowley brings together a wealth of scholarly expertise and pastoral experience to shed light on the complex gender and sexual politics of black churches. *Queering Black Churches* is rich with practical and academic insights that move the conversation forward in such important ways."
—Josef Sorett, Henry L. and Lucy G. Moses Professor, Professor of Religion & African American and African Diaspora Studies, and Dean of Columbia College

"*Queering Black Churches* is one of the most important works of practical theology in the last decade. In addition to its considerable research on Black churches that welcome and affirm LGBTQ communities, this book does the real work of prophetic ministry: it provides culturally relevant practices for healing sacred siblings in the human family who have been harmed by cruel Christianity. Leaders and educators from diverse cultural backgrounds will benefit immensely from this compelling case study on religion's capacity to foster compassion and inclusion. After reading it, you will do what we often do in Black churches. You will shout, 'Amen!'"

—Brad R. Braxton, President and Professor of Public Theology, Chicago Theological Seminary and Founding Senior Pastor, The Open Church of Maryland

"*Queering Black Churches* is bold, uncompromising, beautifully written, and strategically instructive. Without flinching, Crowley calls us to reexamine 'toxic Black heteronormativity in Black churches' and to celebrate queering our congregations as a sacred and divine act and witness of compassion and love. Crowley moves beyond the normative apologetics discourse and provides bold models for queering Black churches in the twenty-first century. This labor of love is a must read for reimagining the intent and promise of a beloved community."

—Renee K. Harrison, Associate Professor of African American and U.S. Religious History, Howard University School of Divinity

Contents

Dedication and Acknowledgments   ix
A Note on the Cover   xi
Preface   xiii
Foreword by Peter J. Paris   xix

    Introduction   1

1. A History of Heteronormativity, Transphobia, and Homophobia in Black Congregations   9
2. An Introduction to Black Ecclesial Queering   44
3. Models of Black Ecclesial Queering, Part I: The Congregational Model—Union United Methodist Church   81
4. Models of Black Ecclesial Queering, Part II: A Pastoral Model—Mount Nebo Missionary Baptist Church   123
5. A More Excellent Way: A Black Ethogenic Report   154

    Conclusion: A Bright Side Somewhere   200

Appendix 1: Another Example of Congregational Queering by the Covenant Baptist-United Church of Christ   221
Appendix 2: The Eight Phases of Black Ecclesial Queering   223
Notes   227
Index   257

Dedication and Acknowledgments

This book is dedicated to Niankhkhnum, Khnumhotep, Mabel Hampton, Marsha P. Johnson, William Dorsey Swann, and a freed enslaved African named Luke. Niankhkhnum, Khnumhotep, Mabel, Marsha, William, Luke, and countless other Black Queer ghosts and spirits, I love and honor you for speaking to me individually and in chorus through body possession, impartation, revelation, and incantation. May the fierceness of your legacies forever "read" and haunt the heteronormative while simultaneously inspiring Black Queer persons born and unborn.

I also dedicate this book to my great cloud of witnesses, the immortal-dead. I honor and remember my late great-grandmothers Jennie V. Crowley, Lillie Bell Porter, and Mamie Lou Phillips; my late great-grandfathers Leon Porter Sr. and Leroy Phillips Sr.; my late grandfather Thomas Crowley Jr.; my late other-mother Elizabeth Montgomery Crowley; my aunt Earnestine Ellis; my cousin J-2; and so many others whom I knew, loved, and adored. I am grateful to God for you for being my choir invisible.

Special thanks to my loving and supportive husband Tyrone Sutton; my immediate and extended family members, Mommy Robyn, Daddy Scott, Mama Emma Crowley; my beloved Williams grandparents; Grandma Charlene Montgomery; and my loving siblings, aunts, uncles, and extended family. I praise God for the caring and supportive members of the Historic Myrtle Baptist Church of West Newton, Massachusetts. I thank my pastors, the Reverends Edward and Judge Penny Brown Reynolds, and my mentors and former professors Lawrence Edward Carter Sr., Peter J. Paris, Pamela Lightsey, Mark Jordan, Delmon Coates, Esther Schultz Vaughn, John Lawson Vaughn Jr., and the late Reverend Peter John Gomes. I am forever indebted to my editor and mentor, the Reverend Martha Jean Simmons, Esq. Your sacrifice of countless hours to bring this ten-year project to completion during the pandemic will never be forgotten. I also offer appreciation to Theodore Calderara and Alexandra Rouch of Oxford University Press. Your belief in this project made the publication of this book possible.

Over the years, I have been blessed to work with some of the most brilliant research assistants, whose feedback and contributions I will never forget.

Thank you to Elijah Gipson-Davis, George Anthony Pratt, Devon Jerome Crawford, Kyle Stevenson, Achille Vann Ricca, Micah Williams, Phillip Valdes, Ciarra Jones, J.J. Warren, Brandon Booth, Darcey Mercier, E. Doctor Taylor, and my good friend George Washington Williams. I also thank the president, deans, faculty, staff, and students of my Queering Congregations seminars at Harvard Divinity School and the Episcopal Theological Seminary of the Southwest in Austin, Texas. Your feedback was highly valued, and I hope you recognize the results of your constructive criticism within this manuscript. Then there are my many colleagues, friends, church members, and students who assisted and supported me in completing this manuscript: Ayeesha Monique Lane, Alicia Marie Johnson, Peter Goddard, Judge Sonya Spears, Inez Dover, Gerald Jay Williams, Jeremy Williams, Otis Brandon Byrd Jr., Lawrence Waters, Sean McMillan, Maurice Wright, Quincy James Rinehart, Michael Wilson, Jonathan-Newell Roberts, and last but not least, my beloved and loyal dog Bishop.

I also thank Union United Methodist Church, Rev. Theodore L. Lockhart, and the countless other pastors, churches, and congregants who welcomed me into their homes and churches as a researcher and friend. I am also grateful to the following organizations and institutions for funding the research for this book: the Forum for Theological Exploration, the Louisville Institute, the Calvin Worship Institute's Teacher-Scholar Vital Worship Grant, the National Resource Center for Domestic Violence, the African American Lectionary Inc., and numerous sponsors who wish to remain nameless.

A Note on the Cover

For the cover of *Queering Black Churches*, I chose a portion of the stained-glass depicting Philip, a diaconate leader in Jerusalem's early Christian community, baptizing an Ethiopian eunuch in Acts 8:26–39. The soaring iconographic façade has illuminated the altar of the Myrtle Baptist Church of West Newton, Massachusetts, for 124 years. The image perfectly captures the message of this manuscript: that the early church affirmed Queer persons. Myrtle is one of America's oldest Black congregations, founded by formerly enslaved people at the end of Reconstruction, and one of a few open and affirming historically Black churches in the United States. On October 22, 1897, a fire destroyed the original church. Within a year, the edifice was rebuilt on the site of the original structure. At the building dedication, a beautiful stained-glass window depicting Philip baptizing the Ethiopian eunuch was unveiled by Rev. Charles Morris, who served as the church's pastor from 1896 to 1899. The design and building of the window are attributed to the studios of George W. Spence of Spence and Bell, a prominent stained-glass artist in Boston's old Scollay Square. According to oral history, the window was brought to Myrtle on the bed of a horse-drawn wagon. It is believed to be a gift from Mr. Edwin B. Haskell, a Newton resident who was then owner of the *Boston Herald*. The photograph of the window was taken by Richard Jefferson.

Preface

It was the second Sunday of March 2015. The worship service was charged with exuberant praise, and the church was on fire with the Holy Spirit. On this particular Sunday, I was not preaching. I sat as my assistant pastor, Alicia Marie Johnson, delivered a sermon about the five daughters of Zelophehad. In the sermon, she contended that Mahlah, Noah, Hoglah, Micah, and Tirzah boldly petitioned Moses before the entire assembly at the tent of meetings to grant them the hereditary holdings of their father's kinsmen instead of transferring them to a male relative simply because he had no sons. According to Numbers 27:1–11, Moses took the matter to God, and God said to Moses: Their plea is just, transfer their father's share to them, and if any future men die without sons, transfer their properties to their daughters as well. Reverend Johnson's sermon concluded with the acknowledgment that the boldness of Zelophehad's daughters "changed the culture, changed the law, changed Moses, changed the people, and changed the whole assembly. That's why we must be bold. God wants to change the world through our boldness."

When she said these words, God sent a surge of apocalyptic revelations, prophetic visions, and moral convictions through the core of my inner being. I had experienced God in my soul before but never this strongly. This particular incantation materialized unblemished. The feeling of liberation was so intense that I could feel it in the air like spiritual condensation. Afterward, God confirmed what I felt. God said, "Brandon, share your gift of queerness with the congregation that I called you to serve."

I froze in fear, clinching my sweating hands to the arms of my chair.

As I began to conceptualize and envision what making a statement about my identity would do or mean for my congregants, I told God, "I can't do this. What would I say? How would I say it? Will they think I planned this? What if they think I am selfishly trying to push my personal life into a sacred space set aside for worship? I've never really been in a closet anyway, so, God, what is the purpose of me doing this?" These questions floated and cluttered my mind throughout the conclusion of my assistant pastor's sermon through the offertory selection.

By the time God revealed these words to my spirit, I had served as senior pastor of the Myrtle Baptist Church for nearly six years. I grew to love Myrtle, and Myrtle grew to love, trust, and support my pastoral efforts; as a result, our pastoral-parish relationship grew more substantial and more profound with each passing year. Elected to serve this thriving congregation at the tender age of twenty-two, my initial years of pastoring were filled with many joys and even more learning experiences. I was living an answered prayer I had in a childhood dream—pastoring a historic Black Baptist church. I describe it as a dream because Black churches and Black church culture were my worlds. My entire philosophy of life was shaped and molded by the communal power of Black churches. I felt safe and most comfortable as a Black person when I entered their sacred naves. As the son of two young college students being raised by two sets of grandparents, the soundscapes and communal power of Friendship Baptist Church, my great-grandparents' church, and Lovejoy Baptist Church, my grandparents' church, gave me a sense of grounding and belonging. Pastors, preachers, the mothers' board, and the deacons were like a magical superhero pantheon in my adolescent mind.

My craving for God, Gospel music, Black preaching, and Black liturgical expressivism extended beyond the physical buildings of churches and into my personal life. As a child, when everyone else was playing house, video games, or recreational sports, I was in the living rooms or dens of my grandparents' home having church in the Black tradition. My grandfather would always tell me, "Son, you will be a pastor up north somewhere one day." And now that my grandfather Thomas Crowley's vision had come true, God was telling me to share my truth—which could end my dream come true with great disaster.

For twenty minutes, my Spirit waned with fear about sharing my truth with Myrtle because the fear of rejection and the possibility of losing it all seemed eerily conceivable.

But then, midway through the offertory song, beneath Myrtle's huge glass-stained window depicting Philip baptizing an Ethiopian eunuch, God instantly winnowed the chaff of fear from my soul with a memory.

At my great-grandmother Mamie's house, she allowed me to play church in her high heels with an old wooden spoon as a microphone in one hand and a stiff, air-dried dishcloth as my preaching handkerchief in the other hand. She always permitted me to do so in her heels because that made me feel comfortable. My cousins and people in the neighborhood would laugh and call me a sissy, but my great-grandmother told me to ignore them. Once while playing church on the front porch in her black patent leather funeral pumps, I vividly remember neighborhood kids throwing gravel at me, calling me "gay" and "weird" while I was in the middle of my sermon.

I immediately ran into our modest home crying and threw my King James red-letter Bible with frayed edges on the old veneer but well-polished coffee table and grunted when the screen door shut with a thump. My great-grandmother immediately ran from the kitchen, wiping her flour-caked hands with the end of her apron. She didn't even ask what was wrong; she knew. It had happened before. But this time, she took the edge of her apron, wiped the tears from my eyes, grabbed my shoulders, turned me about-face 180 degrees, and opened the screen door. She put her old Bible back into my hands and sent me right back to the front porch to fearlessly preach in her heels while she stood in the doorway with her arms crossed and lips perched to ensure that no one said a word while I preached. After that moment, she told me, "Baby, you are different. It won't be easy for you, but never hide it. Be who you are, Son, and don't care about what people or church folks have to say. Church folks almost made me hurt myself when I got pregnant at fourteen in the early 1900s. But I woke up and realized that God didn't care about their foolishness. So I did it my way. And you have to do the same, Son. I always knew you were different, so I loved you, so you'd know it's okay."

Consequently, when I heard God tell me to share my truth, I knew what God meant. In fact, I heard the voice of God as my great-grandmother. God was telling me to do on a Sunday morning the same thing that my grandmother told me to do on her old green cement porch as a child: to be me and never to hide it.

So, without a second thought, I stood up when the choir concluded, walked to the podium, and began my morning announcements. But at the end of reading my announcements, I took off my glasses, and I extemporaneously said, "Myrtle, I want you to know that it is my honor to serve as your pastor, servant, and teacher. And as a proud Black Queer Christian, I unselfishly share my truth with you this morning as a testimony of what God can do and has done for me. I pray that my truth-telling will help further the ongoing movement to help Black churches be more inclusive and affirming of all persons." And with tears in my eyes, I took a deep breath and returned my black frames to my young face to see what the end might be.

But before I cleared the tears from my eyes, I could see the colorful, wide-brimmed church-lady hats moving toward me. One of the first persons to touch my shoulder was Sister Evette Layne, our church clerk at the time. She hugged me with a radiant smile and whispered, "Pastor, we love you; we already knew. This is all in God's timing." When I turned around, the majority of the congregation had risen to its feet with celebration and tears. Young and old clapping their hands freely, yelling praises to God. A spirit of worship hit the room, lifting every spirit of heaviness with a rush of reviving jolts. Deacon Walter Cooper sporadically rang out in an original hymn, which he often did when emotions were high during the altar call and intercessory prayer services. While he sang, parishioners flooded the altar, moving in as close as possible, touching each other and simultaneously laying hands upon me, praying for me, as I did for them on many occasions. At first, I wanted to stop them, but I resisted my ego and submitted to the movement of God. After that moment, I never said a word until I greeted every parishioner with a thank-you and a hug after worship.

We lost some beloved parishioners whom I still miss, but the vast majority of the congregation remained. As time went on, several deacons encouraged me to initiate a season of discernment so that the community could process my statements and think more deeply about its ecclesiology outside of such an emotionally charged Sunday morning occurrence. At first, when Deacon Goddard and others approached me with this idea, I was reluctant to pursue it because I did not want to give off the impression that I was pushing too much Queer stuff into parishioners' faces. A well-meaning investor in the church congratulated me and urged me to "move on and just pastor. We got the message loud and clear that day, so move forward." Many of my closeted colleagues saw my pastoral continuation at Myrtle as a modern-day Black church miracle, telling me that I should leave well enough alone and be quiet. With these messages replaying in my subconscious, I hesitated to initiate a congregational queering process. But my reluctance shifted when several LGBTQIAP+ persons joined the church after my announcement, and the behavior of specific critical stakeholders in the church made it apparent that my "coming out" did not automatically queer or prepare my congregation for the future toward which God was rapidly transitioning it. The church did not automatically become open and affirming because I shared my truth. My truth-telling only turned Myrtle into a Black church with an openly Queer pastor instead of a church with a discreet Queer pastor. After much prayer and contemplation I grew to see my evasions as selfish and cowardly betrayals of my original intent on the second Sunday of March.

So, in good Baptist fashion, I appointed an LGBTQIAP+ task force and brought it to the church body to officially vote the committee and its mission into existence. After the initial vote, the church went through a two-and-a-half-year period of intentional discernment, reflection, and learning about sexuality, gender identity, gender expression, clobber texts, and Black Queer life. Myrtle's self-initiated queering process, which I was not a part of, culminated in a vote to become the first historically Black Baptist church in our metropolitan area to declare itself an open and affirming congregation.

During our congregational discussions, the leadership and I discovered a great void. Resources and curricula to teach Black churches how to become open and affirming are virtually nonexistent. Most of the resources that we encountered were written from the perspectives of liberal white Protestant denominations and white Queer theologians.[1] These materials predominantly displayed photographs of white Queer persons. These socio-ecclesial and photographic differences created certain psychosocial barriers for many of our more conservative congregants who subconsciously interpreted these materials as proof of a "negative white Queer agenda to feminize Black men and masculinize Black women." We also found it difficult to acquire African American Christian resources to address our inquiring Black congregational needs.

In this book I reimagine and converge the theories of Dale Andrews, Kelly Brown Douglas, Horace Griffin, Patrick S. Cheng, Robert E. Shore-Goss, Pamela Lightsey, and E. L. Kornegay to create an ecclesiological strategy for adaptive Black churches to use that desire to subvert and queer their heteronormative ecclesial contexts. Unlike the plethora of literature on white congregational methodologies for becoming open and affirming, my point of departure centers on the intersections of Black liberation theology, Womanist theology, Black Queer theology, and Black subversive hope.[2] This research serves as a constructive theological tool to guide Black churches, pastors, and seminarians through communally co-creating nonbinary brave spaces where Black queerness is regarded as sinless and sacred.

In the words of E. Patrick Johnson, "Almost everything I know about Queer studies I learned from my grandmother."[3] And for that reason, I write. I wrote this book to share with the Black church and the world what I learned from my great-grandmother Mamie Lou Phillips. She taught me that "God is love, not religion; God is love, not a church; God is love, not a preacher's opinion; God is love." Queering Black churches is an attempt to winnow the chaff of toxic Black heteronormativity to prepare the way of the Lord for all of God's children whom God loves.

Foreword

I first met Brandon Crowley, the author of this book, in 2013 while I was serving as the Walter G. Muelder Visiting Professor of Social Ethics at Boston University School of Theology. He was assigned to me as my teaching and research assistant. Because of his excellent work in both tasks, I did not hesitate a year later to accept his invitation to serve as the second reader on his PhD dissertation committee. That experience afforded me the privilege to expand my knowledge regarding a relatively new subject matter in African American theological studies, namely, the response of Black churches to their members who identified with the LGBTQIA+ community. My association with him has greatly expanded my knowledge of that subject matter, and I am grateful for the honor to write the Foreword for this book, which is the first ethnographic study of Black churches engaged in the process of ecclesial transformation through various forms of institutional "queering": a term that signals one of the major contributions that the LGBTQIA + community has bequeathed to the world by providing a new language relative to itself as a whole and its diverse membership.

Since dominant societies invariably speak derisively about the specific minority groups they oppress, one of the first things the latter must do in resisting that oppression is to devise their own language for self-identity and self-respect. In doing so, they may take over their oppressor's derisive language and invest it with new meaning in the process of making it their own. That is what the post–civil rights Black Power movement did with the word "Black," which it changed from a term of opprobrium to one of self-affirmation that exuded beauty and joy. Similarly, the LGBTQIA + movement has given positive valuation to the word "queer," which they now use both as an indicator of self-identity as well as a descriptive term for various actions of social transformation while celebrating themselves as valued people.

Throughout most of my own lifetime the term "queer" was used as a verbal instrument of disrespect and hatred toward those who displayed mannerisms or behaviors that did not conform with the gender stereotypes of the dominant culture. Thus, calling a person "queer" implied their exclusion from the predominant group. Bullying of children was commonplace.

Young boys were often called "sissies" or worse, and young girls were called "butches" or "tomboys." Since a culture of silence attended that issue, the victims of such verbal abuse invariably experienced feelings of insecurity, anxiety, self-loathing, and social isolation that often resulted in tragic consequences. Hopefully this book will serve as an essential guide for all clergy, laity, seminarians, and others in their various strivings to include all of God's people in their sacred spaces and to render them all the dignity and respect they rightfully deserve in our common world.

Peter J. Paris
Elmer G. Homrighausen Professor Emeritus
Princeton Theological Seminary

Introduction

On June 26, 2015, the US Supreme Court ruled that the fundamental right to marry should be granted to all same-sex couples under the Equal Protection Clause of the Fourteenth Amendment. The landmark *Obergefell v. Hodges* verdict struck down all existing state bans and legalized same-sex marriage in all fifty states. Although such legalization could never absolve America of its deplorable history of heteronormative violence, the decision did create a general sense of relief in the emotional health and well-being of many Black Queer persons. However, the majority of religious institutions in America remained wedded to their heteronormative ideals that prohibit same-sex marriages and condemn LGBTQIAP+ persons as abominations.

From the announcement of the ruling to the present, all of the major Black denominations refuse to affirm Black Queer persons as sinless and sacred images of the *imago Dei*. Consequently, many Black Queer Christian folk end up bereaved and disinherited, living in exile, longing to be received by their own. James Cone, a foreparent of Black theology, once stated, "No theological issue is more potentially controversial in the Black church and community than sexuality. Preachers and theologians tend to ignore it, apparently hoping homosexuals will go away or remain in the closet."[1]

In contrast to the widely perceived innate homophobia and transphobia of Black churches, a few historically Black churches unashamedly provide unprejudiced pastoral care, spiritual formation, and radically affirmative ecclesial settings where Black Queer persons learn and thrive.

No ecclesiological or practical theological research has been conducted on the affirming praxis of these rare open and affirming Black congregations. But as Pamela Lightsey stated in *Our Lives Matter*, I do not want silence to be interpreted by anyone as meaning that Black churches that affirm Black Queer persons do not exist, do not care, or have no impact in these contexts.[2]

This book tells the stories of how historically Black churches queered their ecclesial contexts despite the repugnant history of heteronormativity within Black Christianity. I wrote it because I do not want the lack of research on inclusive Black churches to lead future individuals to believe that all Black churches are innately homophobic and incapable of practicing ecclesial inclusivity. The churches discussed in this book represent the future of Black congregationalism. For this reason, I felt called to preserve their histories and bring attention to their successes and obstacles because their methods of queering are historically ripe with narratives that other Black churches can glean from as culture continues to evolve.

This book describes how these churches successfully redefined, reimagined, and subverted the puritanical nature, mission, and practices of Black churches and the Christian church universal. The book's constructive components evolve from open and affirming Black congregations' recurring themes and approaches to queering. From these insights, I present a methodology for queering Black congregations that I created after studying nearly all of the existing opening and affirming Black churches in North America.[3] It is called Black ecclesial queering. Black ecclesial queering centers on the Black Queer body as an ecclesiological sight of sacred worth. Black ecclesial queering (BEQ) is an ecclesiological theory that analyzes and proposes how African American congregations should go about the process of intentionally subverting their heteronormative and puritanical ideologies and, in the process, also transform their traditional spaces into open and affirming congregations.

This book was not written to convince conservative Black cisgender pastors or laity to pursue queering as an ecclesial cause. Nor is it a work of Black Queer apologetics written to change the hardened hearts of Black Christian fundamentalists. I wrote this work for Black churches, Black Queer Christians, pastors, students, and scholars in the fields of Black religious studies, Black church studies, Queer theology, and Black Quare theory, who want a constructive theological tool to guide Black ecclesial spaces through a process of dismantling heteronormativity. Queering Black churches is a product of, beneficiary of, and contributor to the sacred field of Black practical theology.

Black practical theology is a praxis of Black religious folk and an academic method used by scholars of Black religious contexts to transdisciplinarily engage and critically enrich the theologies, religious practices, traditions, and spiritual experiences of Black folk. Black practical theology explores the interrelationships between Black religious practices and the embedded Black theoretical and theological concepts within the practices as a means of processing, examining, describing, analyzing, evaluating, questioning, and preserving the historical sacredness of Black congregations, mosques, spiritual and religious groups, and virtual ecclesial communities with integrity and dignity.

In this book I utilize both the theoretical arguments of Black practical theologian Dale Andrews and the practical theological methodology of Don Browning to extrapolate critical reflections on how African American human experiences and the rituals of Black churches shape and affect the praxis of Black heteronormativity in ecclesial spaces. After that, I present a theory-laden practice of Black ecclesial queering as a response to the injustices caused by Black heteronormativity. The development of this theory-laden practice is the result of my allegiance to the cyclical commitment and responsibility of Black practical theologians to make concrete, practical, and constructive contributions to the communities we research. The Black practical theological method does not just consist of theoretical analyses for the sake of academic inquiry and discussion alone. Black practical theology is not a contemporary scientific form of analysis that is solely in dialogue with classical theological disciplines for the sake of preserving the politics of white Western academic ideology, which reinforces and undergirds whiteness, patriarchy, and heteronormativity. For this reason, the book is not solely a theoretical examination of the intentions of the mentioned theologians, sociologists, and theorists on their own terms. Instead, it is an attempt at applying aspects of their thinking and theories to communities that they may have never imagined. I use theories and theologies in ways that liberate them from the frameworks of their own canons. The aim of my Black practical theological work in this text is to present practical usages of Black and Queer theologies and theories that Black religious folk can use to creatively transgress Christian social and white academic forms of knowing and being for the sake of formation.

Black practical theology is not concerned with appealing to whiteness or fetishizing what J. Drexler-Dreis describes as the Eurocentric loci of rationality, which has historically been an extremely unhealthy and toxic preoccupation of Black theology and Black liberation theology proper.[4] Instead of bowing in servitude to be accepted by white theology, Black practical theology uses the tools of critical race theory, Black liberation theology, Black feminism, Womanism, and Black Queer theory to subvert the systems of whiteness, racism, sexism, homophobia, transphobia, xenophobia, and othering. Black practical theology centers its prophetic work on the analysis, betterment, and edification of Black religious folk, Black sacred spaces and congregations, and Black Queer persons. Thus, Black practical theology and its theologians must resist the temptation to see itself solely as a counter- or subdiscipline of white practical theology, which is often seen as the more dominant discipline. Black practical theology is practical theology. As an academic discipline, Black practical theology is concerned with theologizing and sustaining the prophetic edge of Black resilience while speaking with prophetic urgency about the future of living Black religious and spiritual persons.

Black practical theology speaks conceptually about and constructively to the theological realities of real Black people and real Black communities. Therefore, a Black practical theology must do more than address the academic guilds of the academy. It must rise above its professional interests and resist the temptation of impracticality to see the inextricable links between practice and theory as mandatory for the survival of Black people, the discipline, and theological education itself. Black practical theology begins with the experiences of Black people, it theologizes on said experiences, and lastly, it must construct more intricately nuanced practical theologies that are accessible and beneficial to Black religious folk and folk traditions.[5] Black practical theology is more than just applying Black theological concepts to a Black social context. Black practical theology and Black religious folks are interdependent, and they are fundamentally transformed by each other. As a discipline, Black practical theology always commences the theological enterprise from within the conditions under which Black people of faith are living in order to participate in shaping a better Black future.

According to R. Ruard Ganzevoort and Johan Roeland in their article "Lived Religion: The Praxis of Practical Theology," the work of practical theology should be seen as a sort of "spiritual gardening."[6] Gardeners care for the soils to which they tend because their work aims to induce floral growth, the production of healthy vegetation, or both. Likewise, the praxis of Black practical theology should be regarded as the spiritual gardening of the Black religious landscape. As Black practical theologians, our job is not to damage or destroy the gardens of our foreparents whose blood, sweat, and tears fertilized the now stale or dying grounds of North American Black churches. Instead, Black practical theologians have been called to examine the damaged soils of our Black faiths and to construct fresh theological methods that barely living Black religious communities could use to bring life into their dying situations. This is what I have tried to do in this book. I realized that the Black ecclesial treatment of Black Queer persons was antithetical to the gospel it espoused. Black heteronormativity is all about power, and it angers me. But instead of further dichotomizing and polarizing the issue of sexuality in Black churches by writing another scathing critique of the problem, I chose to construct an innovative and practical way of thinking about Black sexuality that would enlighten and educate both the inclusionist and the questioning on alternative ways of finding common ground.

Queering Black Churches provides a systematic approach for dismantling heteronormativity in Black congregations. Using the lenses of practical theology, ecclesiology, Womanist Queer theology, Black Queer theory, and gender studies, this book examines the cultural backgrounds, beliefs, morals, values, and heteronormative structures of Black churches while proposing methods for restructuring, reimagining, and subverting the heterosexist paradigms and binary assumptions that perpetuate oppression in Black ecclesial spaces. The book examines how open and affirming Black congregations understand what it means to be a church while paying close attention to the similarities and differences in their congregational queering approaches. I describe these congregations as reimagined Black ecclesial brave spaces where sexuality and gender are reimagined to prohibit discrimination against Black Queer persons. This book also provides something that no practical theological work has to date; an ethogenic examination of the radical ecclesiologies and theologies of inclusive Black churches. In this work I share how and why these churches chose to practice a more radically inclusive form of church and how they did it.

The Chapters

Chapter 1, "A History of Heteronormativity, Transphobia, and Homophobia in Black Congregations," is a Black practical theological reflection on the history of heteronormativity as a praxis in Black churches. It employs a sociotheological approach to discerning the cultural and theological meanings embedded within Black Christian heteronormativity that guide, provoke, and animate Black homophobic and transphobic practices in Black churches. By examining the sexual narratives and histories of Black folk, the chapter provides an analysis of the theory-laden practice of homophobia and transphobia within Black churches. The chapter concludes by critically employing this analysis to reflect on the twentieth-century theory-laden homophobic practices of the historic Abyssinian Baptist Church in Harlem, New York. The chapter brings attention to the normative theories within the heteronormative practices of many Black churches by discerning the impetus behind Reverend Adam Clayton Powell Sr.'s 1911 Abyssinian campaign against homosexuals.

Chapter 2, "An Introduction to Black Ecclesial Queering," decolonizes, reclaims, and redefines the words "Queer" and "queering," after which the history of queering by and for Black folk is chronicled to explain why Black churches should live into their inherent ideological queerness. To aid Black churches in living into their fundamental missions, the chapter introduces a methodology for queering Black congregations called Black ecclesial queering. Black ecclesial queering continues the historic Black church tradition of being transgressive and moves beyond ontological Blackness in the tradition of Victor Anderson.[7] Black ecclesial queering compels Black congregations to reimagine the exclusivist nature, incestuous institutional mission, and inequitable practices of the ecumenical Christian empire worldwide. Lastly, the chapter argues that Black ecclesial queering is already happening. This final argument serves as an introduction to the ethogenic data on queered Black churches that the following chapters present.

Chapter 3, "Models of Black Ecclesial Queering, Part I: The Congregational Model—Union United Methodist Church," uses the theories and historical analyses from the previous two chapters to survey the queered ecclesial contexts of Union United Methodist Church in Boston, Massachusetts. I selected Union United Methodist Church as a flagship example of queering because it is the oldest congregationally queered and open and affirming historically Black church in the United States. Union's queering process was celebrating a decade of inclusivity at the time of my research. The longevity of Union's inclusivity makes it a ripe sight to investigate congregational queering. The questions, ideas, and practical theological commitments discussed in the previous two chapters are placed in the experiences of one congregation. This chapter considers how this congregation understands what it means to be a Black church—the defining characteristics of its ecclesiology, theology, and praxis. This chapter describes the Union Church as a congregationally queered congregation because it did not queer its ecclesiology through the pastor's executive decision but through collective conversations, compassionate engagement, and a majority vote.

Chapter 4, "Models of Black Ecclesial Queering, Part II: The Pastoral Model—Mount Nebo Missionary Baptist Church," describes Mount Nebo Missionary Baptist Church as a pastorally queered congregation. The town, state, and church names and identities of all research subjects in this chapter have been pseudonymized for the sake of confidentiality and anonymity. The senior pastor obligated Mount Nebo to become Queer affirming. This decision arose not from congregational conversations but rather through hierarchical decision-making. Nevertheless, the senior pastor, Reverend Franklin, was subtle in how he conducted the process. I argue that the pastor solely queered the church's ecclesiology by first teaching the congregation that women should not be discriminated against. He later made a connection between sexism, racism, and homophobia. Their willingness to follow him was due to Mount Nebo Baptist's deep entanglement with the politics of personality: many of the congregants loved the senior pastor. They were willing to accept his decisions as long as they came with his continued presence in the church.

Chapter 5, "A More Excellent Way: A Black Ethogenic Report," argues that the most excellent way to Queer a Black church is contextual. It contends that while the open and affirming Black congregations discussed in chapters 3 and 4 may be spaces of safety and bravery, they also replicate some of the oppressive structures, teachings, and practices that exist in heteronormative Black churches. By critiquing the very churches in the previous chapters as models of congregational queering, this chapter posits that ecclesial accountability is distinctly different from congregational bravery and safety. The more appropriate way of queering a Black congregation will require open and affirming Black churches to move beyond mere security and courageousness and toward true structural transformation and ecclesial accountability. This chapter also presents a pastoral approach for teaching Black congregations about pronouns and how to know if a church is queerable.

Chapter 1 should be read as a survey of what scholars have said about Black sexuality, the history of Black sexual trauma during slavery, and the history of homophobia, heteronormativity, and transphobia. Chapter 2 presents what scholars have said about Queer theory, Queer theology, Black theology, and the history of subversion by Black churches and Black folk in America. Throughout these two chapters I intentionally put the scholarship experts in the fields into conversation with each other to wield a more excellent way of responding to the tragedy of Black heteronormativity. Simply put, chapter 1 is an explanation of the problem. Chapter 2 is an academic survey of queering that yields a hypothesis and proposes a solution to Black ecclesial heteronormativity. The case studies in chapters 3 and 4 are intensive and detailed systematic investigations of affirming Black churches. The aims of these chapters are to generate quantifiable results to prove the validity of the queering methods discussed in chapter 2. Chapter 5 is an ethogenic report on nearly two hundred open or affirming Black churches resulting from roughly one thousand congregant interviews.[8]

In the conclusion, titled "A Bright Side Somewhere," I share practical steps for effective congregational queering and what the future of congregational queering must entail.

This book is not a work of biblical interpretation that wrestles to persuade heteronormative persons that queerness is divine, sacred, or holy. Capable biblical scholars have already written fresh and Queer biblical exegetical works on clobber texts. Unlike that scholarship, this book begins its work from the belief that Queer persons are already sacred and holy without repentance. This book teaches Black congregations how to go beyond mere apologetics to develop a practice of inclusion that reinforces the biblical principles of hospitality and love without making the interrogation of texts the sole focus of the queering process. Although I do speak about studying the Bible, throughout this book readers learn that congregational queering is not about biblical proof-texting but about love, compassion, and communal inclusivity.

1
A History of Heteronormativity, Transphobia, and Homophobia in Black Congregations

Introduction: Understanding Black Christian Heteronormativity

Morphed into existence within the envelope of white heteronormative society, Black Christian heteronormativity is an embedded patriarchal ideology that has shaped the lives of countless Black church folk since the inception of Black ecclesial institutions. As an institutional sin that plagues many Black congregations, Black Christian heteronormativity is a toxic form of religious indoctrination that propagates the presumption that heterosexism and Christianity are indivisible institutions. Influenced and sustained by the evil progenitors of racism and sexism, Black Christian heteronormativity informs Black homophobia, transphobia, and Black sexual ethics, dictating the role of gender in Black churches. It reinforces the categories of male and female as the only moral gender identities in God's design for humanity. Black Christian heteronormativity is an evil theological ideology that institutionalizes and standardizes heterosexuality through a myriad of practices like homophobic preaching and teaching that affirm patriarchy and justify heterosexism as the only moral sexual conduct.

This chapter argues that Black Christian heteronormativity was born out of a Black quest for civility, puritanicalism, a preexisting posttraumatic sociotheological dependence on biblical inerrancy, and fear. Although the Bible is used by heteronormative Christians to substantiate their beliefs in the Divine disdain of Queer persons, the cultural contexts out of which heteronormativity was born is a more theologically thick space from which to draw broader conclusions. Scriptural references and verses such as the Sodom and Gomorrah story in Genesis 19:1–38; the Levitical laws in Leviticus 18:22 and 20:13; the pederasty laws in 1 Corinthians 6:9–11, Ephesians 5:5, and 1 Timothy 1:9–10; and the indictments against cult prostitution in Romans

1:25–27 are all examples of clobber texts that Black heteronormative churches have used to marginalize Black Queer Christians, but their literal reinforcement is a matter of personal ethics and culture.[1] While these verses are the theoretical bedrocks of Black Christian heteronormativity, their praxis is a much deeper matter than simple misinterpretations of texts. Black Christian heteronormativity is a symptom of a problem much deeper than any form of apologetics could repair. For this reason, chapter 1 does not focus on scriptural interpretation as a true understanding of the history of Black Christian heteronormativity. Instead, it centers on a history of Black sexual trauma, the perversion of Blackness by white sociotheological terrorism, the oversexualization of Blackness by enslavers and white supremacists, and the Black survival tactic of civility-seeking as the precursors of Black Christian heteronormativity. I do this by tracing the history of Black homoerotic trauma at the hands of white fetishizers and the evolution of Black homophobia and heterosexism as means of survival. The early history of Black Christian heteronormativity is synonymous with the history of Black communal heteronormativity itself. The intertwining of religious and recreational life makes it hard for one to trace the beginnings of Black Christian heteronormativity without examining the culture of Black understandings of sexuality in response to trauma. This chapter argues that Black Queer identity began before slavery. Queer persons existed and thrived in many West African villages prior to the trans-Atlantic slave trade. Hence, an understanding of Black Christian heteronormativity has to begin with an explication of white terrorism. Within this chapter I survey the arguments of scholars to construct a history of Christian heteronormativity in Black life and thought.

In this chapter a Black practical theological approach is employed to discern the history of heteronormativity as a praxis in Black churches. I employ a sociotheological approach to discerning the cultural and theological meanings embedded within Black Christian heteronormativity that guide, provoke, and animate Black homophobic and transphobic practices in Black churches. Since Black ecclesiologies exist within contexts that preserve the cohesion of Black identity and Black liturgical expressivism, the heteronormative praxis of many Black churches marginalizes Queer persons in a manner that is sinful. By examining the sexual narratives and histories of Black folk, I provide an analysis of the theory-laden practice of homophobia and transphobia within Black churches. In turn, I employ this analysis to reflect on the theory-laden twentieth-century homophobic practices of Abyssinian Baptist Church in Harlem, New York. This chapter brings attention to the normative theories within the heteronormative practices of many Black churches by discerning the impetus behind Reverend Adam Clayton Powell Sr.'s 1911 Abyssinian crusade against homosexuals.

A History of Black Queer Existence

Molefi Asante, professor of African American studies at Temple University, argues that Black homosexuality is a byproduct of the prison industrial complex.[2] He contends that the recent outburst of homosexuality in Black communities results from the "prison breeding system," which, he believes, distorted the relationship between Black male friends in single-sex prison units.[3] Asante's assertion that Black homosexuality is in some manner less prevalent among Blacks before the phenomenon of mass incarceration is problematic for the following reasons. First, to suggest that the display of cultural evolution is the result of the "prison breeding system" assumes a male perspective of Black queerness that centers on male prisoners, thereby ignoring the lives of Black lesbian, bisexual, transgender, queer, intersex, asexual, pansexual, and others who do not identify as male. Second, he believes that the inmates he interviewed had never had same-sex curiosities prior to their imprisonment. Despite Asante's statement, his data did not yield such findings. The scope of his research proved to be limited in its ability to undergird such a generalized presumption about the "straight" sexual identities of all Black male prisoners.

Furthermore, his assertion ignores the dynamics of silence and secrecy that are often associated with Black Queer sexual expression. These dynamics alone would have prevented Asante's subjects from speaking about any same-sex curiosities they may have had before their imprisonment. Contrary to Asante's argument, Black Queer bodies are not new phenomena, nor are they the production of private prison breeding or raw sex among Black men. Black Queer bodies have always been present, even before the end of the nineteenth century. Hence, the existence of Black queerness predates mass incarceration.

Chronologizing and tracing the history of homophobia and Black Queer experiences within Black communities and Black churches are arduous tasks. Like most Black folk narratives in the United States before the nineteenth century, the records and historical documentation of enslaved Africans with same-gender attractions or homo-traumatic sexual pasts are quite rare. In the secret hush-harbor religious gatherings of the enslaved, the concept of

Black ecclesial homophobia and the categorizations of persons as gay or lesbian did not exist.

A handful of sodomy accusations from the seventeenth century document the accounts of homoerotic behavior between masters and male servants, and most of the homoerotic slave narratives from the eighteenth and nineteenth centuries fail to identify any same-sex interactions as gay, lesbian, or bisexual activity. Most of the homoerotic activity during slavery consisted of acts of molestation, rape, gender-based violence, and human trafficking. As Abdur-Rahman points out in his article "'The Strangest Freaks of Despotism,'" the homoerotic references in the testimonies of enslaved Africans are vaguely written and often only insinuate same-sex sensuality.[4] This glaring reality problematizes all historical pursuits to analyze and interrogate the cultural practice of Black homosexuality and Black homophobia, but all is not lost.

The lack of empirical data creates an opportunity for Black Queer theorists to wrestle with the idea that the LGBTQIAP+ gap in American slave literature is ripe for innovative forms of theoretical inquiry and historically congruent imaginativeness. For example, many enslaved Africans came from West African territories where "the existence of male homosexuality was not a threat and transvestite homosexual men were allowed to equally live alongside heterosexual men and women."[5] From the Zulu transgender persons in precolonial South Africa to the West African same-sex guardians, Black Queer expression predates European influence and oppression.[6] As a huge continent, Africa is not monolithic. Africa is filled with vastly distinctive cultural understandings of gender and sexuality that include Queer identities and expression. For example, in Uganda, many "mudoko dako" of the Langi people, who were extremely effeminate, often married other men.[7] There are tombs in Egypt that depict two male lovers by the names of Niankhkhnum and Khnumhotep in 2380 BCE. The painting is believed to be the oldest piece of Black Queer art known to date. In the painting, Niankhkhnum and Khnumhotep are portrayed in the traditional Egyptian funeral style, like a man and a woman kissing with touching noses. And although their wives and children are depicted at the far ends of the ossuary, the wives are not depicted as family but as perfunctory surrogate spouses.[8] In Zimbabwe, ancient paintings chronicle the history of men engaging in normative penetrative sex rituals with other men.[9] Black Queer persons and Black queerness predate African colonialism, the slave trade, the trans-Atlantic passage, and American chattel slavery. But after arriving on North American soil, the normativity of gender fluidity became harder to express. Hence, it is hard to chronologize the history of Black Queer expression in America prior to the audacious self-identified "first Black queen of drag" and Black Queer liberationist known as William Dorsey Swann. Swann was born into slavery in 1858, but by the 1880s and 1890s he had organized and been arrested for holding several drag balls in Washington, DC.[10]

While it is safe to assert that no single American historical event or circumstance produced Black queer identities, slavery and the white abuse of enslaved Black bodies are the precursors of Black heteronormative practices and behaviors. Hence, a thick theological description of the history of Black homophobia must begin with an investigation of Black enslavement, oppression, sexual trauma, and suffering. The institution of American chattel slavery is undoubtedly the original birthplace and progenitor of Black homophobia and heteronormativity. Many of the enslaved Africans who were raped feared speaking to officials or other enslaved Black folk about their homosexual encounters for fear of being killed by their sexual predators. The same fear that forced enslaved women to hold their narratives of molestation by their male masters in secrecy shrouded the enslaved men and women who endured the same gender terrorization at the hands of their male and female masters. The fear of being killed or beaten forced sexually abused enslaved folk to remain silent about their forced same-sex encounters. On the other end of the spectrum, the fear of having their homosexual desires discovered by their wives or colleagues forced white enslavers to act out their homosexual curiosities with their Black enslaved men. "Male victims of slave rape left behind no biological record in the form of offspring, and given the gender roles in their cultures, were even more constrained than female slaves from verbalizing the experience of sexual abuse."[11] Black same-sex interactions, both involuntary and voluntary, were formed within and birthed out of a system of perpetual silence, fear, and secrecy.

In his book *The Delectable Negro*, Vincent Woodard asserts that patterns of silencing and the dismissal of the physical needs and desires of enslaved persons were powerful mechanisms of slave control that grew out of the homoerotic and sensually consumptive appetites of many American enslavers.[12] Upon the immediate arrival of enslaved Africans in the Americas, enslaved Black bodies and sexual identities were never respected or regarded as sacred sites of dignity. These occurrences greatly traumatized and trivialized the enslaved Africans' understanding of Black sexual health and Black sexual formation. Many enslaved Africans refrained from expressing themselves sexually for fear of being raped, abused, or killed by their white masters. During the era of slavery, Black men were frequently labeled as sexual predators and rapists of white women, and Black women were regarded as sensual sites of white erotic pleasure. To gain acceptance into the larger white heteronormative society, many enslaved Africans, especially Black men, sexually repressed themselves to avoid extreme traumatic social experiences.

Enslaved Africans often held their traumas in and never spoke of their oppressive sexual experiences. They essentially remained silent and secretive as a means of survival and self-preservation. In a sense, the shame, secrecy, and rarity of pleasure among the enslaved coupled with the internalization of Black sexual trauma became the precursors to Black homophobia and the Black cultural closet. Secrecy, fear, shame, and disparagement were survival techniques. Such secrecy caused nonheteronormative Black narratives to be intentionally left out of the history of Black peoples.

However, there are narratives out there that tell Black queer stories. For example, as early as 1890, a known gay male sociologist by the name of Augustus Granville Dill worked with W. E. B. Du Bois to write *Efforts for Social Betterment among Negro Americans* in 1909, *The College-Bred Negro* in 1910, *The Common School and the Negro* in 1911, *The Negro American Artisan* in 1912, and *The Morals and Manners Among Negro Americans* in 1914. In his memoirs, Du Bois remarked:

> In the midst of my career, there burst upon me a new and undreamed aspect of sex. A young man, long my disciple and student, then my co-helper and successor to part of my work, was suddenly arrested for molesting men in public places. The young man in his charge was Augustus Granville Dill, whom Du Bois's biographer described delicately as a "fastidious and a predestined bachelor." Much to Du Bois's dismay, Dill was arrested in 1928 for having gay sex in a subway toilet. Although Du Bois said he "never contemplated continuing my life work without you [Dill] by my side," Dubois nonetheless terminated his protégé. Apparently troubled by this decision for the rest of his life, Dubois wrote in 1958, "I had before that time no conception of homosexuality. I had never understood the tragedy of Oscar Wilde. I dismissed my coworker forthwith and spent heavy days regretting my act."[13]

The above reminiscence from Du Bois's memoirs reveals that ignorance and invisibility are essential facets of homophobic praxis in Black communities. Du Bois writes that, before that time, he had no conception of homosexuality, which suggests that he was oblivious to the existence of gayness of the Black persons around him. Because of his lack of awareness and subsequent compassion, he spent most of the later years of his life regretting that he allowed his lack of knowledge about the lives of homosexuals to force him to dismiss his coworker. However, after he was made aware of the tragedy of being both Black and gay in America, Du Bois's entire approach to handling Black Queer persons changed from ostracization rooted in ignorance due to invisibility to a type of acceptance rooted in regret. At least for Du Bois, a significant aspect of Black homophobia is rooted in ignorance about queerness and the lack of exposure to the humanity of othered persons. This passage also reveals that the issue of LGBTQIAP+ rejection and acceptance is not new. It was also a matter of concern for early Black thinkers like Du Bois as early as the 1930s, which demonstrates that Black homosexuals and Black homosexual activity did not begin, as Asante asserts, with the twentieth-century prison breeding phenomenon.

A White Rape Culture of Buck Breaking, Castration, and the White Obsession with Black Dick: A Precursor to Black Homophobia

While many thinkers like Molefi Kete Asante describe Black Queer identity as a harmful byproduct of coercive European influence, I see same-sex slave rape and sexual trauma during the era of American slavery as progenitors of Black homophobic and transphobic praxis. The molestation and rape of Black enslaved persons by their white enslavers did not create the Black homosexual. On the contrary, their rape produced the assumption that same-gender sexual pleasure was a problematic human expression because it was used as a form of reprimand and control of the enslaved. When enslaved African males posed a threat to the sexual prowess or power of their white masters, a process known as "buck breaking" would be imposed to force the "Blackbuck" into subordination.[14] Also used as a form of discipline for enslaved men seeking freedom by way of escape, buck breaking was a practice that involved sodomy, castration, lynching, public anal penetration in front of the enslaved man's family members, and other homotraumatic forms of terrorization. The lynching tree, auction block, and the swinging phalluses of "buck-broken" bodies exhibited the destructive nature of white male homoeroticism on the Black sexual psyche. According to Wooten, buck-breaking castration and "the willingness to observe and handle another man's penis certainly has homosexual overtones. They (white men) weren't happy with just shooting Black men, hanging Black men, or burning

Black men at the stake. These men always had to go for the Black penis."[15] Even the American Freedmen's Inquiry Commission of 1863 reported that white male enslavers often found homoerotic solace in the beating, whipping, and raping of their slaves.[16] This form of white terrorism traumatized the psyche of the enslaved.

Although most Black homoerotic abuse during slavery went undocumented, some Black male slaves were bold enough to speak of their abuse. Connecticut court records contain accusations of white males molesting their Black male slaves as early as the 1600s.[17] In 1677 Nicholas Sension, an affluent and married immigrant settler from England, was put on trial for raping his enslaved Black males. During the trials, dozens of Black men told narratives like the one below:

> Nicholas Sension spoke to me to lodge at his house. Daniel Saxton coming [to stay over as well] when that night I lodged with him, Nicholas Sension came into the next room and came to Daniel Saxton and took off the [bed] clothes from off Daniel when he said Daniel was asleep and lay down by him and caused the bed to rock much and then rose up and kneeled on the chest and wiped something off from Daniel. And then he went to the next room to pray and prayed to God to turn him from this wicked sin that he had lived in a long time.[18]

The sexual prerogative of Nicholas Sension, a privileged white man, over his enslaved male dependents proves that southern plantation owners used the enslaved for economic gain as well as for sexual pleasure. According to American abolitionist Solomon Northup, the primary author and the featured character of the 2015 media memoir *Twelve Years a Slave*, "the 'gastronomical enjoyments' and excesses of whites included the sexualized treatment of men such as himself at the hands of slave catchers, overseers, and masters."[19]

For enslaved persons like Solomon, despite the public nature of the previously interrogated slave narratives, their sexual and homoerotic trauma was never spoken of, nor was meaning ever made of the abusive sodomy that they endured. Instead, same-gender-loving expression became synonymous with public ridicule and social embarrassment. Silencing and secrecy destructively prohibited the healthy development of a Black sexual ethic and politic in the traumatized psyches of the enslaved.

Interrogating Black Same-Gender Sexual Trauma

At the end of the Civil War, formerly enslaved persons in America, like Harriet Jacobs, began recounting and writing North American slave narratives. According to Jacobs's 1861 biography, *Incidents of a Slave Girl*, homoerotic torture existed on southern plantations. In her memoirs, she tells the short narrative of an enslaved Black man who was often tortured and molested by his white male owner. She states,

> I was somewhat acquainted with an enslaved person named Luke, who belonged to a wealthy man in our vicinity. His master died, leaving a son and daughter heirs to his large fortune. In the division of the slaves, Luke was included in the son's portion. This young man became prey to the vices growing out of the "patriarchal institution," and when he went to the North to complete his education, he carried his vices with him. He was brought home, deprived of the use of his limbs, by excessive dissipation. Luke was appointed to wait upon his bed-ridden master, whose despotic habits were greatly increased by exasperation at his own helplessness. He kept a cowhide beside him, and, for the most trivial occurrence, he would order his attendant to bare his back and kneel beside the couch while he whipped him till his strength was exhausted. Some days he was not allowed to wear anything but his shirt, in order to be in readiness to be flogged. A day seldom passed without his receiving more or less blows. If the slightest resistance was offered, the town constable was sent for to execute the punishment, and Luke learned from experience how much more the constable's strong arm was to be dreaded than the comparatively feeble one of his masters. The arm of his tyrant grew weak and was finally palsied; and then the constable's services were in constant requisition. The fact that he was entirely dependent on Luke's care, and was obliged to be tended like an infant, instead of inspiring any gratitude or compassion towards his poor slave, seemed only to increase his irritability and cruelty. As he lay there on his bed, a mere disgraced wreck of manhood, he took into his head the strangest freaks of despotism; and if Luke hesitated to submit to his orders, the constable was immediately sent for. Some of these freaks were of a nature too filthy to be repeated. When I fled from the house of bondage, I left poor Luke still chained to the bedside of this cruel and disgusting wretch.[20]

While it is inaccurate to prescribe modern notions of sexual identity to Luke, his narrative forces us to consciously grapple with the reality of homosexual rape, racism, and gender-based violence on American slave plantations. Luke's abusive sexual experience with his master gives us a quick look into the evil ramifications of rape culture during American chattel slavery. His rape was the byproduct of the overtly sexualized white American constructs of racism, the economics of human trafficking, and power. Regardless of the early occurrences of these historical moments, Luke's and all other violent homoerotic slave narratives are inextricably linked to the current Black disdain for Queer expressions in all of their varieties. African American scholar of literature and gender studies Aliyyah I. Abdur-Rahman argues that Luke's sexual and racial identity formation suggests that "the era, culture, and terror of slavery shapes the emergent models of what constitutes Black sexual difference in America."[21] Luke's narrative proves that same-sex practices were weaponized against the enslaved.

Historian Thomas Foster also argues that the white male molestation of enslaved Black men reveals that racism and the sexual abuse of Black bodies share a common rootage: the white fetishization and obsession with Black skin, Black hair, Black reproductive organs, and Black genitalia.[22] Although we have few accounts of homosexual abuse due to cultural norms that forbade discussing it, the abundance of biracial enslaved persons frees one to assert that many slave plantations were sites of white erotic exploration and Black erotic torture. Despite the lack of support due to the prevalence of sexual secrecy and silence, many enslaved Africans who endured sexual trauma survived. According to Harriett's slave narrative, one day, when she was running an errand for Mrs. Bruce in the North as a formerly enslaved person, she was hurrying through the back streets when she saw Luke. Seeing him on northern soil caused her to rejoice because she remembered the extreme homoerotic hardships and brutality he endured on the plantation. After Harriet and Luke greeted each other, Luke explained how he had resisted and used his agency to get enough money from his dead master to run toward freedom. How could Luke and the countless other Lukes whose bodies had been sexually battered in secrecy live through such trauma? When did they acquire the desire to resist and strive toward freedom? According to Alfred Adler, an Austrian physician, psychotherapist, and founder of the school of Individual Psychology, feelings of inferiority are the sources of human striving. In other words, human beings have an instinctive drive to resist oppression. He contends,

> To be a human being means to possess a feeling of inferiority which constantly presses towards its own conquest. The greater the feeling of inferiority that has been experienced, the more powerful is the urge for conquest and the more violent the emotional agitation.... Difficult questions in life, dangers, emergencies, disappointments, worries, losses, especially those of loved persons, social pressures of all kinds may always be seen as included within the framework of the inferiority feeling, mainly in the form of the universally recognizable emotions and states of mind which we know as anxiety, sorrow, despair, shame, shyness, embarrassment, and disgust.[23]

In this excerpt, Adler proposes that human agency is born and discovered in helpless environments where inferiority complexes are formed. However, Adler's theory fails to consider that how humans strive for freedom or display their agency is solely predicated upon the oppressive environments within which they live. For example, how Luke, the enslaved African enduring homosexual rape, channels his perceived cultural status and how his paralyzed white enslaver channels his inferiority are entirely different. Even though both are culturally inferior in one way or another, the white enslaver still has the upper hand because he is free, and Luke is enslaved. Adler is correct in his assessment that all humans have an instinctive drive to resist oppression, even when that resistance may be a mental form of resistance or the infliction of sexual pain. Luke appears to have mentally resisted by not internalizing his oppression, while the white owner dealt with his inferiority by inflicting homoerotic torture upon Luke's Black body. The brutal sodomizing of Luke may have made the white enslaver feel somewhat superior despite his paralysis. Mental resistance was, therefore, the first form of human striving displayed by enslaved African victims of sexual and physical violence like Luke. M. Shawn Copeland characterizes what I am describing as "closeted resistance" and "mental resistance" as enfleshing freedom.[24]

Because the sexually battered bodies of enslaved persons, like that of Luke, primarily functioned as a site of amusement in the service of white male privilege, Copeland proposes that the only way Black enslaved persons endured and resisted was to turn inward. She argues that although the bodies of sexually battered enslaved persons were seen as objects of property, production, reproduction, and sexual violence, many enslaved persons, like Luke, literally and metaphorically refused to internalize the white devaluation of the Black self. In essence, they reclaimed their own bodies. That is how Luke survived homosexual brutalization. In contrast to the abused bodies of Black women—and in our case, Luke, who endured the slave trade and sanctioned slavery in the United States—Copeland sees the sexually abused Black body as a site of divine revelation. She argues that the Black body is "the medium through which the person, as essential freedom, achieves and realizes selfhood through community with other embodied selves."[25] Many sexually abused enslaved persons freed their minds with education and their spirits with slave religion, while others redeemed their souls with self-induced death or an attempt to flee north.

The phenomenon of mental resistance among enslaved Africans was often the first act of rebellion, because it demanded minimal risk on their part. Even though the enslaved desired to resist the violent actions of their owners, acquiescence was inferred because the humanity of the enslaved was a nonfactor for enslavers. The enslaved had no choice but to endure violation because at least endurance guaranteed an anesthetized physical survival. Some Africans who endured enslavement and sexual abuse responded to their trauma by adopting a comatose-like facade of immobility and compliance. This outward appearance created an illusion of cooperation, serving as a coping mechanism to mitigate and endure the risk of additional sexual terror. However, in the case of a young man like Luke—who, because of the nature of his sexual abuse, could not conceive a child as proof of his rape—silence and secrecy appear to have been his only solace. Some of the more public sites of homoerotic trauma for enslaved Africans were auction blocks, horse harnesses, lynching trees, and cabins. These sites produced a homoerotic mixture of white male gazing, touching, forced anal penetration, forced oral sex, and the bloody mutilation of Black genitalia, biceps, triceps, and hands. Some of the earliest Black recollections of homosexual activity are interrelated with Black molestation, the white abuse of power, and male-on-male rape. Acts of sexual violence undoubtedly affected how Black people understood same-sex interactions before and during the post–Civil War and post–Reconstruction eras. Noted in *Recreating Africa*, by Sweet,

> A Mina slave named Luís da Costa confessed that one day while he and his master were out in the woods, his master forced him to submit to anal sex. Cabral threatened to shoot his slave if he did not comply. Luís unwillingly surrendered to his master on this one occasion but claimed that it never happened again because he fought against his master's continued advances. Perhaps the most violent sexual assaults of slaves occurred in

Pará in the late 1750s and early 1760s. Francisco Serrão de Castro, heir to a large sugar *engenho*, was denounced for sodomy and rape by no less than nineteen male slaves, all Africans. Among those who were assaulted were teenage boys and married men. As a result of these sexual attacks, a number of the victims suffered from "swelling and . . . bleeding from their anuses." Francisco Serrão de Castro apparently infected his slaves with a venereal disease that eventually took more than a quarter of his victims to their graves.[26]

According to Abdur-Rahman, the vulnerability of enslaved male and female Black persons to nearly every conceivable violation has "produced a collective 'raped' subjectivity" that has left an indelible mark on Black understandings of sexuality.[27] Thus, any form of Black sexuality, especially heterosexuality, must be regarded as an extension and response to something. In the instance of Black heteronormativity, such must be regarded as a survival mirroring, indoctrination, and reproduction of the white American puritanical worldviews of its context. If Black LGBTQIAP+ existence preexists slavery and Black heteronormativity does not, then Black homophobia and transphobia must be regarded as an American phenomenon birthed during slavery.

A Black Practical Theological Examination of Black Heteronormativity

In *A Fundamental Practical Theology*, Don S. Browning proposes that the only way to understand a particular religious community's theology is to begin and end with an examination of its practices. Browning offers an extensive practical philosophy of religion that uncovers how religious communities exercise practical reason. He describes practical theology as a critical and constructive reflection on a religious community's praxis and lived experiences and rituals in its own context. Browning contends that theology is not just a configuration of biblical studies, church history, and systematic theology. He argues that theology is a process of understanding that goes from "present theory-laden practice to a retrieval of normative theory-laden practice to the creation of more critically held theory-laden practices."[28] Browning argues for the reorganization and reconceptualization of how we intellectually perceive theology. In his view, theology should move from practice to theory and back again, which he perceives as the most sensible formula because it follows the nature of human thought. Browning argues that "practical theology describes practices to discern the cultural and religious meaning that guide a particular community's way of life and thinking."[29] Although theory is distinct from practice, for Browning, it cannot be separated from practice because theories are embedded within practices. He further contends that all practices contain beliefs about the nature and value of things. He argues that when one describes a particular practice in a specific community of faith, one must understand that beliefs are embedded within practices. Browning describes fundamental practical theology as a critical reflection on the church's dialogue about experiences and practices within the community. He uses Hans-Georg Gadamer's theory, which defines understanding as a "moral conversation shaped throughout by practical concerns about application that emerges from our current situation."[30] Browning's emphasis on the interrelatedness of theory and practice can help us see that Black Christian heteronormativity is an intentional theory-laden practice with theological and ethical convictions.

Heteronormative Black Christians use these moral convictions to authorize and rationalize the subjugation of Queer bodies even when heteronormative Black Christians are not aware of the matrix of theories and theological beliefs that ground their heteronormative claims. Many heteronormative Christians, who are products of the evangelistic enterprise of religious education, are intentionally uninformed about the historical complexity of human evolution and the spectrums of gender identity and expression. Ignorance around the topics of Black gender identity and expression does not divorce the embedded heteronormative theories of Black Christian culture from the Black ecclesial practices of homophobia and transphobia, which share this common progenitor. The firmly fixed heteronormative theories of Black Christian culture and the Black ecclesial practices of homophobia and transphobia are intersectional and inextricably linked. Both feed off each other, and neither can exist independently of the other. However, this assessment has its limitations. Because Browning's practical theology is rooted in a white perspective, it cannot adequately navigate the complexities of heteronormativity within Black congregational life and experience. It is essential to recognize that while Browning's insights are foundational in practical theology, queering Black congregations cannot solely rely on his white scholarship. Instead, Black ecclesial queering, which I will describe in greater detail in chapter two, must grapple with Browning's practical theological method of inquiry while simultaneously incorporating Dale Andrews's perspective on Black practical theological inquiry.

Black Practical Theology

The theological contributions of Black practical theologian Dale Andrews and the practical theological methodology of Don Browning have been instrumental in my evolving theology of Black heteronormativity. Their works have aided me in extrapolating critical reflections on how traditional Black Christian understandings of gender and Black homophobic practices in Black churches shape and reinforce the praxis of Black ecclesial heteronormativity. This theory-laden understanding of the practice of Black ecclesial homophobia is the result of my allegiance to the cyclical commitment and responsibility of Black practical theologians to make concrete, realistic, and constructive contributions to the communities we research.

But before this, one must first have a clear and historically accurate Black theological understanding of the praxis of Black Christian heteronormativity.

The Black Queer Struggle

In "Circum-Religious Performance: Queer(ed) Black Bodies and the Black Church," Ashon Crawley argues that Black constructs of sexuality and gender are best understood as performative and contextual.[31] Since cultural spaces dictate and control what is and is not a normative gender expression, Black ecclesial heteronormativity essentially pushes Black Queer persons into preestablished closets of Black heteronormativity, preventing Black Queer persons from self-actualization. Due to this constant reinforcement of heteronormativity in Black churches, many Black Queer Christians internalize their subordination with continual feelings of inadequacy, guilt, and low self-esteem. For this reason, the safety of the closet, not Black churches, is the initial and often the only space for Black Queer Christians. The majority of Black churches have not created an atmosphere of self-actualization for Black Queer persons as they have for Black heterosexuals. According to Riggins Earl Jr., this is the "anthropological problem of Christianity" for nonheterosexual Black bodies.[32] Both Earl and Crawley describe this phenomenon as a type of religious institutionalization of Black-Queer vilification. This type of sexual institutionalization informs both the narratives and practices of Black heteronormativity and Black homophobia. At least two kinds of Black Queer persons exist: the Black Queer person who has internalized Black-Queer vilification as the only way forward and the

Black Queer person who is working toward delivering themselves from Black-Queer vilification, which is a lifelong journey. Both exist in highly complex and layered realities. However, there have been and are Black Queer persons who are bold and socially prophetic enough to bring their antiheteronormative views into the mainstream.

Before examining the difference between these Black Queer bodies, I want to reiterate that the following examination does not aim to determine which is moral or immoral. Instead, I want to interrogate both as forms of Black Queer survival. One must be careful not to demonize the intentions of Black Queer persons held captive by heteronormative contexts. Because of the systemic nature of Black homophobia and Black heteronormativity, the self-acceptance of one's Queer self is often an unfathomable option. For this reason, the nestling of one's Queer self within heteronormative contexts and even the denying of one's own queerness should be respected as a form of survival. While this assertion might appear to create a social justification for Black Queer persons held captive by heteronormativity, my intent is quite the opposite. I am not suggesting that the closet is a safe or healthy space. Instead, my intention in shedding light on this issue is to reveal the complexity of both sides of the dichotomy that I have drawn between Black Queer persons. Both are Black bodies striving to survive in a heteronormative world. Whether surviving by discreetly being or denying one's true self or fighting to survive by striving for familial or ecclesial respect and recognition, the Black Queer stride to survive is real, contextual, and risky. Both the Black Queer soul held captive by heteronormativity and the self-accepted Black Queer soul living with subversive hope seek survival. By framing the question as a form of survival, we equate Black Queer survival with the basic human will to survive. According to Paul Tillich, protecting one's existence from nonbeing is the ultimate concern of humanity.[33] However, they are different. The difference is that Black Queer persons held captive by heteronormative contexts seek survival by staying in the closet. In contrast, self-accepted Black Queer souls living with subversive hope either seek to survive through resistance by queering or subverting the heteronormative context(s) in which they exist or they leave them altogether. Both are forms of queer resistance. Some Black Queer Christian persons remain wedded to heteronormative contexts because they have internalized the toxic theologies of their childhoods. This is what M. Shawn Copeland means when she describes the bold and prophetic self-disclosive acts of Black Queer persons questioning their heteronormative contexts, resulting in repression, expulsion, and sometimes death.[34] These penalties exemplify the toxicity of Black heteronormativity.

The Anti-Black Nature of Black Heteronormativity

As a sinful Christian praxis in many Black churches, Black homophobia, transphobia, and heteronormativity transgress the innate Blackness in Black churches. According to Peter Paris, the one common characteristic of Black churches is that they center on being antiracist spaces where white racist theologies and ideologies were antithetical to the Black ecclesial mission.[35] Therefore, if Horace Griffin is correct that Black Christian hostility toward homosexuality is a product of America's racist history and racism, then homophobic and transphobic churches with Black congregants are not Black churches because Black churches center on being antiracist spaces. Heteronormative Black churches are not Black churches but radicalized white, puritanical, Christian cults populated by Black persons. In *Enfleshing Freedom*, Copeland describes this same phenomenon—the Black heteronormative perspective—by addressing human sexuality under the rule of what she calls the white heteronormative empire. Copeland argues that, in an empire, homosexuals are forced to undergo intense rebuke and disdain.

> Empire entices and intimidates its ordinary subjects, and perhaps especially its most wretched subjects to react to gay and lesbian people with panic, loathing, and violence (malevolent homophobia). Empire permits its privileged subjects to respond with curiosity, experimentation, and tokenism (benign homophobia). In the empire, self-disclosure and self-disclosive acts by gay and lesbian people are penalized by repression, expulsion, and sometimes death.[36]

According to Copeland, the church teaches that gay and lesbian people should repress their sexualities, thereby denying them the opportunity to appreciate their bodies within faith communities. Copeland argues that the church and Queer people must grow to realize that "the vulnerability and marginality of gay and lesbian people" gives them the ability to make a definitive claim on the body and narrative of Jesus.[37] Here Copeland gives us the ability to assert that Black churches are not just centered on being antiracist spaces but must also be spaces where the vulnerable and marginalized have a claim on the body of Jesus, meaning Black Queer folk have the right to claim solidarity with Christ. A pre-existing example of this assertion can be seen in Black theology, which argues that Jesus is Black, revealing Christ's solidarity with impoverished Black folk. Likewise, LGBTQIAP+ Christians striving to deliver themselves from marginalization have a right to identify with a Queer Christ who heals the "anthropological impoverishment of homosexual bodies."[38] Some Black churches deny Black Queer persons the right to develop and practice a Queer Christology that is inclusive of Queer concerns and bodies. But as Copeland states, "If Jesus of Nazareth, the Christ of God, cannot be an option for gays and lesbians, then he cannot be an option."[39] To prove her point, she uses the works of Robert Goss, who constructs a Queer Christology to reveal the inclusive, transcendent, and adaptable dimensions of Christ. Goss says "when queer churches, synagogues, and groups decenter heterosexual presumptions and readings that often suppress diversity, gender, race, class, ethnicity, and sexual alternatives."[40] Copeland uses Goss here because he argues that for people to completely detach themselves from all forms of homophobic and transphobic hegemony and ideology, they must free themselves from the rigidity of cultural and sexual codes and concepts of God and religion that are rooted in heteronormative constructs of theology.

Copeland also discusses Goss's Queer biblical hermeneutic that sought to "befriend the text" by deflecting textual violence and tracing the negative apologetics that is often misapplied. She argues, as does Goss, that the only way to set a completely inclusive welcome table in the household of God is to develop a different Christological interpretation, in which all who hear and follow him are given the freedom to recognize ourselves as the body of Christ. She says, "If the risen Christ cannot identify with gay and lesbian people, then the gospel announces no good news, and the reign of God presents no real alternative to the 'reign of sin.'"[41] Doing acts of justice, critiquing the empire, and standing in solidarity with othered persons is what brings life to the body of Christ.

While there are many like-minded critiques of Black Christian homophobia, the analytical methodologies of Shawn Copeland, E. L. Kornegay Jr., Horace Griffin, Kelly Brown Douglas, and Patricia Collins Hill provide distinctive descriptions that reveal the cultural complexity of preexisting theories embedded within the Black heteronormative perspective. From their historical assessments evolved five Black heteronormative perspectives: the Augustinian perspective, the Black heteronormative perspective, the white Christian normative perspective, the puritanical heteronormative perspective, and the Black civility perspective. The Black civility perspective will be used to analyze Abyssinian's homophobic practices.

The Augustinian Perspective

Black practical theology examines practices by conversing with Black Christian sources, traditions, and thinkers for social and personal transformation. Augustinian perspectives on gender and sexuality have heavily influenced Black heteronormativity. Augustine is a progenitor of many normative theories within Christian practices and traditions about moral or immoral sexual performance, taboos, and ritualized repression. His sexual theories constitute a theo-cultural perspective that shrouds postcolonial and puritanical Black sexual theology. Augustine's demonization of sensual pleasure and eroticism was rooted in his own sexual frustrations with constricted sexual expression. Augustine argued that sexual desire, passion, lust, and the desire to share one's body with another subvert the attention of humans away from God.[42] He believed that persons who gave in to their sexual urges became contaminated with moral illness—that Christians live in the danger of being overpowered by what he describes as the sexual sickness of the body.

In his writings on marriage and virginity, Augustine contends that virginity is a great gift from God. Although it should be regarded with humility, it is the most superior of sexual states for human beings because it is how we share in the lives of the angels. He does not see marriage and virginity as equal; instead, he admonishes that virginity is the more perfect gift. Augustine does contend that marriage is both necessary and reasonable because it is the ultimate remedy for sexual perversion and lust. He argues that marriage is a preventative step that keeps men and women from falling victim to temptation. For proof, Augustine leans heavily on the writings of Paul, which state that "it is better to marry than to burn" (1 Cor. 7:9).

Augustine argues that three essential benefits are associated with marriage: it allows humanity to procreate, it enforces fidelity, and it creates a sacramental bond, which is exclusive to two persons.[43] But, the sexual human body was not always a site of sexual perversion. For Augustine, the pre-antediluvian era of humanity represented a time when humankind was submitted in absolute obedience to God. This Augustinian presupposition implies that all pre-antediluvian sexual relations were sinless and procreative.

In other words, for Augustine, all sexual relations before the fall of humanity fulfilled God's commandment to be fruitful and multiply.

The primary good that Augustine saw in marriage was that it allowed humanity to procreate, thereby fulfilling God's command to be fruitful. Because most LGBTQIAP+ relationships are not procreative, Augustine would regard such relationships as reprehensible. In his *Confessions*, Augustine perceives homosexual sex as objectively wrong because those who engage in it are connected to the crimes of the men in Sodom as a type of distorted loving of one's own sexual kind.[44] He closely linked this concept with the letter of Paul to the Romans, which argues that individuals who become lovers of themselves are under the auspices of a reprobate mind (see Rom 1:18–32).

Horace Griffin argues that Augustine displayed a special disdain for homosexuals because he believed homosexuality was an evil spirit that "men" were constantly in danger of acquiring.[45] The first problem with using such reasoning in the modern era is the fact that Augustine's writing is male-centered, thereby leaving out parallel discussions about other gender variants and identity expressions. In Griffin's view, this fear caused Augustine to create rules for monastic orders that restricted them from going to the public baths in pairs. Augustine even denied monks from being able to select whom they wanted to have as a travel companion for fear that they might indulge in sexual explorations together. Griffin contends that the contemporary African American Christian understanding of sexuality and homosexuality is bound to the beliefs and opinions of Augustine.[46] Augustine was a historical custodian of early Christian perspectives on sexuality and heteronormativity. His heteronormative perspective lives on in many Black and non-Black churches as homophobic and transphobic practices.

The Black Heteronormative Perspective: A Product of Church and Culture

The dehumanization and rejection of Black Queer persons in Black churches have contributed, at least in part, to the existence of Black heteronormativity, homophobia, and transphobia in Black culture at large. Additionally, the white racist culture has had a determinative influence on the heteronormative practices of Black churches and cultures. Horace Griffin argues, "In an effort to receive acceptance from a homophobic society, Blacks strongly condemn and deny homosexuality within Black communities and churches."[47]

Here, Griffin offers that acceptance from a homophobic society is the prevalent factor in homophobia in Black culture. Griffin contends that Black communities and churches embrace(d) strict sexual codes of the Victorian era to counter the perception of Black sexuality as perverse and lewd. He suggests that Black homophobia evolved from a Black desire to protect Black male bodies from having to endure further defamation in the racist societies of America. Griffin also contends that the homophobia of the Black heterosexual majority is rooted "in a biblical indictment that identifies gays as immoral."[48]

Indeed, Black ecclesial heteronormativity is influenced by the social practices of Black communities. These practices are situated within specific social realities of Blackness, which are often influenced by Black theology(ies). Black churches and Black communities play a pivotal role in constructing and reinforcing Black heteronormative practices. Black homophobia is both a determinative influence that is theologically and biblically constructed by Black churches, and it is a socioculturally reinforced construct of existing binary attitudes and ideals. Black homophobia is best understood cyclically: Black churches' practice of homophobia is influenced by the established attitudes and standards of Black culture and vice versa.

For sociologist Patricia Hill Collins, the Black understanding of sexuality and gender must be examined as a system of ideas and social practices that are based upon the social inequalities of Black people. She argues that because ideas about Black sexuality are so intertwined with the ideology of Black gender, all discussions about Black understandings of sexuality and gender must begin with examining what she calls "Black sexual politics (BSP)." Collins describes BSP as a set of ideas and social practices shaped by gender, race, and sexuality that frame Black men and Black women's treatment of one another, as well as how African Americans are perceived and treated by others."[49] She contends that it frames how persons treat one another, dictates how others see persons, and is rooted in the Black struggle for empowerment and validity. It is an "analysis claiming that systems of race, social class, gender, sexuality, ethnicity, nation, and age form mutually constructing features of social organization, which shape Black women's experiences and, in turn, are shaped by Black women."[50] Collins further argues that the traditional Black understandings of sexuality and gender create a Black sexual politic that essentially reproduces racism, poverty, rape, HIV, and sex negativity. She contends that most Black social problems stem from Black sexual politics and will never be resolved until we examine and critique Black understandings of sexuality and gender. Essentially, Collins's approach to the Black understanding of sexuality and gender hinges on the idea that race, class, gender, and sexuality are not competing frameworks but intersecting frameworks that mutually construct systems of power and understanding that permeate all social realities and relationships. Because Collins disagrees with the traditional descriptions of sexuality as restricted to male and female biology and gender as the social construct of masculinity and femininity, she rejects the conventional enterprise of defining sexuality and gender. She offers three interrelated meanings of sexuality. Sexuality, in her eyes, can be viewed as an entity that is manipulated by race, class, and gender oppression; a site of intersectionality that demonstrates how oppressions converge; and a freestanding form of heterosexist oppression that is similar to and shares like goals and practices with racism, sexism, and classism.[51]

To believe that the Black understanding of sexuality and gender is merely a copy of white approaches for self-preservation is a mischaracterization of Collins's undertaking. Her intersectional theory also critiques Black hegemonic masculinity and Black heteronormativity as equal contributors to the systems of Black sexual ethics and gender. Collins argues that the traditional Black understandings of sexuality, gender, hegemonic masculinity, and heteronormativity are systems of power that suppress heterosexual and homosexual Black bodies. According to Collins, these power systems foster the Black sexual subordination of Black Queer persons. Black homophobia is best characterized as an intersectional issue resulting from the social convergence of racism, religious indoctrination, gender bias, and power.

The White Christian Heteronormative Perspective

Black sexuality scholars like Kelly Brown Douglas, Horace Griffin, and Patricia Collins critique and describe Black hegemonic masculinity and Black heteronormativity/homophobia as a direct response to American slavery, racism, and white heteronormative structures of power. The Black internalization of white hegemonic terror has morphed into a Black disdain for themselves and their Black "othered" bodies. In actuality, whites used Black sexuality to devalue Black bodies; consequently, the Black community has subconsciously taken an oath of silence regarding Black sexuality.

Douglas describes the silence of Black churches on sexuality as concerning. For her, this silence is partly due to its conscious and unconscious desire to maintain "white hegemonic, racist, sexist, classist, and heterosexist structures."[52] She argues that the most critical discourse needed in Black communities is "a sexual discourse of resistance to help Black Christians recognize how the white exploitation of Black sexuality has corrupted Black people," besmirched Black churches, and tainted the Black liberationist understanding of God.[53] In her book *Sexuality and the Black Church*, Douglas contends that Black churches often reinforce white representations of Black sexuality by treating Black Queer persons with disdain for fear that they may destabilize the Black family and Black communities.

Griffin argues that the Black religious heterosexual majority has historically demoralized Black Queer persons because of their allegiance to the white hegemonic and patriarchal tradition of literal biblical interpretation—and continues to do so. Griffin argues that racist attitudes about Black men after slavery described them as sexual predators and rapists of white women. Black men, and all Black folk for that matter, soon realized that their survival depended on dissociating themselves from any sort of "sexual perversions" that could cause them extreme hardship or death. Griffin suggests that this is where the suppression of the Black sexual self began. To survive and gain respectability and acceptance by the white majority, Black communities and churches embraced the strict sexual codes of the Victorian era. Griffin further contends,

> Much of Black heterosexuals' anti-homosexual sentiment exists as a means of countering the perception of Black sexuality as perverse in order to survive and gain respectability and acceptance by the majority. Thus, it is understandable that African Americans would approach homosexuality with more dread and disdain than others, often denying a Black homosexual presence to avoid being further maligned in a racist society.[54]

This cultural ethos and these already established attitudes and ideals about human sexuality created the practice of homophobia within Black communities. Black homophobia is essentially driven by preestablished cultural perspectives arising from literalist readings of Scripture, human sexuality, respectability, and the quest for Black civility. Griffin contends that the Black understanding of sexuality and gender should be examined as a direct emulation of white heteronormativity. Black homophobia evolved out of a

Black desire to protect Black bodies from having to endure further defamation in the racist society of America.

While both Griffin and Douglas accuse Black churches of being silent about Black sexuality, Victor Anderson argues that Black churches, on the contrary, have been quite vocal about sexual difference, as evidenced by the countless homophobic sermons delivered from Black pulpits. He contends that Black churches have vocally and culturally stereotyped the Black sexual other as "the poor sissy choir director" or the "butch-dyke truck driver."[55] Anderson argues that these stereotypes dehumanize the people at whom they are directed. Still, they also dictate how Black heterosexuals understand and speak about Black sexual categories and Black Queer presence. Anderson contends that it is dangerous and detrimental to Black life when Black religious leaders describe the sexuality of Black Queer persons as a problem that needs to be corrected. He supports his claim that the generative care and creativity of Black Queer persons helps foster and nourish Black churches, Black communities, and Black culture. Anderson contends that any threat to Black Queer sexuality is also a threat to the creative flourishing of Black culture and Black churches. He further states that the demonization of Black Queer sexuality by Black communities and churches is, in fact, hypocritical because Black Queer persons are responsible for writing the hymns and songs that nourish the spirits of Black heterosexuals; serving as Sunday school teachers and publishers who aid Black folk in learning about their Christian faith, preaching the sermons that compel us to be Christ-like; and serving as deacons, ushers, and trustees. Anderson acknowledges that even in Black communities, Black Queer persons are responsible for nurturing Black youth as educators from preschool to college.

The Puritanical Heteronormative Perspective

When tracing the legal roots and cultural genesis of Black homophobia, one must also consider the overarching practice of American puritanism, which shrouded Black existence in the early eighteenth century. E. L. Kornegay Jr. argues that the overarching practice of American Puritanism is the primary heteronormative perspective within which Black Christian homophobia finds its roots. Many of the Euro-American ideals of Puritanism are rooted in a specific type of religious interpretation that employs a "hermeneutic of 'conquest and suppression' concealed behind a veil of noble religious motivations."[56] Protestant Puritanism privileges the white male heterosexual stereotype as normative while utilizing oppressive theologies that reinforce whiteness in ecclesial spaces. These oppressive theologies presently live in Black churches. According to Kornegay, the middle-class, white American puritanical society presents an inescapable heteronormative perspective and is a progenitor of Black homophobia and gender oppression. This perspective is inescapable for Black Queer persons because Black Queer bodies exist in all the pockets of American puritanical society. Even in many Black religious communities, the middle-class, white American puritanical ideal is reinforced to ensure that Blacks attain the same social, economic, political, sexual, and religious standing as their white counterparts. Kornegay describes this phenomenon as a "psychological collision between Puritan ideology and Black bodies."[57]

Significantly Puritanism was also enforced religiously, culturally, and legally. Even as early as 1791, constitutional amendments made sanctions to legalize the castration, imprisonment, and execution of homosexuals in America. Before the 1962 Illinois ruling to decriminalize sodomy, homosexuality was a punishable offense in every state in the United States. The word "sodomy" in the laws above illustrates the interwoven relationship between religion and law. Kornegay characterizes homophobia and the Black ecclesiological allegiance to Protestant Puritanism as the quintessential moral flaw of Black theology.[58] For him, this moral flaw within Black ecclesiologies lies in the fact that the Puritanism many Black churches subscribe to often ignores the social underpinnings and cultural traditions of Black religion and Black identity. Black churches that are steeped in puritanical ideals sublate Blackness into a caricature of white cisgendered heteronormativity, which creates a massive contradiction in Black churches because their distinctive characteristics are supposed to center on their nonracist histories and orientations. Black churches with allegiances to white racist puritanical ideals are oxymorons.[59]

An Analysis of Abyssinian Baptist Church's Homophobic Practices

One of the most prominent Black leaders of the twentieth century was the Reverend Adam Clayton Powell Sr., pastor of Abyssinian Baptist Church in Harlem. In 1929 Reverend Powell launched a crusade against homosexuality. "The stated purpose of this crusade was to protect the Black family. Powell warned that the sin of homosexuality threatened to eat the vitals out of America."[60] As a representative character in Black leadership at the turn of the twentieth century, his stance provides an analytic and hermeneutic lens to examine Black theological and communal homophobia.

As the oldest recorded documentation of an official church crusade against homosexuality, Abyssinian—one of the most prominent and historic Black churches in America—becomes the best location to examine and critique the history of heteronormative rhetoric within Black churches. Reverend Powell and the 1929 Abyssinian crusade present an opportunity to critically engage with and interpret questions about sexuality in Black churches. His homophobic notions are quests for civility and the residual effects of Black respectability and assimilationist politics that have plagued Black churches since Reconstruction. Although one could argue that Powell's quest for civility was transformative because it upheld Black heteronormative Christian ideals, it was also dysfunctional and destructive because it was rooted in a Black survivalist preoccupation with white notions of civility.

Civility is commonly thought to be solely associated with manners, social etiquette, moral sensibilities, and class orientations. Beginning with certain habits and virtues institutionalized by systems to gain social capital, civility pertains to the individual's social dignity within a structure. It is also used as a framework for understanding the role of social capital within the context of the lives and practices of public leaders. Additionally, civility is not and cannot be limited to attaining social capital. Civility indicates a far more extensive social-historical script by which citizens of a particular system negotiate being within the context of a much larger society. According to Walter Fluker, "Civility is the psychosocial ecology of the individual; a certain understanding or self-referential index of the individual's place within a social system as it relates to character."[61] This study investigates three types of civility: subversive, dysfunctional, and transformative.

According to Jeffrey Goldfarb, subversive civility contributes to democratic life with civilized political contestation and facilitates public deliberations about problems buried by the norms of civility.[62] When a particular leader of a system fails to speak to the existence of destructive practices to maintain good civil relationships with persons within the system, this is an example of dysfunctional civility. On the other hand, transformative civility is a subversive practice "that exposes unjust practices and calls upon the highest within the leader's character."63 For instance, a leader who realizes a moral flaw in the fabric of their system and ignores it is practicing dysfunctional civility. A leader who addresses it is practicing a method of transformative civility. In the eighteenth and nineteenth centuries, civility was tied to class and the bodily survival of the Black race. Civility has historically been linked "to the insatiable need for social dignity and respectability."64 This need often manifested itself in a desire to be recognized by the dominant culture. According to Orlando Patterson,

> Confronted with the master's outrageous effort to deny him all dignity, the enslaved person, even more than the master, came to know and desire this same attribute passionately. For dignity, like love, is one of the human qualities that are most intensely felt and understood when they are absent—or unrequited.65

One of the significant challenges for many Black religious leaders during the nineteenth and twentieth centuries was this need to be recognized, justified, and approved by the white establishment. This need for recognition begins with consciousness or a focused awareness of dominant frames of reference. After one is aware of these dominant frames, they will often start to mirror the dominant structure, thereby developing a recurring need for justification and approval from others. "Mirroring refers to self-reflection on and transference of one's deepest past emotional experiences onto others and in situations that are provoked by memory."66 Mirroring leads to masking, which "compels leaders to begin to remake themselves or excessively adapt the ideas that others give value or relevance, thus dismissing their life's purpose and sense of self."67 As the practices of mirroring and masking intensify, they can cause leaders to feel isolated and frightful of being who they are, losing touch with their inner selves. This is what Harold Cruse means when he argues that Negro intellectuals and the Black elite tend to gravitate toward the social dynamics of white American society as a form of signifying their arrival and resting on their laurels. Negro intellectuals and the Black elite end up feeling isolated and frightful of being who they are when they mask and mirror the social dynamics of white society. For Cruse, the masking and mirroring of Negro intellectuals is an illusion because such acceptance is tentative.68

As it pertains to Reverend Powell's crusade against homosexuality, the quest for civility did not just pertain to etiquette, manners, and social graces; it was also an adaptation to specific social-historical scripts and contracts. For a Negro intellectual and member of the Black elite such as Reverend Powell, the quest for civility concerned the development and social acceptance of certain social dignities within the system of white normality. This framework for understanding and negotiating life worlds and systems was Reverend Powell's way of attaining social capital while creating and sustaining a civil community.[69] When Reverend Powell launched a crusade against homosexuality, it was a form of recapturing, reappropriating, and maintaining a set of sexual norms, habits, and practices that he believed were essential for the survival and uplift of the Black race in 1920s' white heteronormative America. While it is indeed evident that Powell did, in fact, reappropriate or retrieve, he was doubtlessly limited by the dominant thinking of his era. Therefore, how could he have reframed the Black cultural script within his historical context? In a sense, Powell's failure to retell or reframe the story led him to imitate and perpetuate the larger drama of Black emasculation and oppression. Of course, he was a man of his time. However, by asking analytical questions about his practices as a leader, we will hopefully learn how not to repeat them, as many are doing in the present.

Harlem in the Early Twentieth Century

From 1910 to 1970, millions of Black folk relocated from the South to the northern cities like New York, Detroit, Chicago, and Boston during an era known as the Great Migration, and Harlem's Black population grew tremendously. Blacks had to compete for jobs and housing with Irish and other white Americans in Manhattan—and because of the history of race riots in New York City, leaders of the growing Black middle class in Harlem sought to combat all notions of anticivility. They sought to suppress all stereotypes that would allow others to question Black respectability.

At the same time, in the fall of 1929, drag balls became extremely popular among the Black homosexual working class in Harlem. The presence of Black nightlife in Upper Manhattan did not sit well with Harlem's white community. The Committee of Fourteen, an all-white moral reform society that originated in 1905 to close New York saloons where prostitutes openly solicited proprietors, released a report naming Harlem "the most vice-ridden neighborhood in New York City."[70] An editorial complaint in the *New York Age*, a Harlem newspaper, accused lesbians and gay men in Harlem of hosting rent parties. These parties, where drag performers entertained, were fundraisers held in the apartments of lesbians or gay persons to help the party promoters and entertainers pay their rent.[71] According to the article,

> One of these rent parties a few weeks ago was the scene of a tragic crime in which one jealous woman cut the throat of another because the two were rivals for the affections of a third woman. The whole situation was on par with the recent Broadway play [about lesbianism, *The Captive*], imported from Paris, although the underworld tragedy occurred in this locality. In the meantime, the combination of bad gin, jealous women, a carving knife, and a rent party is dangerous to the health of all concerned.[72]

In response to these publications and to reclaim the civility of the Black neighborhoods of Harlem, Black preachers and civil rights leaders teamed together to launch a crusade against homosexuality and drag balls. Reverend Powell took the lead in organizing this initiative because he also served as the president of the National Association for the Advancement of Colored People (NAACP) and the Urban League. As the standard-bearer for the Black middle class of Harlem in the 1920s, Reverend Powell was concerned about whites' perception of Harlem's Black community. As attested by his sermons published by the *New York Age* in November 1929, he worried that sexual perversion was "steadily increasing" in large Black American neighborhoods like Harlem.[73] According to Powell, the individual pursuit of pleasure over obligations to the community was both the cause and consequence of homosexuality. Indulgence in the sensual pleasures that were newly available to the great numbers of recent Black arrivals in the cities was "causing men to leave their wives for other men, wives to leave their husbands for other women, and girls to mate with girls instead of marrying."[74] Homosexuality, one of "the powers which tend to debase the race," was a rejection of the familial responsibility that held Black communities together and made them a viable political enemy.[75]

As a Black pastor who frequently condemned homosexuality as sexual immorality that displeased God, Reverend Powell appealed in his crusade to biblical literalist claims that homosexuality was not a practice sanctioned in the Bible and that it was a sexual perversion that "threatened to eat the vitals out of America."[76] Responding to those who opposed his crusade, Reverend Powell said, "Why did I preach against homosexuality and all manner of sex perversions? Because, as every informed person knows, these sins are on the increase and are threatening to destroy the Black family."[77] Reverend Powell's activity against homosexuality is an example of how a charismatic religious and political figure of the church can tie the notion of the model of the Black family to inflexible categories of sexuality and gender. Reverend Powell's crusade raises several questions: Why does Powell understand homosexuality as an attack on the family, and why is this sociocultural assessment rooted in the Bible? Are there deeper reasons behind Powell's ideological and cultural precedents that inform the discursive features and practices of his quest for civility?

To answer the first question, we must first understand the history of the Bible's usage in Black culture and Black life. As stated in the introduction, most Black churches have remained wedded to premodern, nineteenth-century white Evangelical, and post-Reformation beliefs in the exclusive authority, infallibility, clarity, self-sufficiency, internal consistency, and self-evident meanings of the Bible. The Bible serves as the archetypal source of ethical and moral instruction for most Black Christians. Griffin says of this view of the Bible,

> The Black church has historically been and continues to be an institution of support, nurture, and uplift. Unfortunately, however, Black church leaders and congregants have been resistant and even closed to treating gay and heterosexual congregants equally or, in many cases, offering simple compassion to the suffering of gay people. The Black heterosexual majority is presently engaged in a biblical indictment that identifies gays as immoral.[78]

The fact that literalist methods of biblical interpretation are a portion of what undergirds the theology and sociology of most Black preachers, like Powell, cannot be overstated, especially as it relates to understanding homosexuality as an attack on the Black family. For scholars such as Horace Griffin, this type of oppression created by Black persons often fulfills the oppressed's unconscious need to imitate their oppressors. Consequently, anyone identified as "other" in the Black community, either female or gay, is often denied inalienable rights, the respect of personhood, equality, and the experience of comfort in their otherness for the sake of Euro-American conformity. Thus, Black males become guilty of dehumanizing those they consider their subordinates in the same way white men dehumanized them. According to Griffin,

> In an effort to receive acceptance from a homophobic society, Blacks strongly condemn and deny homosexuality within Black communities and churches. While Black church leaders and congregants tolerate a gay

presence in choirs, congregations, and even the pulpit as long as gays cooperate and "stay in their closeted place," gays quickly experience the limits of this tolerance if they request the same recognition as their heterosexual counterparts.[79]

From this same critical standpoint, Professor Patricia Collins argues,

> Domination always involves the objectification of the dominated; all forms of oppression imply the devaluation of the subjectivity of the oppressed. Individual subjectivity is another concern for marginalized groups. Differences can be used as a weapon of self-devaluation by internalizing stereotypical societal views, thus leading to psychological oppression.[80]

This inverted and internalized logic has informed how homosexuality has been interpreted in Black churches.

Scripture, Sexuality, and Gender

The Bible contains only seven passages about homosexuality, and none condemn same-sex couples for being in long-term sexual relationships. As it pertains to the texts in Leviticus and the Pauline epistles, most of these texts are only relevant to most heteronormative readers when discussing the topic of homosexuality. Given that societies and traditions determine the significance of sacred texts for their communities, it is crucial to acknowledge that prevailing homophobic attitudes in Black churches are often substantiated biblically through the social enforcement of normative Levitical codes that label same-sex pleasures as abominable. Interpreting the enforcement of heteronormative Levitical codes as a choice rooted in nurture and enculturation rather than a reinforcement of Divine nature is essential. Such heteronormative choices and enforcements are contradictory because they selectively overlook certain forms of cultural transgressions and their corresponding punishments elsewhere in Leviticus. This is done by applying a hermeneutic of suspicion to some passages while simultaneously isolating same-sex pleasure as an abomination. For example, people in Black churches generally do not believe it is sinful to eat shrimp (Lev. 11:10) or pork (11:7) or to wear clothes with mixed fabric (19:19), even though the Levitical code forbids these actions along with same-sex affection. However, the problem is more extensive than just a matter of biblical interpretation and apologetics. Deeper cultural questions about ideological and cultural precedents informed Powell's quest for civility.

In *God, Sex, and Politics: Homosexuality and Everyday Theologies*, Dawne Moon, a sociologist of religion, explores the social components of religious beliefs in the life of a person searching for the coexistence of theology and a plurality of sexualities. The book considers how members of Protestant congregations distinguish between polarities, including good and evil, right and wrong, and righteousness and sinfulness. Moon argues that the problem is more extensive than interpretation: historical-critical tools and nuanced exegesis of biblical scholars that validate the inviolable dignity of homosexuals will not single-handedly solve the issue of homophobia in the church.[81] Scholar Jay Emerson Johnson agrees with this view, saying that new biblical sociological, ethnographic, and cultural studies may

> offer a fresh voice to the conversation, clarifying various aspects of the debate and perhaps expanding the theological and spiritual vision of all the parties involved, but they will certainly not resolve the sexuality debates in our churches or provide an adequate explanation of the type requested by the Lambeth Commission.[82]

For this reason, Moon contends that the social components of a person's everyday theology cause them to oppose changing their opinions about homosexuality—even when the change is grounded in new interpretations of the Bible. However, it would be naïve for me to situate my critique of Reverend Powell's crusade against homosexuality upon the claim that he is misinterpreting Scripture because, theologically, this interpretation was a reflection of, in the words of Moon, "his every day."

According to Moon, the Bible is not the only source of religious and cultural attitudes that fuel homophobia.[83] She believes that the attitudes and social components of religious beliefs shape biblical interpretations that have traditionally caused people to condemn homosexual persons. Moon contends that "anyone who uses Scripture as a guide for life uses both literal and contextual readings to some extent. The difference seems to come from the experiences that shape the members' everyday theologies."[84] She defines "everyday theologies" as those beliefs that a person has already considered "natural" in their socially constructed and ordered world. Like the Jungian understanding of the psyche, which was an integration of conscious and unconscious components, the theological framework of many Christians also integrates consciously and unconsciously affirmed cultural norms of a socially constructed and ordered world. Moon describes the usage of Scripture as a sort of defense mechanism because "expressing something in a language of emotion forecloses debate, and therein lies its rhetorical power."[85] Moon's argument that the way in which already-established attitudes and social components of religious beliefs shape biblical interpretations is an example of how the Black perception of homosexuality is influenced by the social conventions of the cultural milieu of Black communities. Still, these same practices are also situated within social contexts influenced by Black theology(ies). Biblical interpretation and Black culture have both played a pivotal role in formulating and concretizing Black homophobia. Black homophobia is both a determinative influence that has been theologically and biblically constructed by Black churches and a socioculturally reinforced construct of the already-established attitudes and ideals of Black culture.

Similar to Griffin's argument that Blacks strongly condemned homosexuality within Black communities and churches to receive acceptance from the greater heteronormative society, Reverend Powell's crusade against homosexuality and the drag balls was an attempt to reclaim the civility of Black neighborhoods and families in Harlem in order to receive acceptance from the larger heteronormative society, and the all-white moral reform society known as the Committee of Fourteen. This leads to two additional questions: Where did Reverend Powell's already established attitudes and ideas about human sexuality and homophobia originate, and from where did his pursuit to reclaim the civility of Black neighborhoods and families in Harlem derive?

The 1929 popularity of drag balls among the Black working class in Harlem tarnished the heteronormative and white assimilated images of the Upper Manhattan Black community. As a result of these alternative forms of entertainment, the Committee of Fourteen, an all-white moral reform society, named Harlem "the most vice-ridden neighborhood in New York City."[86] This negative portrayal of Harlem in written publications threatened to tarnish the images of civility and respectability in Black neig hborhoods. Therefore, Reverend Adam Clayton Powell Sr.'s campaign against homosexuality resulted from his desire for social uplift and his quest for civility to preserve and promote the white heteronormative concept of family in his Black context. He believed that homosexuality threatened to destroy the Black family. He was concerned that if what he termed sexual perversion continued to increase steadily in large predominantly Black neighborhoods like Harlem, it would debase the race and tarnish the white perception of Harlem's Black community.

Reverend Powell's biblical understanding of homosexuality might be best understood as the product of an already-established system of attitudes and ideas about human sexuality and homosexuality or habitus. Powell's attitudes about homosexuality were inherited principles rooted in the Black middle-class aim for social uplift. Reverend Powell's homophobia was not just driven by his literalist readings of Scripture but also by attitudes and ideas about human sexuality, respectability, and the quest for Black civility. Likewise, his campaign against homosexuality and the drag balls was an attempt to reclaim the civility of Black neighborhoods and families in Harlem to receive acceptance from the greater heteronormative society and the Committee of Fourteen.

As a Negro intellectual, Reverend Powell was a member of Du Bois's Talented Tenth; therefore, he believed his responsibility was to function as a race manager and serve as a model "of Negro gentility for the dominant white society and subordinated Blacks."[87] Reverend Powell's leadership in the crusade against homosexuality was a self-appointment whereby he served sacrificially on behalf of what he likely believed was the impulsive and irrational behavior of the Black middle class who attended the drag balls and Black Queer persons themselves. He thought he was shaping the Black masses by molding values managing the theology of Harlem's Black churches.

Similar to the social uplift ideology of Anna Julia Cooper,[88] Reverend Powell's crusade against homophobia was rooted in Western ethnocentrism, staunch religious piety, and Victorian standards. To gain respectability and acceptance by the white majority, Reverend Powell, whether subconsciously or consciously, embraced the strict sexual codes of the Victorian era for fear of Harlem's Black community being associated with any sort of "sexual perversions" that could cause them extreme hardship or death. According to the liberal standards of twenty-first-century pro-gay activists, Reverend Powell's crusade appears to be an unethical indictment of the moral and cultural deficiency of gays and lesbians in Harlem during the 1920s. It is important to note that his strategy, albeit rooted in his faith in a white, patriarchal "god," was one that he likely believed was a strategic form of social uplift that sought to help Blacks acquire social capital within the context of white society. For Reverend Powell, the attainment of civility for Blacks in Harlem during the 1920s was about more than just learning manners, social etiquette, moral sensibilities, and class orientations.

Reverend Powell's quest for civility indicates a more extensive social-historical script that Blacks in Harlem had to follow if they wished to navigate safely the white world that surrounded them. This social-historical script was the white heteronormative family structure. During the 1920s, when Harlem's homosexual community was thriving and actively participating in the Harlem Renaissance, civility was synonymous with heterosexuality.[89] The psychosocial ecology of Black people in Harlem in the 1920s had to disassociate itself from anything that appeared homosexual to fit within the social system. In an attempt to reclaim the civility of Black neighborhoods and families in Harlem and to receive acceptance from the greater heteronormative society, Reverend Powell argued that homosexuality was a moral flaw in the fabric of his heteronormative system. He spoke out against the existence of these destructive sexual practices to maintain civility and respectability, which in hindsight we now see as dangerous and destructive. Reverend Powell's crusade against homosexuality mirrored premodern, nineteenth-century white Evangelicalism.

Griffin argues that the Black Christian condemnation and denial of LGBTQIAP+ identities within Black communities and churches is inextricably linked to the white American otherization of Black persons since 1619.[90] For Reverend Powell, the objectification of homosexuality was simply a mirroring of white heteronormative familial structures to help Blacks gain acceptance into the larger white heteronormative society. However, this mirroring supported his unwillingness to guide Black religious folk in Harlem toward a more precolonial African ideal of gender fluidity. Historically, Black churches have been institutions of support, nurture, and uplift. However, because of Reverend Powell's quest for civility, his strivings for social acceptance within the system of white normality, and his adaptation to specific social-historical scripts and contracts, he engaged in a biblical indictment that identified Harlem's gays and lesbians as immoral. Like Du Bois, Reverend Powell was merely attempting to establish a system of social uplift whereby all Blacks could participate in a multiracial democratic America.

Summary

Many Black churches remain homophobic spaces where white heteronormative systems and beliefs are reinforced. Black homophobia and transphobia are sins that animate Black heteronormativity. When Black folk begin to question their socially cultivated heteronormative perspectives, a disruption will occur between the questioner and the heteronormative perspective that enshrouds them. In the next chapter, I describe this disruption as a type of queering.

2
An Introduction to Black Ecclesial Queering

"Ain't 'Queer' a Bad Word? Why You Wanna Use That?"

Queerness is not usual or typical. It exists and thrives outside of the norm. It is a way of life that cannot and should not be reduced to the categories of pleasure, identification, or a way of expressing one's self alone. Queerness is much more than a category of personal specification about with whom a person has sex. Queerness is a worldview, a liberative way of living and subversive confidence that breeds a personal, theological, and political intolerance for heteronormativity and the ridiculousness of gender rigidity. Queerness is a fluid form of human existence that cannot be contained or restrained by conformity. As an ever-evolving state of consciousness, queerness denotes freedom and inner peace within the innermost being of oneself. It is a recurrent transmutation of liberation and freedom that ebbs and flows with unfettered rearrangements and imaginative ways of thinking, being, and nonbeing. Queerness is not static, nor solely the opposing end to a more normative way or thing. Queerness is the grey, the not yet understood, and a budding realization of the self, the other, and the world that perpetually undergoes repeated changes and transformations that evolve in tandem, indicating its fluid and ever-expanding nature. Moreover, each manifestation of queerness is intricately tied to liberation, emphasizing its relentless pursuit of autonomy, self-expression, and the fundamental right to live authentically. Once queerness appears to be fixed, it will rearrange itself in response to current and future oppressive measures. Queerness is a spiritual state of movement and steady evolution of self-awareness that gradually lessens the grip of an oppressive measure over time, especially heteronormativity.

As a methodology of subversion, the praxis of queerness is queering. Queering is the process of making the normal odd and the familiar strange. The queerness of queering pushes it to be more than just a theory. Queering is a prophetic enactment, embodiment, and realization of the universal ideals of equity, liberation, and soul freedom. Christian queering is a work of the Spirit that breathes life into what Jonathan Walton calls the homophobic valley of dry bones.[1] Moreover, akin to Ezekiel, queerness, when viewed through a theological lens, serves as a methodology rooted in the belief and determination to actualize the will of God, demonstrating that even dry bones can be brought back to life. Queerness is about possibility because it is synonymous with openness, potential, and departure from the normative and the restrictive.

As an identity, to be Queer means to be made in the image and likeness of God.[2] Self-accepting Queer Christian folk are freed children of God who resist conforming to the heteronormative ways of the world because their minds have been renewed and transformed by the affirming power of God. "Queer" is a divine and sacred description of a soul whose inward journey has pushed them to embrace an anti-Augustinian awareness of the innate goodness of the unchristianized original self. Queerness is good, and while pleasure is not precluded from it, queerness is not about sex. It is a sainted state that centers on love for the Divine within one's own authentic self and a love for and ability to see the Divine within the varying expressions of God's creation. Queer persons are whole and holy beings whose ability to see the *imago Dei* within themselves is their daily bread. Queer Christian folk are those whose rejection of self has been washed away by the love of Jesus. They have been energized and empowered by the Holy Ghost in a way that mirrors Pentecost. The Christian liturgical season of Pentecost is a reminder that the indwelling of God's spirit manifests an eradication of the oppressive social categorizations that plague human existence.

Humanity has historically divided itself into numerous categories based upon the concepts of geography, religion, ethnicity—or the socially constructed term of race—socioeconomic status, gender, identity, and sexuality. But in Pentecost, there is a queering of these categories. The coming of the Spirit creates unity and eradicates the social division caused by language. This eradication should not be understood as an obliteration of culture because Acts states that everyone heard in their own language. This means that the Spirit of God unifies humanity while acknowledging the importance of cultural expression: this is the personification of queerness. It is a movement with a means of subversion that ends in unity and solidarity. As Peter's sermon indicated, the Spirit was poured upon all flesh, and the social constructs of gender and identity were no longer qualifiers of the called. Everyone received the outpouring of the Spirit; all beings were recognized as being part of God's creation. Christian queering is akin to the collapse of differentiation during Pentecost. The coming of the Holy Ghost queered human categories. The ministry of Jesus queered those who were gathered in the Upper Room and around the room to do the work of Jesus because, as I discuss in greater detail in this chapter, the works of Jesus were Queer. Therefore, the indwelling of the Holy Ghost rightfully brings about a queeruption in the lives of self-accepting Black Queer Christians who believe in a God within whom there is no condemnation. Queering is a constructive eruption of God's innate queerness that must come out. God's image is imprinted upon the entire world without reproach. The acceptance of such is Queer.

The word "Queer" evokes a variety of sentiments. For some, "queer" is an umbrella term that denotes the identity of LGBTQIAP+ persons. Queer is also an explicitly derogatory referent that many LGBTQIAP+ persons found offensive at the beginning of the twentieth century. Academic guilds also disagree on the meaning and efficacy of the word "Queer." Queer is also a pluri-disciplinarian academic theory of subversion that advocates for gender fluidity, gender abolition, and non-binarization. Judith Butler, who never explicitly defined Queer theory but is a major contributor to the field due to their work in gender studies, describes the enterprise as "the point of departure for a set of historical reflections and futural imaginings, it will have to remain that which is, in the present, never fully owned, but always and only redeployed, twisted, queered from a prior usage and in the direction of urgent and expanding political purposes."[3] Here Butler lays the foundation for queering as a theoretical tool to deconstruct the social constitution about the problematic social natures of sex and gender.

On the other hand, many Black LGBTQIAP+ scholars, like E. Patrick Johnson, have decolonized Queer theory by developing intersectional Quare theory, which centers on the convergence of race, gender, and sexuality.[4] In light of these different academic and social views about queering, it should come as no surprise that the usage of the word "Queer" in Black congregational settings is even more complex. Many illusions to Queer anything in Black churches give immediate rise to questions like What does this word mean? Throughout this chapter I chronicle the history of queering by and for Black folk to explain why Black churches should live into their inherent ideological queerness.

Some Black Quare scholars might wonder why I have selected the term "Queer/queering" to describe my endeavors to reclaim the original ecclesial aims of pre-Reconstruction Black churches. First, I use "Queer" as opposed to "Quare" not as a means of disrespecting or disassociating my new work from the groundbreaking work of my Quare foreparents but rather as a personal matter of theoretical reasoning, analysis, and preference. Queer theories that are not innately Quare are not Queer. When theories employed by Queer folk reinforce whiteness, patriarchy, sexism, transphobia, classism, or resistance toward Womanism for the sake of gender demolition alone, it is no longer Queer but white.[5] Queer theory is Quare if it is genuinely Queer.

For this reason, I do not give racist white LGBTQIAP+ scholars the rights to a discourse that they do not own or deserve the sole rights to. Queerness is ours! And in that same vein, I do not neglect the right of Quare persons to demolish the temple with our own tools. But I choose, as I have done with Christianity and America, to decolonize, reclaim, and redefine the words "Queer" and "queering" for the good of the worldwide movement to help the Church universal to be more liberative and loving. To aid Black churches to live into their fundamental missions, I coin an original phrase and methodology for queering Black congregations called "Black ecclesial queering." Black ecclesial queering is not a new enterprise. It continues a type of historic Black church tradition that is focused on being transgressive and unapologetically Black. Black ecclesial queering compels Black congregations to reimagine their exclusivist theologies, their incestuous institutional preoccupation with whiteness, and its inequitable practices of Christian empire. This chapter argues that Black ecclesial queering is already happening. This last argument in this chapter serves as an introduction to the ethogenic data on queered Black churches presented in chapters 3 and 4.

What Is Queering?

Since the US Supreme Court ruling legalizing same-sex marriage in 2015, the concept of queerness has become popularized by the mainstream media and marketed by corporations as a vogue and chic utility for profit. The hypothetical and performative queering of corporate America and the American public has been less about true queering and more about the performance and maintenance of some resemblance of diversity, belonging, and inclusion. These catchphrases, which have been formulated into positions, titles, and entire departments, have been huge buzzwords within American public discourse since the mid-1990s. Many diversity, equity, and inclusion (DEI) employees and managers are expected to queer their contexts through event planning, which can often come off as nonsubversive acts of performative allyship. In the American public square, performative queering can best be seen in the tokenization of living LGBTQIAP+ figures, the erection of Queer statues of sages like Marsha P. Johnson in New York's Christopher Park across from the Stonewall Inn, and shows like POSE and the series Legendary. These are all forms of performative societal queering that increase LGBTQIAP+ visibility while often exploiting Queer persons. The powerfully transformative and subversive artistry of Black Queer underworlds have become marketable because of their undeniable grip on cultures globally.

However, despite the newfound visibility of Black Queer culture, the heteronormative and racists tenets of American society and corporate America continue to prevail against Black Queer folk. Hosting corporate Pride celebrations, sponsoring Pride floats, and acknowledging homonormative LGBTQIAP+ persons are not examples of queering. The aforementioned scenarios are examples of the hetero-appropriation of Queer culture, a phenomenon that frequently results in the erasure of the authentic Queer essence inherent in the appropriated cultural practices. The heterosexual celebration of queerness during Pride should not be the means or the ends of queering but an annual recommitment to a corporate, organizational, or governmental commitment to true equity. The heterosexual celebration of queerness without a subversive education is merely a license to practice performative and nontransformational allyship. Corporate and governmental Pride celebrations should only happen after extensive training and intense dialogues on the historically toxic effects of heteronormativity within the American societal and corporate landscapes. Corporate, organizational, and governmental queering processes should expose persons to the narratives of LGBTQIAP+ persons while working to collectively agree upon a set of principles and moral guidelines that will be used to subvert the culture of heteronormativity, sexism, racism, xenophobia, ableism, and inappropriate religiosity in public and corporate spaces. Then and only then should organizations and public institutions celebrate Pride, Black History Month, Women's History Month, Transgender Awareness Day, or the International Day of Persons with Disabilities (IDPD). Performative queering does not qualify as a productive or genuine form of queering. Queering is a subversive praxis that challenges norms and systems rather than merely adopting a performative allyship.

For the context of this book, we must consider the following questions: How can Black churches reimagine the rhetorical devices that have been used heteronormatively to condemn Black Queer persons for decades? How can Black churches reimagine Scripture as a basis of compassion for Black Queer persons who have been traditionally harmed by fundamentalists' methods of biblical interpretation? How can Black Christians reconfigure queerness as a nonpathological identity that emphasizes compassion and relationship as opposed to loathsome affection and degenerate promiscuity? If E. L. Kornegay Jr. is right in his assertion that queering is the answer to Black theological homophobia, how can a Black church queer itself, what does it mean to queer a Black church especially considering the fact that Kornegay believes that anything that is Black is already queer. So and why is it important?[6] It is important because queering, in Black ecclesial contexts is a calling of the Black church back to its innate queerness, its Blackness.[7] Queering normalizes LGBTQIAP+ folk and queering is, as Kornegay argues, a method or system for normalizing blackness. The status quo has purged Black churches of their Blackness and innate queerness. But without its innate Queerness Blackness cannot be Black.[8] In his book *Radical Love: An Introduction to Queer Theology*, Patrick Cheng defines the process of queering as follows:

> To "Queer" something is to engage with a methodology that challenges and disrupts the status quo. Like the function of the court jester or the subversive traditions of Mardi Gras, to "Queer" something is to turn convention and authority on its head. It is about seeing things in a different light and reclaiming voices and sources that previously had been ignored, silenced, or discarded. It is proudly asserting a worldview for which LGBTQIA+ people have been historically taunted, condemned, beaten, tortured, and killed.[9]

Cheng contends that the enterprise of queering Christian theology is important because it intentionally challenges and unsettles the conventional and authoritative norms of the status quo. The queering of Christian theology winnows heteronormativity out of the gospel by redefining what it means to be a whole person reflecting on the cultural and theological oppression of Queer persons and calling into question the hegemonic institutional structures of the Christian enterprise. Christian theological queering is an imaginative process that erases boundaries and creates new languages, ideas, and frames of reference that are nonbinary and subversive.[10] The act of Christian queering also obliges the queerer to thoroughly understand the institution's heteronormative history and culture, and its oppressive theological ideologies that need to be subverted. This type of historical understanding is crucial because it aids the queerer to most effectively disrupt and challenge the status quo in a way that helps the Queer person to destabilize and reexamine heteronormative interpretations of texts, stories, and institutional notions of normalcy.[11] This is why I began this book with a chapter that serves as a thick description of the history of heteronormativity in Black congregations and culture. To queer Christian theology is to assert a Queer worldview that turns the Christian notion of decency and the politics of respectability on their heads. Queering creates brave spaces for persons to freely see things in a different light and listen to marginalized voices and sources that have been ignored, silenced, and discarded.

Practical theological queering begins with what Don Browning describes as the enterprise of deep descriptive theologizing. Practical theological queering commences with an examination of the lived experiences, histories, sacred texts, interpretive traditions, rituals, and faith symbols of a heteronormative Christian community that is governed by a homophobic Christian praxis. Therefore, when people endeavor to queer Christian theology, they must begin their enterprise of queering with Browning's first movement, descriptive theology. Furthermore, similar to Browning, who contends that practical theology can lead to social and personal transformation, Cheng argues that the queering of Christian theology endeavors to challenge and deconstruct categorical binaries with radical love to establish a more fluid and malleable understanding of gender and sexual identity.[12] He also argues that Christian theology itself is an innately Queer enterprise.

In *A Queering of Black Theology* E. L. Kornegay Jr. describes queerness or the process of queering as that which does not derive from "an overarching Queer subjectivity" that solely benefits and represents homosexual persons.[13] For Kornegay, queering is not an exclusively LGBTQIAP+ enterprise. Rather, it is concerned about the liberation of all persons who have been marginalized due to racism, gender constructs, othering, and social inequities. Any movement or reconstruction of Christian theology that challenges heteropatriarchal privilege, questions the use of traditional whitewashed Christian sources, or fosters theological discourse that disrupts the norm is an example of queering. Hence, Horace Griffin argues that Christian reformers like Martin Luther, Richard Allen, Martin Luther King Jr., and Jarena Lee are examples of persons who arguably queered the hegemonic and oppressive structures of White American Christianity.[14] Therefore, I assert that the process of queering Christian theology and its churches is a profoundly Black Christian undertaking.

Queering Ain't New: A History of Black Christian Queering

The idea that queering is a profoundly Black Christian undertaking forces us to wonder if Christian queering is a reinvention of the Christian faith or a retrieval of ancient Christian insights—or both? Kornegay argues that queering can be categorized as a movement or reconstruction of Christian theology that challenges heteropatriarchal privilege, racism, gender constructs, othering, and social inequities. One example of queering is Richard Allen, one of founders of the African Methodist Episcopal denomination. The founding of African Methodism exemplifies how Christian queering reinvents and retrieves the ancient insights of the Christian faith while re-creating and refashioning a new world of meaning. When Richard Allen left St. George's Methodist Church because of its racial discrimination against Black bodies, he reinvented and reconfigured Christian Methodist theology by arguing that individuals' access to grace and their right to worship and pray to God should not be predicated upon their race. Allen's assertions drastically reinvented and challenged the landscape of American religious and racial structures. According to Anthony G. Reddie, Professor of Black Theology, University of Oxford,

> In the United States, Christian ministers and activists such as Richard Allen used Christian teachings and a nascent Black existential theology to respond to the need for Black subjectivity. Henry McNeal Turner, a descendant of Allen in the A.M.E. church, began to construct a clear African-centered conception of the Christian faith, arguing that aligning with Africa should become a primary goal for Black Americans. This focus on African ancestry would enable subjugated objects of Euro-American racism to find a suitable terrain for the subversive activism that would ultimately lead to the steady path for political, social, cultural, and economic liberation and transformation.[15]

For the white racist Methodists at St. George's Church, Mother Bethel AME Church emerged as a new Christian enterprise that challenged the social inequity of America's racialized culture. Furthermore, not only did Richard Allen reinvent

Methodist ecclesiology, he also retrieved, reconfigured, and reinvented the ancient insights of the white Christian faith. For example, Horace Griffin argues that Richard Allen hinged the reinvention of Christian Methodism on retrieving the ancient Christian insight that Jesus Christ himself crossed social barriers and eschewed exclusionary laws rooted in religious culturism.[16] Likewise, when Queer activist Troy Perry queered white American Christian ecclesiology by founding the first Christian denomination for gay persons, the Metropolitan Community Church (MCC), he essentially reinvented the Christian church by developing a reimagined religious consciousness that acknowledged the spiritual, social, and religious needs of LGBTQIAP+ folk.[17] Perry's reinvention, much like Allen's, hinged on the retrieval of the ancient Christian insight of radical hospitality. Therefore, in the context of queering Christian theology, queering should not singularly focus on reinvention without rescue. This is what Chang means when he argues that the act of Christian queering obliges the queerer to copiously understand the histories, cultures, and theological ideologies of the institution or methodology to retrieve or rescue and call Christianity back to its original insights rooted in love, radical hospitality, and liberation.[18]

According to Kornegay, the inability of Black churches to render love, liberation, and salvation to all persons despite their sexual desires directly contradicts the original missions of Black churches. This is why many Black churches are grappling with contradictions, navigating the tension between conflicting claims of freedom and liberation on the one hand and a historical backdrop marked by gender-based violence and discrimination based on sexual orientation on the other. Kornegay argues that faced with the irreconcilability of religiously sanctioned liberation and oppression, along with the Black Christian responsibility to adhere to a history meant to "keep" Queer folk "in place," Black Queer individuals, as did James Baldwin, are choosing to disassociate themselves from Black churches.[19] He argues that the church has essentially thrown away James Cone's "God of the oppressed" and replaced it with a "god who oppresses."[20] For Kornegay, this sort of replacement is sinful because in stands in stark opposition to Cone's original intent. Kornegay contends,

> By annexing the systematic approaches of European theologians like Barth and Tillich, James Cone queers black theology into existence. This annexation (as I outlined) allows him to address his concerns surrounding the inequities caused by the mismatches created by the social construction of race/racism and remain unapologetically Christian. This is what I think makes black theology queer by definition.[21]

For this reason, a Black church that harbors fear and hatred of the effeminate or butch others cannot at the same time offer safety and liberation for all.[22] Kornegay offers that the enterprise of queering Black theology requires the queerer to reinvent the sacredness of the body and sexual desire as good and holy by retrieving the ancient insights of the Christian faith that command us to love ourselves and other selves equally. He describes the reinvention and retrieval process of queering Christian theology as God's call for the church to be the incarnational site of love, affirmation, growth, maturation, and liberation where "the closet door of sexuality is swung wide open, and all are welcome."[23] In his literary analysis, Kornegay also argues that James Baldwin is a perfect theoretical example of how the reinvention and retrieval process of queering Black theology redeems Black churches of their hypocritical white evangelical ideology of puritanical terror. Therefore, for Black Queer persons, the queering of Black theology is not just a process of reinventing and retrieving but also a method of reclaiming the Christianity that rightfully belongs to Black Queer persons.

Christian Theology's Contribution to Queer Theorizing and Queer Theorizing's Contribution to Christian Theology

In a similar vein, Dawne Moon characterizes Queer theory as an endeavor that delineates how sexuality influences societies. She describes it as a process of restructuring principles and subverting hegemonic structures.[24] Queer theory challenges the normative understanding of identity and questions heterosexual privilege. From Moon's point of view, Christian theology contributes to the ongoing development of Queer theorizing for Queer-identified Christian persons; *and* Queer theorizing in equal measure contributes to the continuing development and expansion of Christian theology as a whole. Therefore, if Christianity is to be more inclusive of Queer persons, Christian theology must prayerfully engage the perspectives of Queer theory to most successfully challenge the systems of cultural homophobia in the Christian faith. In this light, Christian theology should not only contribute to but also employ Queer theories to begin the self-reflexive, creative, and research-oriented enterprise of queering the minds and hearts of people within churches.

To answer how Christian theology and Queer theory mutually benefit from and contribute to each other, I turn once again to Kornegay's *A Queering of Black Theology.* Kornegay argues that Queer theories and theorists such as James Baldwin unearth the ideologies of racial rage and sexual phobias that exist in Christian theology.[25] In Kornegay's view, Queer theory forces Christian (Black) theology to acknowledge the codes of race, sexuality, gender, hegemony, rigid heterosexist identity, and indoctrinated hatred that has laced its creeds, doctrines, and ideologies since the Constantinian period.

Furthermore, Queer theory reveals, just as Michel Foucault argues, that contrary to popular belief, Christianity did not invent a code of sexual ethics.[26] Foucault further shows how Queer theory helps Christian theology to understand that sexual norms are not transmitted from God but through religious, familial, cultural, institutional, and educational discourse. Foucault contends that sexual discourse within religions and theologies regulates proper and improper conduct, licit and illicit behavior, and produces and reinforces power.[27]

What Is Black Ecclesial Queering?

In this study, "Black ecclesial queering" refers to a specific type of prophetic action that only emerges at the intersection of Black ecclesial, Black theological, Black sociological, and Black sexual discourses on oppression and liberation. Black ecclesial queering seeks to employ the disciplines of Black theology, Black ecclesiology, and Black Queer theory as praxis. Namely, Black ecclesial queering utilizes Patricia Collins's Black sexual politics and Kelly Brown Douglas's Black sexual discourses of resistance as tools to cultivate brave spaces for transparent and inclusive sexual dialogues in Black churches.[28] Black ecclesial queering must always be understood, first and foremost, as that which disrupts oppressive forms of ecclesial and theological normality within Black churches. The term oppressive in the definition above is important because Black ecclesial queering should never be interpreted or implemented as a subversion of all that is or has been. Instead, Black ecclesial queering is only focused on queering and subverting the oppressive components of ecclesial and theological normality within Black churches.

This distinction is quite important when considering that most Black homophobia is rooted in fear of Queer persons turning everything and everybody "gay." Black ecclesial queering is not a quest to turn every person in the Black church gay. Queering recognizes and honors the full diversity of humanity. Hence, it is not a quest to inappropriately introduce children or youth to sexual actions or molestation. Finally, Black ecclesial queering is not an attempt by Black gay men to effeminize the Black church. Instead, Black ecclesial queering is a new Black quest for civility that, unlike the Abyssinian Church's homophobic quest for civility, seeks respect for all Black folk. Black ecclesial queering also strives prophetically to hold Black churches accountable to the liberative praxis embedded within their ecclesial heritage. According to Dale Andrews, any remodeling, or what I refer to as Black ecclesial queering, of Black ecclesiologies must first bridge the divide between the refuge and liberation functions of Black churches.[29] Therefore, Black ecclesial queering is an attempt to reclaim the liberating aspects of Black ecclesiologies while also extending the invitation for refuge to once-excluded Black Queer persons.

Discovering a Call to Queer in Dale Andrews's Refuge-versus-Prophetic Dichotomy

In *Practical Theology for Black Churches: Bridging Black Theology and African American Folk Religion,* Dale Andrews contends that the present divide between the Black church and Black theology is the result of the inability of either entity to understand that the terms "liberation" and "sanctification" are indivisibly linked for battered Black bodies. Many Black theologians fail to see how sanctification, religious piety, and self-fulfillment through the paths of personal devotion were, in fact, a form of protest for many battered Black religious bodies. Andrews describes this phenomenon as the "refuge function" of the Black church.[30] He contends that the Black church became a place of refuge and peace for African Americans to use religious practices to protest the white notion of Black inferiority without the fear of torture or death.[31]

Andrews describes the refuge image of the Black church's ecclesiology as a practical intervention that may have started with personal spirituality but led to the formation and institutionalization of Black denominations, Black sources of social welfare, the education of Blacks, and a style of Black preaching that used pastoral care to empower people to overcome personal sin and the oppressive ills of society.[32] Andrews argues that although the Black church had lost its militant edge by the turn of the twentieth century, its turn toward a more personal spirituality was a way of making empowerment more practical and accessible to the average Black person. He reasons that although the militancy of the pre–Civil War Black church brought about the emancipation and the civil liberties of African Americans, it did not make civil power accessible to Black people.[33]

Andrews argues that the Black church's turn toward personal spirituality and collective "refuge" was not in opposition to, but a part of, the Black quest for liberation and the Black prophetic. Therefore, Andrews contends that Black theology's inability to see the refuge function of the Black church as a quest for freedom reveals a significant misdiagnosis on the part of Black theology that must be corrected. Andrews describes this misdiagnosis as the single most crucial mistake in the entire field.[34] He offers that Black theology's underestimation and adversarial disregard for Black religious life limit its ability to redefine the Black church because it is neither in dialogue nor standing in solidarity with the Black church.[35]

According to Andrews, Black theology's primary challenge is to be found within its resistance to repositioning itself as a discipline whose impetus is a Black religious experience.[36] He argues that the new starting point for Black theology must be Black folk religion because it is the only way to shrink the gulf between the Black church's tradition of pastoral spirituality and Black theology's prophetic campaign for wholeness and freedom. Andrews's admonishment to Black theology is a perfect example of what it means to do practical theology. Andrews makes clear that the only way for Black theology to fulfill its prophetic call is to ground its theologizing in the methodology of practical theology. He posits that Black theologians should always begin their theologizing with a thorough investigation of praxis within Black ecclesial settings. Andrews also contends that Black theology's obsession with non-Black understandings of liberation, Eurocentric theology, the Black Power movement, and apologetics has caused it to ignore the substance that lies within the lived experiences of Black religious persons.

Andrews further offers that Black theology's resistance to examining Black religious experience is rooted in its claim that pre–Civil War Black churches saw liberation as the fundamental tenet of the Christian gospel. In contrast, the post-Reconstruction Black church subscribed to a more "otherworldly" understanding of the gospel. Because of this claim, Black theology has typically confined itself as a field to only theologizing about the pre–Civil War Black church, thereby ignoring the lived experiences of Black religious folklife in the present. Additionally, many Black theologians have engendered adversarial relationships with post-Reconstruction Black churches because they believe that they have abandoned their ecclesial understanding of protest, gravitating toward a more escapist ecclesiology that focuses on personal devotion, religious piety, personal sin, and religious emotionalism. The primary ecclesiological issue within Andrews's articulation of the relationship between the Black church and Black theology is the question of the nature and mission of the Black church. According to Andrews's argument, the post-Reconstruction Black church views its nature and mission as a place where personal devotion, sanctification, emotionalism, individual piety, practical empowerment, the education of the Black masses, and the preaching of healing and self-fulfillment through the gospel of Jesus Christ are a part of the overall Black pursuit for liberation.

On the other hand, Andrews argues that Black theologians understand the nature and mission of the Black church to be a place where prophetic teaching and preaching are mandatory, liberation is the essential message of the gospel, disobedient protest is the only mode of rising above racial discrimination, and the aggressiveness of the Black Power movement serves as the primary sociopolitical tactic for the freedom and wholeness of Black persons.[37] Andrews suggests that Black theology's survival hinges on its ability to readdress Black theology to Black churches by redirecting its methodology. This is what the queering of Black churches must look like. The queering of Black churches is a form of prophetic teaching and preaching where liberation is the essential message of the gospel. Queering Black churches is a form of Black prophetic protest that transgresses against and rises above the Black Christian tradition of heteronormativity as a sociopolitical tactic of freedom and Black wholeness.[38] The queering of Black churches is the reinvigoration of the lost Black ecclesial prophetic dimension that centers the lived experiences of Black folk on the margins of the Black ecclesial frontier.

Like Andrews, James Cone maintains that Black churches should strive for a more prophetic ecclesiology. In *Black Theology and Black Power*, Cone defines the church as a people who are called into being by the love of God to do revolutionary acts to liberate humanity. The church, for him, is where Christ is, and Christ is only present with the hurting and the oppressed. If the church is to be the church, then the church must, like Christ, identify and become one of the oppressed.[39] Hence, Cone reasons that the only way for the white church to be the church is for the white church to become Black. Cone's Black ecclesiology is rooted in the ideas that hope for freedom, liberation from white supremacy, and a Christian hermeneutic of suspicion make up the nature and mission of the Black church. Cone is a perfect example of a Black theologian's understanding of Black ecclesiology. Notably, Cone began his work during the civil unrest of the late 1960s. Cone merged Black power with Black theology in the same way Dale Andrews hinged his Black practical theology on the fringed relationship between Black folk religion / Black churches and Black theology.

Black ecclesial queering uses Black theology, Queer theology, and Black Womanist theology to constructively respond to the desires of some Black Queer Christians to be affirmed by their ecclesial homes. Many Black Queer persons no longer need Black churches because they have found meaningful community in other ways. Still, there are Black Queer persons who have left Black churches and they want to come home, but they are afraid to because ecclesial affirmation is not prevalent in American Black churches.

Just as enslaved Black folk depended on the bravery of white supporters of the Underground Railroad to risk their privilege to affirm their humanity by welcoming them, many Black Queer Christians need more Black churches to practice ecclesial courage to welcome and affirm them before they will return home. This would require the dismantling of "manhood Christianity." Cisgender and heteronormative understandings of manhood Christianity have a long history in Black churches and still exist in many Black churches today. According to Paris,

> The early records of many of the Black church conventions and conferences refer frequently to their "manhood Christianity" because the experience of slavery and subordination raised in most Blacks themselves doubts that they had the capacity to form and maintain institutions and to exercise the normal functions of citizenship and social responsibility.[40]

This type of hypermasculinity, which was best seen in the pastoral performativity of Black machoism in the late bishop Eddie Lee Long in Atlanta, is what Jonathan Walton describes as that which fosters and undergirds a "homophobic valley of dry bones" in Black churches.[41] Manhood Christianity promotes a type of hypermasculinity that is extremely toxic and oppressive for Queer and transgender persons, robbing them of the opportunity to feel safe in the communities where they seek to be pastorally cared for as whole persons. For this reason, many Black Queer and Transgender persons leave the Black churches they love. This is a moral problem and mental mental health crisis becausemany Black Queer and transgender Christians in exile need communities of refuge for their mental health and well-being. The souls of Queer folk who long to worship in churches need heterosexual Christians to answer the call of God to critique and challenge the deep-seated heteronormative Christian beliefs, systems, doctrines, and theologies that have often characterized Black churches. Griffin argues that pastoral care and the Christian community are vitally important for the sexual and psychological healing of Black Queer persons.[42] Exiled Black Queer Christian persons could also benefit from the soothing sounds, moans, and cadences of the Black ecclesial as-if world. While Du Bois called it the "frenzy" and Dale Andrews referred to it as the "otherworldliness" of Black churches, I describe empathic and emotional Black worship as the "as-if world" of Black ecclesiology.[43] On the surface level, a person may find the expressiveness of the as-if world of the Black church to be excessive and nonsensical. When this dramatic quality is examined deeper, one may see an undeniable sense of theodical meaning-making during these worship services that supersedes the theatricality of the worship genre. The as-if world of Black ecclesiology creates what Puett calls an as-if world that aims to provide hope for its hopeless partakers.[44] African Americans have been marginalized and disenfranchised for centuries. Nevertheless, their indignation and frustration were often filtered through their faith in God. The pain-influenced theodicies of Black ecclesiologies inclined them to form an expressive worship style to channel their social and economic hardship.

The as-if character of Black ecclesiology "builds a world that, for brief moments, creates pockets of order, joy, and inspiration." It constructs an imaginative world where personal emancipation and eternal peace are conceptualized as if they were attainable in one's present reality. For the oppressed ears of Black Christian Queer persons born in Black churches, the soothing soundscapes of a Black church in which they are loved and welcomed can cause them, in Bennett's non–Black church terms, to be figuratively and "simultaneously transfixed in wonder and transported by sense and caught up and carried away."[45] This can be seen in joyful moments when the energy of Black worship leads worshippers into what W. E. B. Du Bois calls the frenzy. This is what Jane Bennett would call "magical refrains," or "meditative and worshipful trances," or "spell casting sounds."[46] Although their reaction may seem strange to outsiders, in their world of homophobic rejection, this radical expressiveness or enchantment becomes somewhat of an escape from their everyday troubles. During these worship services, the as-if world of Black churches allows Black Queer Christians to exchange their hypothetical inadequacies and pain for tranquility and acceptance as if those were realities outside of the church. While many may consider this to be a false hope because it does not change the heteronormative context outside of the church, this is where the refuge ideology of the Black church ends, and the prophetic begins.

According to Paris, the Black church was created to provide a non-racist refuge for all battered Black bodies, which was an undoubtedly subversive phenomenon in nineteenth-century white American slave culture. Hence, the primary duty of Black ecclesiologists is to remind Black churches of their original purposes and prophetic callings, emphasizing the need to reaffirm their foundational mission. This foundational mission is what Peter Paris describes as "the equality of all persons under God regardless of race or any other natural quality. This doctrine has been the essence of the Black Christian tradition and the most fundamental requirement of its churches."[47] For this reason, instead of creating another separatist-meaning-making imagery, many Black Queer Christians would rather call upon Black churches to be its inherently Queer self and queer that which resembles oppression and whiteness within its ranks. The truth is, Black churches can become surrogate spaces of safety, converted wildernesses, and spaces of transcendent meaning-making for Black Queer persons. Paris argues that "the Black Christian tradition stands in opposition to the Western Christian tradition."[48] Here Paris is asserting that Black churches must first be characterized by their anthropological principle and indistinguishable pursuit of equality, freedom, and justice for all Black persons. He contends that "although Blacks are guilty of oppressing other Blacks, the churches generally give their attention to the fact that all Blacks are oppressed by the greater force of white racism, which is considered the greater evil and possibly the source of all sin."[49] Black heteronomativity and Black homophobia, which I often use interchagebly, are forms of Black oppressing other Blacks white Christian tactics.

This brings us to the question: W, what is the source of Black homophobia? Are Black people the source of the Black heteronormative perspectives, or is it just a symptom of the overarching structures of American racism? If Paris's assertion that the empirical African American referent for the doctrine of sin is white racism;, and if the empirical African American referent for the doctrine of virtue is Black resistance to white oppression by Black people and Black institutions, then Black ecclesial homophobia is best understood as a Black ecclesial praxis responding to white theological oppression.[50] This is why Black ecclesial queering is as a purging of the white ecclesial sin of oppression with the virtue of prophetic Black resistance.[51]

Black ecclesial queering is also explicitly focused on embracing, acknowledging, and theologizing the experiences of Black Queer bodies that the church often ignores. According to Anthony Pinn, "Poor attention to bodies has produced bad church policies and practices that literally and figuratively kill African Americans."[52] Lee Butler also insists that Black people will never "be able to restore our [their] full humanity if we [they] maintain this split" where "the body has frequently been identified as what is bad."[53] In other words, Black churches must retrospectively reclaim and dismantle the separation of body, spirituality, and sexuality. This transformation is needed in Black churches if Black Christians wish to become "wholly (holy) human."[54] The pursuit of sexual and spiritual wholeness is a significant aspect of the Black Queer Christian's life journey.

Expanding and Reimaging the Pre-Reconstruction Black Church Image of Refuge

In 2012 constructive theologian and Black religious scholar Keri Day published *Unfinished Business: Black Women, the Black Church, and the Struggle to Thrive in America*. In her book, Day calls upon Black churches to address the unequal economic structures that hold poor Black women captive to unemployment, underemployment, isolation, and economic disadvantages.[55] Day also acknowledges that it would be inaccurate to describe all Black churches as prophetic communities that denounce and critique structural oppression and injustices. She contends that Black churches were understood as sites of prophetic declaration and hope for political and spiritual freedom prior to Reconstruction. However, as Reconstruction's policies were implemented, many Blacks wondered if the cultural heritage of the Black church, which was tainted with the remnants of enslavement, could remedy the structural evils of American society. Day asserts that prominent Black academicians like W. E. B. Du Bois, Fannie Williams, Carter G. Woodson, and Nannie Helen Boroughs "settled on a consensus that the Negro Church was a failed institution that had plunged into political irrelevancy by the end of the Reconstruction period."[56] However, Day argues that other Black scholars challenged the prevailing popular perception of the Black church's demise. These scholars not only discussed how to reform Black churches, but Du Bois and Boroughs eventually agreed with them that the Black church as a vehicle for "socioeconomic and political liberation for Black communities could work collaboratively with more central political and economic institutions within Black communities, such as Black banks, Black unions, and so on."[57] Day argues that the Black church is more complex and problematic than it is prophetic. However, for Day, the complexity of the efficacy and prophetic relevancy of Black churches raises questions about whether or not Black churches should be seen as solely responsible for dealing with the modern social ills of Black communities.

In chapter 1, Day poses a fundamental question: is the Black church "home" for poor Black women? As a result of the Black church's history of overt sexism, "Some womanist scholars see the Black church as deeply oppressive for poor Black women."[58] Day poses the same question for poor Black women that I am raising for Black Queer persons. Is the Black church "home" for Black Queer persons? Day calls for the Black church to address the social issue of sexism in America. However, the question arises: Did the establishing members of early Black churches have the inclusion of women in mind when they created the Black church as a nonracist "refuge" for Black bodies? The direct answer is no. Day agrees with scholars such as African American ethicist Peter Paris. According to Day,

> While Paris is undoubtedly correct to describe the Black churches of the late nineteenth century as surrogate worlds that provided a sense of refuge for oppressed Blacks, many Black Queer persons do not feel safe or understood within modern Black churches. I question whether the Black church as a surrogate world remains an accurate metaphor for how some Black folk experience Black churches today.[59]

To respond to the tensions and ambiguities of the mission of Black churches, Day depicts a new image of the Black church that expands and builds upon Black ecclesial history with accuracy and integrity while simultaneously addressing the circumstances of Black female existence in the twenty-first century. She argues that some Black women view the Black church as a community of transcendence: "For them, the Black church is less about being a surrogate world or wilderness and more about how its context enables them to be hopeful despite the contradictions they experience within and without these institutions."[60] Day expands the mission and meaning of Black churches while acknowledging the historical situatedness of the institution emphasized by Paris. Day defines the transcendent image of the Black church as the quintessential element of Black ecclesiology that enables and ecclesiologically empowers persons to act as agents and make new meaning "despite debilitating, inhumane socioeconomic conditions."[61] Day offers that Black ecclesial thought must make room for different and new religious interpretations of God and church to remain alive and relevant.

Up to this point, I have posited that the distinctive ecclesiology of Black churches centers on their nonracist refuge orientation as brave spaces for weary Black bodies. However, much like Day's argument, this historical distinction stands in stark opposition to the current theory-laden practices of sexism, classism, colorism, elitism, homophobia, and transphobia in many twenty-first-century Black churches. The nonracist orientation of Black churches lends itself to two different interpretations. The first is that Black churches began as nonracist institutions, but this has no bearing on the nature, mission, or modern social responsibilities of Black churches in the twenty-first century. In other words, the nonracist history of Black churches is solely a historical fact about racism and is therefore inexpansible. By inexpansible, I mean that the historical distinction of Black ecclesiology is restricted from any forms of theological amplification or prophetic gleaning of the general nature and mission of Black ecclesial settings in the evolving future.

The second possibility, the one undergirding this book, is that we interpret the nonracist distinctiveness of Black churches as an indication of an ongoing mandate of Black churches to continue being brave, nonexclusive spaces for all Black folk. By nonexclusive, I do not mean that the Black church was not or should not be solely populated by Black people. Instead, I use this word to maintain that all types of Black bodies were and should be welcomed into Black churches without any form of Black-on-Black exclusivism. This second interpretation enables Black churches to interrogate the tradition and history of Black ecclesiologies to expound upon them in ways that may have been foreign to the enslaved themselves.

However, an alternative argument about the implicit nature of Black ecclesiologies problematizes my previous Queer reasonings. For example, Black churches that were created as nonracist institutions during slavery never had the inclusivity or exclusivity of Black Queer persons in mind. Therefore, the assertion that *because Black ecclesiologies were founded as nonracist institutions of social uplift for Black bodies traumatized by white hands, Black churches should be the leading citadels of hope for Black Queer persons* could be interpreted as historically incorrect. Many Black religious historians might, for that reason, consider my Queer expansion of the nonracist orientation of Black churches to be an ahistorical reading of Black ecclesiology. While my deductions are based on the actual historical distinctions of Black churches, they intentionally disrupt the conventional race-oriented images of Black ecclesial history as solely racial and nonexpansive. My conclusions could be described as a Black Queer stretching of the Black ecclesial narrative that promotes false ideas about pre-Reconstruction Black churches and how they were composed. It is true that enslaved Africans may have never envisioned queering as a futuristic extension of their nonracist ecclesiologies.

Additionally, during slavery, the concept of Black ecclesial homophobia and the categorizing of persons as LGBTQIAP+ were nonexistent. However, in the pre-Reconstruction Black churches founded by and led by enslaved persons, homosexuality was also never identified as something that prevented one from being part of an early Black church. The sexual identities, orientations, or interests of the enslaved were no doubt varied, but such would have been undiscussable. However, such undiscussablity should not be misconstrued as an indication of the nonexistence or impossibility of Black Queer enslaved folk. The possibility and probability of Black Queer enslaved folk, despite the gaps in archival evidence, is a logical and conceivable proposition when considered through the prism of Alfred Kinsey's human percentages claims.

Additionally, it could be argued that early Black churches were filled with enslaved persons whose physical bodies had experienced or been used for a myriad of intense, traumatic sexual abuse scenarios and consensual enslaved pleasure.

The fact that the bodies of enslaved Black folk belonged to their masters created a toxic ecology of secrecy about sex. Few enslaved Black folk openly spoke about the sexual aspects of their ownership or identities. They were taught to comply with every white sexual advance, regardless of gender. Hence, early Black churches were filled with enslaved Black folk whose bodies had experienced numerous types of sexual engagements and traumas.

These reflections are not an attempt to superimpose sexual identities onto the enslaved members of early Black churches. Instead, I shared these reflections to expose the innately welcoming and affirming nature of early Black churches as true citadels for all types of battered Black souls and bodies, even those eclipsed by history because of secrecy. Early Black churches were spaces where all enslaved Black folk could find spiritual care amid objectification and white terrorism. Such an expansion of the Black ecclesial narrative helps us to see pre-reconstruction Black churches as innately nonracist spaces that predate the innate whiteness of Black Christian homophobia and heteronormativity. With these expansive understandings, it becomes easier to make a case for the connection between the historical image of the Black church as a refuge and the actualization of the Black church as a refuge for Black Queer persons in the current era. Suppose Black ecclesial spaces were indeed founded as nonracist institutions of social uplift for Black bodies traumatized by white hands. In that case, Black churches should be the leading citadels of hope for Black Queer persons whose oppression also finds its rootage in white terrorism.

It's Happening Elsewhere: Father John J. McNeill, Queering in the Catholic Church

In *Justice, the Church and the Homosexual*, Father John J. McNeill discusses the injustices, persecutions, and suffering of homosexual Christians in the Catholic Church. In the concluding chapter of his book, McNeill uses the 1971 International Synod of Catholic Bishops' statement on justice to prove that Catholic gays and lesbians deserve ecclesial justice. His book offers several practical and responsible solutions to the dilemmas faced by homosexuals who decided to remain in the church despite the homophobic theologies that drove many away from Catholicism. Father McNeill demands the recognition of the dignity and rights of one's othered neighbor. The fact that homosexual Catholics are denied admittance into the "Holy Catholic Church" or the "communion of saints" reveals that "they have been deprived of their rights as a condition for their continued association with the Church. Among these rights are the right of association and the right to be heard in decisions which affect their lives."[62] Father McNeill argues that the church's attitude toward homosexuality is an example of what he describes as "a structured social injustice." He perceives structured social injustices as moral viewpoints and operational attitudes based on the interpretation of Scripture, prejudice, and blind adherence to human traditions. He contends that most Catholics and Christians are

> inclined to see "laws of nature and of God" in what are purely human creations. Consequently, Church members tend not to accept responsibility for the social structures that embody and make operational attitudes of prejudice and blindness. The homosexual community is inclined to see the unconscious univocal heterosexual structuring of society precisely as a human creation mistakenly accepted as the law of nature and of God, which results in prejudice and blindness.[63]

According to McNeill, "The life of a Catholic homosexual is a constant negotiation of social structures, the ecclesiological oppression of human dignity, and the ecclesial maintenance of gross inequality."[64] He cites slavery and the inferiority of women as examples of structured social injustices that were once defended by social values, economic prosperity, and ecclesial reasoning. He says, however,

> Once the Church arrived at a clear consciousness that these supposed values were being maintained only by the perpetuation of essential injustice and disregard for the dignity and rights of certain of its members, it was obliged in conscience to reject these structures and do everything in its power to bring about a more just social order.[65]

For this reason, in the late 1970s Father McNeill called upon the Catholic Church to reject structured social injustice; overturn operational attitudes based on the interpretation of Scripture, prejudice, and the blind adherence to human traditions; and rethink its ecclesial segregation. Essentially, Father McNeill sought to queer Catholic ecclesiology. Although he never used the verb "queering" to describe his ecclesial challenge, his espoused methodology exemplified queering at its best. The most significant aspect of Father McNeill's proposal to queer Catholicism for the evolution of Black ecclesial queering is his recommendation to only queer an element of the church when the time is right and ripe for fruitful discussion. He argues that the first step toward ecclesial inclusivity is for the heterosexual Christian and the homosexual Christian to understand that the church needs to learn and not merely teach that what is required is sexual justice. By making this claim, he frees the church from needing to have all of the answers by opening up the possibility for the church to learn. Additionally, this first step prevents homosexuals from expecting more from their ecclesial setting than they can give, due to their ignorance about homosexual pastoral care.

Father McNeill's second step toward ecclesial inclusivity states that "homosexuals within the Church have an obligation, and therefore a right to organize and attempt to enter into dialogue with Church authorities."[66] Here, McNeill places the charge to begin the conversation in the hands of the Catholic homosexual. I have great difficulty adapting Father McNeil's theology of Queer suffering into my concept of Black queering. It is unethical for Black churches to obligate Black Queer persons to solely dismantle heteronormativity to the detriment of their mental and physical well-being.

Black Queer persons should not have to suffer to redeem the souls of Black churches. If Christ is the ultimate sacrificial lamb, Black Queer persons should never be obligated to organize or enter into retraumatizing toxic dialogues with homophobic religious authorities. McNeill's second step is a dated and flawed form of queering that should be avoided because it calls upon the Christian homosexual to take up their cross and face the possibility of ridicule and rejection.

Moreover, while he argues for heterosexual Catholic authorities to display a Christian demeanor of reflection, listening, dialogue, and prophetic action, the effectiveness of their Queer efforts would always be hinged on the questionable willingness of the empowered to hear or even address the sinful nature of heteronormativity. In light of McNeill's efforts to carefully and timely queer Catholic ecclesiology, it is vital to raise the following questions: When is a Black ecclesiology ripe for Black ecclesial queering? Who is responsible for beginning discussions about Black ecclesial queering? How should Black ecclesiologists and ecclesial spaces respond? Like McNeill's admonishment to the Catholic Church, the Black church cannot be seen as an authority or teacher but must instead take on the role of listener and learner, and Black Queer persons and members of Black churches need to be aware of such. Therefore, if a Black church is not ready to listen, learn, and hear, Black ecclesial queering will never be able to teach Black churches what is required of them in response to Queer injustice.

Second, Black Queer persons within Black ecclesial settings have a right to organize and dialogue with church authorities. Following McNeill's assertion, Black Queer persons should not only have the right to organize an effort to queer their Black ecclesiologies, but they are often the first persons to initiate and attempt the dialogue with Black churches. The Queer affirmation in the Black churches often rests on the shoulders of the Black Queer members of the body of Christ, but this is unfair. A Black ecclesiology is ripe for Black ecclesial queering when heteronormative members of Black churches are ready to listen, learn, and face their complicity in the system of heteronormativity. The cross of inclusion into the Black church rests on the shoulders of heterosexual allies, not "out" Black Queer members of the body of Christ. I speak more about this in chapter 5.

In light of my previous argument that Black Queer persons are not responsible for beginning the process of queering, I also wish to define Black ecclesial queering as a reclaiming and owning of Black churches by Black Queer persons. Black ecclesial queering calls upon Black churches to resist the homophobic temptation to turn a deaf ear to the wounds of Black Queer persons. Instead of hiding Black Queer persons or further wounding them with conversion therapy, traumatizing altar calls, homophobic sermons, or theologies that exclude them, Black ecclesial queering not only welcomes Black Queer persons into Black ecclesial spaces but also works to subvert all forms of heteronormativity and power that threaten the permanence of queering. Black ecclesial queering converts Black churches into inclusive affirmatoriums where sexual difference is nonexistent and power dynamics based on gender are subverted to establish gender equality. Much like Robert E. Shore-Goss's "Queering of the White Eucharistic table," Black ecclesial queering refers to a process of exposing the cultural, theological, and ecclesial boundaries around the sexual politics of Black churches. Black ecclesial queering intrudes upon heteronormative theology with Black queeruptions.[67] Queeruptions cultivate and curate spaces for healthy sexual discourse that excludes puritanicalism, heteronormativity, sexism, and power imbalances. Such exclusions aid Black ecclesial queering to strategically subvert, deconstruct, and reconstruct gender; what constitutes a Black family; and Black sexuality while eradicating all allegiances to respectability politics.

Essentially, Black ecclesial queering is a specific type of subversive discourse explicitly for Black churches. However, as a subversive discourse, Black ecclesial queering depends on the willingness of heteronormative and nonheteronormative Black Christians to come together and engage in dialogue. Subversive discourse only works when both parties are willing to have transparent and honest conversations over time. As long as heteronormative oppressors and the oppressed are trapped within the sociological closets that produced the oppression in the first place, any attempt at cross-communal dialogue will end unsuccessfully. Thus, if Black heteronormative and nonheteronormative Christians cannot agree on the basic fact that Black heteronormativity evolved out of the Black quest for civility, then Black ecclesial queering will never be successful.

Are Slave Religion and Black Ecclesiology Queered Forms of White Christianity?

According to Anthony Reddie and Albert Raboteau, the foremost spread of Christianity among enslaved Africans in the Americas occurred during the antebellum period.[68] At first, most of the enslaved attended worship services with their white owners or under the supervision of white missionaries. However, as time went on, many enslaved Africans conducted secret worship services in cabins, brush arbors, wooded areas, old barns, and other spaces undisclosed to their masters.[69] Raboteau argues that attendance at these "invisible institution" services was a huge risk because the enslaved could have been and often were beaten and severely punished for worshiping without white supervision and consent. Therefore, the first essential element of the Black church's historical development is the ecclesiological issue of protest and freedom versus obedience and scriptural literalism.

After the Great Awakening during the early eighteenth century, many enslaved persons sought to worship God in their own way.[70] They sought to publicly establish spaces where their Blackness could be normalized amid America's limiting structures of racism. The origins of Black churches are inextricably linked with the colonization of the United States, the trans-Atlantic slave trade of the seventeenth century, and the racist practices of white churches.[71] Similarly, Reddie argues that the varying ecclesiologies of the many Black churches in America were likewise birthed out of the struggles of Black people who were trying to survive the periods of slavery, Jim Crow, segregation, and overt Black marginalization. Black ecclesiologies evolved out of the Black existential experience of pain and grief.[72] Worship within Black churches was empowering and relieving for its Black participants—a place of healing and joy amid pain and grief.

The establishment of Black churches fostered a notion of Black resilience and self-awareness grounded in liberative concepts derived from the narrative of the exodus of the children of Israel. They believed that they, Black people, were God's chosen people awaiting their exodus from the white Christian American system of inequality and oppression. According to Reddie, this single extension of the exodus narrative historically distinguishes the Black church and its original ecclesiology as unmistakably Christian.[73] Therefore, Reddie argues that Black ecclesiologies' development should be seen as the means by which Blacks in America responded to their existential need to create a brave space to rehearse the rubrics of their Blackness and humanity. Black ecclesiology was established from "a determined and self-conscious attempt to create liminal spaces where the subjected and assaulted Black self could begin to contrast a notion of selfhood that extended beyond the limited structures of the objectified and absurd nothingness of fixed identities."[74] In other words, Black churches are Queer and prophetic alternative worlds of possibility where the discriminatory and racist practices of

Constantinian Christianity have been destabilized to heal and curate the intentional care of Black souls.[75]

The point here is that slave religion, which was characterized by what Albert J. Raboteau would describe as a syncretistic blending of West and Central African religious traditions with elements of Christianity, was itself a Queer formation of religion. Slave religion queered the White American Christianity forced upon the enslaved. Slave religion, which gave way to Black churches and many other Black religions, subverted and converted the blond-haired, blue-eyed white Christ into a Black Jesus who empathized with Black bodies instead of battering them with conversion for free labor.[76] According to James Cone, many enslavers only introduced their enslaved Black folk to Jesus to make them obedient and docile. Christ was initially used to subject Blacks to faithful servanthood.[77] However, despite their lack of formal theological training, enslaved Africans knew enough about the theology of Christianity to recognize the inconsistencies between the gospel and slavery. According to Peter Paris,

> Blacks not only perceived in the White churches a deliberate distortion of the Christian gospel, but they feared a loss of their own self-respect should they continue indefinitely in such association. Thus, from slavery through Reconstruction, Blacks resolved to find ways of separating themselves from the religious and moral corruption endemic in the White churches in order to gain a measure of independence wherein they might affirm their own humanity in the light of a non-racist appropriation of the Christian message.[78]

In *Slave Religion*, Albert J. Raboteau's documentation of the words of John Anderson, a formerly enslaved Black man, best exemplify Paris's assertion that enslaved Africans perceived the distortion of Christianity within white churches. According to Anderson,

> Some folks say slaveholders may be good Christians, but I can't and won't believe it, nor do I think that a slaveholder can get to heaven. He may possibly get there, I don't know, but though I wish to get there myself, I don't want to have anything more to do with slaveholders either here or in heaven.[79]

Anderson's and Paris's quotes exemplify enslaved queering. In the statement, John Anderson subverts the power dynamics of white Christianity by questioning the salvation of his white Christian owner, who more than likely introduced him to Christianity in the first place and the heteronormative world of white Christianity in which he existed. In other words, Anderson and enslaved Black folk of like minds could discern the ethical dissonance between Christianity and the behavior of white, slave-owning Christians. Slave religion's queered interpretation of what a Christian world could be deepened the faith of the enslaved and created for them a new world of Blackness and Black identity. These Black worlds of subversion created Black churches with Black ecclesiologies and Black theologies. The enslaved created their ecclesial setting, within which they employed a hermeneutic of suspicion based on their liberationist interpretations of the Exodus narrative. They chose the latter when it came to the ecclesiological issue of remaining obedient to their enslaver's religion or reenvisioning it for Black souls.

Child, Hush: The Black Church Ain't Queered Nothing

Early Black churches were not created as institutions to queer white churches. Black ecclesial structures were not established to do anything to the structures of whiteness. Enslaved individuals sought to create brave havens where they could worship and observe their own religions. Pre-Civil War Black churches and particularly slave religion(s) embodied distinctly Queer characteristics. It was Queer to create a Black nation within a nation that centered Black religious practices and the spiritual care of Black souls in the shadow of an empowered and oppressive white Christian nation. Nevertheless, the establishment of Black churches should not be misconstrued as an attempt to alter the inherently racist theologies, ecclesiologies, and ecclesial structures of white Christianity. The enslaved African choice to establish their own religious spaces was a response to the racial dynamics of the time rather than an effort to influence white churches to welcome the enslaved back into their white sanctuaries. Once the enslaved started worshiping in their own manner, the majority of them never looked back. Therefore, Black churches should never be interpreted as having an aim or mission to queer the racist ecclesiologies of white Christianity.

However, although Black churches were not created to queer white Christianity, Black ecclesial structures do exist as queered, nonracist inversions of white Christianity. The enslaved Africans encountered racism within white supremacist churches. Many were segregated and restricted to worship from a balcony, while white supremacist parishioners worshiped on the main floor. When the enslaved started their own religious spaces, most were founded as Christian churches. However, their reading of Scripture, their ecclesial missions, and their central concerns with the Black experience differentiated them from their white supremacist counterparts. Early Black churches were fashioned as nonracist versions of the churches they vacated. The enslaved or freed Negroes, in the case of many Methodists and northeastern Baptists, subverted the racist norms of white churches for the sole purpose of creating nonracist churches that denounced white supremacy. The early Black churches may have resembled white Christianity in many ways, but their missions and aims were quite different. Most pre-Reconstruction white churches had ecclesial leanings that reinforced racist ideals and upheld American patriotism. On the other hand, pre-Reconstruction Black churches used the medium of Christianity to resurrect unborn hope as an act of faith and Black religious praxis, and they did so in a priestly and prophetic manner. The key ecclesiological issues and historical elements of the Black church's early evolution in the United States were protest and freedom versus obedience and scriptural literalism; the pain and grief of racism by whites versus Black determination and Black self-consciousness; the oppression of white Christianity versus the beginnings of a Black Christianity of liberation; and the priestly versus the prophetic. From the complex and lived harsh realities of everyday Black life, Black ecclesiologies evolved. These events gave birth to Black ecclesial practices and Black religious life in American life.

The Priestly and Prophetic Aspects of Black Ecclesiologies

According to Lincoln and Mamiya, the Black church exists between a dialectical model: the priestly and the prophetic.[80] This dialectic uncovers a major ecclesiological issue in the historical development of Black churches in the United States. Lincoln and Mamiya indicate that Black churches have priestly functions that are spiritual. Similarly, Dale Andrews refers to the priestly element of preaching and pastoral care in the Black church's ecclesiology as the progenitors of Black ecclesial refugeeism.[81] Many Black theologians argue that the priestly function of the Black church is so concerned with personal piety, going to heaven (the otherworldly), and earthly escapism (the focus on worship as a remedy for long-suffering) that it has lost its this-worldly orientation. The other side of this coin is what Lincoln and Mamiya call the "prophetic functionality" of Black churches.[82] They define the "prophetic" as the ecclesiological element of the historical development of Black churches that produced the Black activists of the abolitionist movement, the leaders of the civil rights movement, the desire for economic empowerment and political change, and the establishment of a Black identity. Lincoln and Mamiya make it clear that an assessment or glorification of either of these two models that is too simplistic or one-sided would be highly problematic because most Black churches are not either/or but both/and. Lincoln and Mamiya suggest that based upon the varying dimensions of a church's location and the period within which it was formed and presently exists, Black churches are not one-dimensional but dualistic regarding their allegiance to the prophetic or priestly traditions of the Black experience.[83] As with all faith communities, on occasion Black churches have leaned too heavily on the priestly side, and on fewer occasions the prophetic side has not recognized the power and impact of the priestly tradition. However, when historically Black churches fully leaned into the power of their prophetic tradition, their subversive activism has been a form of queering that addresses the multitude of injustices that Black folk face in America with righteous indignation. This type of prophetic activism coupled with the priestly functionality of worship and cathartic religious practice is the quintessential example of what it means to be a queered Black church. Black churches that have been queered are both priestly and prophetic. Queerness is a part of the evolution of Black ecclesial purpose and history.

The Civil Rights Movement: A Form of Black Legal Queering

On July 9, 2015, during a same-sex-marriage campaign event, then–vice president Joe Biden argued that gay rights "is the civil rights movement of our generation. This decision is as consequential as *Brown v. the Board*."[84] His comments sparked a series of African American debates. The vice president's remarks raised several questions in the minds of Blacks: Are gay rights synonymous with civil rights? Is it possible for gay rights organizations to associate their struggle with the Black struggle for equality and civility? Is gay the new Black? If gay is the new Black, what does that mean for heterosexual Black persons? What does the association of queerness with Blackness denote? Does queerness harm or infringe upon the Black quest for civility or identity? Questions like these create dichotomous understandings of racism and homophobia in African American culture as unlinked and unaffiliated evils. Socially and culturally, racism and homophobia are often viewed as disparate issues in Black communities. For this reason, most discussions about the civil rights movement, Blackness, the gay rights movement, and homophobia never go beyond reifying Black heteropatriarchal privilege and substantiating homophobic defensiveness.[85]

It would be ahistorical to characterize the civil rights movement as a Black initiative to queer the American legal system while ignoring the elements of homophobia that pervaded the movement. A deeper investigation of Black history would unearth a hidden truth about the civil rights movement. Bayard Rustin wanted to discuss gay rights and civil rights, as did many of his contemporary Black thinkers like James Baldwin and Audre Lorde. However, because Adam Clayton Powell Jr. was caught up in the normative worldview of Black homophobia, he threatened to spread false rumors about King and Rustin being lovers if King agreed to give Rustin leadership and say-so in the movement as an "out" gay man.[86] As a result of these threats, King fired Rustin, one of the most effective organizers of the civil rights movement. King's back and forth with Rustin began as early as 1964, when Stanley Levison, one of King's close friends who aided him as a speech writer among other things, admonished King not to hire Rustin as executive director of the Southern Christian Leadership Conference (SCLC) because of his queerness. This raises several questions about King, Rustin, and the movement's innate queerness or lack thereof. What does Dr. King's apprehension and willingness to temporarily terminate or block Rustin's role in the civil rights movement mean for the civil rights legacy of Dr. King? Was Dr. King's willingness to fire and not hire Rustin rooted in a form of self-preservation or his belief that the intertwining of gay rights and civil rights was too forward thinking of a project at the time? What was King's perspective on gay rights? I believe that Dr. King's apprehension and willingness to temporarily terminate Rustin was a combination of both self-preservation and preservation of the movement. King was aware of the extramarital allegations mounting against him, which posed a threat to his national reputation as a leader of moral integrity. A false claim of homosexuality would have tarnished his reputation which would have also burdened the progress of the entire movement. According to Rustin,

> It is difficult for me to know what Dr. King felt about gayness except to say that I am sure he would have been sympathetic and would not have had a prejudicial view. Otherwise, he would not have hired me. He never felt it necessary to discuss that with me. He was under such extraordinary pressure about his own sex life. J. Edgar Hoover was spreading stories, and there were genuine efforts to entrap him. I think at a given point, he had to reach a decision. My being gay was not a problem for Dr. King but a problem for the movement.... Adam Clayton Powell Jr., for some reason I will never understand, actually called Dr. King when he was in Brazil and indicated that he was aware of some relationship between me and Dr. King,

which, of course, there was not. This added to his anxiety about additional discussions of sex.[87]

This quote exemplifies that sexuality and Black gay bodies were, at times, topics of discussion during civil rights meetings and planning discussions. According to Michael Long's book *Martin Luther King Jr., Homosexuality, and the Early Gay Rights Movement*, although Rustin was King's mentor, professor of nonviolence, administrative assistant, speechwriter, tactician, fundraiser, muse, researcher, and friend, King chose to shun Rustin because even he was too shrouded by the normative worldview of Black homophobia to stand with Rustin against Powell. According to Long, Dr. King's decision to dismiss Rustin was not caused by King taking issue with Rustin's queerness.[88] Instead, King was worried about what people might think and how their perceptions about Black gay equality would impede overall Black equality. For this reason, Thomas Kilgore, the senior pastor of Friendship Baptist Church in Atlanta and King's other trusted advisors admonished King to essentially sacrifice his love for Rustin for Black equality. King loved Rustin, but he could not enact his love through public support.[89] It is important to read King within his own context. But in doing so we must not paint an ahistorical picture. King's motives were also personal. According to both Long and Rustin, King was worried about his own sexual reputation and feared any association with Rustin that might tarnish his character in light of J. Edgar Hoover's accusations. This narrative is another example of how secrecy and the silencing of Black Queer persons have been used to preserve the Black heterosexual image for white and Black approval. Despite the undeniably Queer presence and Queer nature of the civil rights movement, Black heterosexuals in the 1960s sacrificed the narratives and lives of Black Queer persons on the altars of white heteronormativity. However, despite its homophobic hypocrisy, the civil rights movement was successful in queering white racist laws in America.

In "Law and the Regulation of the Obscene," Phoebe C. Godfrey argues that American laws and social norms were constructed based on a specific set of ideas about normality to affirm the ideals propagated by the ruling class. Since these laws are contingent upon the constituents of the ruling class, the laws are bound to change over time. The Black civil rights movement queered white culture and American law by interrogating institutionalized norms and laws, which eventually led to the breakdown of traditional mores and a renewed quest for attaining the basic needs and rights for diverse populations to live in civil society. Godfrey asserts,

> Thus, like all laws and social norms, obscenity and obscenity laws are socially constructed and are linked to more significant ideological and institutional expressions of social control and power. Since they are socially constructed and do not exist in any absolute form outside of a particular context, they have changed over time and will continue to change according to the specific beliefs, tastes, needs, and discriminations of any given society, specifically that society's ruling class. Definitions of obscenity and its codification into laws have been used and continue to be used to control people's behavior, creative work, and sexual expression through the threat of punishment that can vary from social shaming to criminal protest.[90]

However homophobic the civil rights movement was, in fact, it is still one of the most significant and most successful examples of Black legal queering in American history. According to Bayard Rustin's 1950 letter to A. J. Muste, those who wish to reach absolute consciousness in light of the racial frustrations of the world "must be prepared to be looked upon as Queer."[91] He argues that Socrates, Luther, Lincoln, and Thoreau were all looked upon as Queer because their contemporaries perceived them to be "foolish, unrealistic, idealistic, premature and doing more harm than good."[92] Likewise, Rustin perceived his work with the civil rights movement as a subversive form of behavior that sought to idealize a nonracist America. This was a queer enterprise. Moreover, if he or his contemporaries were viewed as Queer for believing in American freedom, Rustin encouraged all who seek to subvert oppressive powers to identify as Queer.[93]

For Rustin, to be Queer was to be in the company of Socrates, Luther, Lincoln, Thoreau, and Christ. Although Rustin was a northerner of Quaker origin, his ties to Dr. King led him to discover the rich religious Christology of Black Christianity:

> [Rustin] saw Jesus as a positive example—"this fanatic whose insistence on love thrust at the very pillars of stable society," he wrote in an "Easter Greeting" to supporters in 1952. Everyone saw Jesus as a lot of trouble, but even crucifixion could not get rid of Him. "Easter in every age ... recalls the imminence of the impossible victory, the power of the impotent weak." Rustin took the opportunity to note that "Jesus' followers need to be reminded that Easter is the reality, and that the awesome structures of

pomp and power are in the process of disintegration at the moments of their greatest strength."[94]

This quote shows that Rustin's Christology is rooted in what Lincoln and Mamiya would define as the prophetic characteristics of Black Christianity. For Rustin, Jesus and Black churches were queer prophetic symbols of strength and the willingness to be troublemakers even under the threat of death. Rustin fueled the civil rights movement using the rich religious heritage of Black churches and the civil disobedience of Jesus. He notes that because "the [Negro] . . . finds the church the center of his life," all African American pursuits of justice must be in conversation with Black religious and Black ecclesiological dialogue about the *Queer* behavior of Christ.[95]

According to Lincoln and Mamiya, Black churches fed, housed, populated, led, marched for, funded, orchestrated, and even birthed the civil rights movement.

Black church members fed and housed the civil rights workers from SNCC, CORE, and other religious and secular groups. Most of the local Black people, who provided the bodies for the demonstrations, were members of Black churches acting out of religiously inspired convictions. Black church culture also permeated the movement from oratory to music, from the rituals and symbols of protest to the ethic of nonviolence. It is estimated that several hundred churches in the South were bombed, burned, or attacked during the civil rights years, with ninety-three of those occurring between 1962 and 1965, with more than fifty in Mississippi alone. The white opposition understood the importance of the Black churches. The civil rights movement is a significant watershed in the annals of Black church history and the nation's history. The role of the Black church in whatever success that movement has accomplished is self-documented.[96]

Essentially, the civil rights movement had strong roots in Black religious and Black theological traditions.[97]

Some Black churches and Black ecclesial leaders organized, populated, and led a civil rights movement to overturn or queer the white racist laws of America. However, to be clear, the civil rights movement was not mainly a Black church movement, nor did it queer the entirety of American culture. While some Black pastors and Christians were involved in the work and execution of the civil rights movement, many of them did so without the full consent of the churches they served. Many Blacks did not support the movement, especially a large portion of the churches associated with the National Baptist Convention of America Inc., which was Dr. King's home denomination led by Rev. Dr. J. H. Jackson. When I speak of the civil rights movement as an example of queering's history in the Black American narrative, I am not suggesting that Black queering in America began with the civil rights movement or that the civil rights movement actually was successful in queering America. In thinking about Black queering as a form of subversive strategizing to radically overturn oppression against Black persons in America, we have to bring up names and organizations such as Marcus Garvey and the National Association for the Advancement of Colored People. These organizations positioned the civil rights movement not as the beginning of Black queering of the American racist landscape but as a defining moment in the pre-existing and continuing Black stride toward American equitability.

In my categorization of the civil rights movement as a type of queering within the Black American narrative I am also not suggesting that the movement was successful in queering all of America. The movement did not queer American culture, white American churches, or the inherently white ideals of American society. The civil rights movement only queered certain aspects of the American law that supported segregation. The evidence of racism after the civil rights movement demonstrates that the movement did not abolish racism or queer the entirety of American culture. The civil rights movement, which arguably paved the way for the passage of the landmark Civil Rights Act of 1964, was a Black initiative to challenge and transform the American legal system in a manner akin to queering. The foundational documents of the United States, particularly the Declaration of Independence and the Constitution, espoused lofty ideals of equality, liberty, and justice for all. However, the lived reality for Black individuals did not align with these principles. The movement aimed to dismantle the oppressive structures of Jim and Jane Crow, compelling America to actualize its professed ideals. This stands as the quintessence of queering.

Conclusion and Summary: What Does It Mean for the Black Church to Become Queer? What Will It Do, and Why Does It Need to Be Done?

If, as I argued at the beginning of the chapter, queerness is sacred and queering is a work of spirit, and if Black Queer persons are able to identify themselves in the personhood of Christ, then Black churches must become queer if they wish to remain wedded to their original Blackness and Black

Christian morals. The idea that Black churches must become Queer to be a part of the body of Christ is somewhat steeped in the sentiments of an argument made initially by James Cone. When faced with the dehumanization of Blacks in the 1960s, Cone argued that "where there is Black, there is oppression; but Blacks can be assured that where there is Blackness, there is Christ who has taken on Blackness so that what is evil in men's eyes might become good."[98] Cone contends that for the white church and Christ to remain faithful to the Word, Christ and the white church must become Black and accept the shame that white society has placed on Black people. Cone argues, "The Church is for people called into being by the power and love of God to share in his revolutionary activity for the liberation of man."[99] He contends that the church should continually derive its purpose and define its existence through the power and love of God. According to Cone, the church is where Christ is, and Christ is present when and where hurting people are present. He says, "Christ is to be found, as always, where men are enslaved and trampled underfoot; Christ is found suffering with the suffering; Christ is in the ghetto—there also is his church."[100] For Cone, the church is only the body of Christ or the continuation of the incarnation of Christ if, just as Christ does, it "identifies totally with the oppressed to the extent that they too suffer for the same reasons persons are enslaved."[101]

In the same vein, if heteronormative Black churches wish to avoid hypocrisy, they too must become Queer. The proposition that Black churches should adopt a Queer identity presents a challenge for certain Black heterosexual Christians, as it inadvertently prompts them to contemplate the idea of a Queer embodiment of Christ. Nevertheless, in reality, it would be inconsistent for Black churches not to undergo a queering process because Black churches themselves can be viewed as Queer phenomena. Arising from, in Raboteau's terminology, a synchronistic merging of Western and Central African religious practices, coupled with elements of white Christianity, known as slave religions, Black churches are queer phenomena. These slave religions were Queer enterprises in that they constituted radical para-ontological counterclaims and complex counter-hegemonic systems of oppositional consciousness that gave rise to Black prophetic Christianity and Black churches. Black churches must do this, first and foremost, as a means of solidarity, empathy, and companionship. They must also acknowledge the Black homophobic practices that have historically taunted, condemned, beaten up, tortured, and killed Black Queer persons. This raises a few final questions. Are Black churches—or the church at large, for that matter—going to die if this does not happen? I would say yes, and they should because homophobic Black churches are actually not Black churches; they are white churches in blackface. What are the benefits of queering Black churches? And, what are the consequences and potential fallouts a Black church could have when acknowledging the innate queerness of Christ and Black churches? These questions are answered in chapter 5. The next two chapters use the Black sexual historical analyses of chapter 1 and the Black queer theories and theologies of this chapter to think theologically about why and how open and affirming historically Black churches queered their ecclesial contexts. The next chapter places the questions, ideas, and practical theological commitments discussed here in the context of congregationally and pastorally queered Black congregations.

3
Models of Black Ecclesial Queering, Part I
The Congregational Model—Union United Methodist Church

A Black Practical Theological Introduction to the Models

The late Dale Andrews longed for Black practical theology to move away from the cultural and academic chasms between Black churches and Black theology and toward a more prophetic exploration of faith claims as they function in the lives of Black religious folk.[1] Black practical theology brings the voices of Black laypersons, pastors, and parachurch leaders into conversation with the disciplines of Black theology. Black practical theology uses systematic theology, ethics, biblical studies, history, and other disciplines to address the intergenerational challenges in Black communities of gender and sexuality, racism and poverty, education and health care, the justice system, housing, and economics. Black practical theology is not a distant or disengaged mode of theological discourse that centers on thoughts and ideas. Instead, it is concerned with better understanding the embedded Black theories of cognizance, social contexts, and living practices of faith in living churches, religious groups, and spiritual communities. As an academic, pastoral, and lay enterprise, Black practical theology is a necessary form of inquiry that utilizes various spiritual and cultural tools and disciplinary partners to examine and situate knowledge, rituals, and practices of faith communities to make Black theological meaning. For those who write and teach about Black practical theology, it is also a spiritual practice and discipline in and of itself that helps us to make theological meaning from our Black consciousness from varying theological perspectives.

The first chapter of this book placed a particular focus on pre-Reconstruction Black churches through the 1920s Black congregational era because, according to Black sexuality expert Patricia Hill Collins, any solution or understanding of sexuality in Black communities must begin with a deeply descriptive articulation of slavery and the African American past.[2] However, this book is not just an excavation of the past; it interrogates the present in conversation with the past to construct a more inclusive Black practical theology for Black churches. This chapter illustrates, in the tradition of Dale Andrews, how Black practical theology is living and thriving inclusively by telling the story of how an open and affirming historically African American congregation queered its congregation. In the previous chapters, I argued that Black homophobia is historically linked to the pre-Reconstruction American slave practice of buck breaking and the 1911 Abyssinian Baptist Church campaign against homosexuality led by Rev. Adam Clayton Powell Sr. in Harlem. Over the next two chapters, I use the theories and historical analyses from the previous two chapters to think theologically about why and how several open and affirming historically Black churches queered their ecclesial contexts.

In this chapter, I consider how a congregationally queered Black church, Union United Methodist Church of Boston, Massachusetts, understood what it meant to be a Black church in 2000 while identifying their defining characteristics, theologies, and praxis. Chapters 3 and 4 clarify how two historically Black congregations practice radical inclusivity, and what church means to them. During my research I was captivated by their defining characteristics and why they chose to queer their Black ecclesial contexts.

This chapter is about Black congregational queering. Black congregational queering is an ecclesial strategy that subverts the heteronormative and Puritan-based envelopes that shroud Blackness. Black ecclesial queering destabilizes the white American judgment that Blackness is an inherently sinful, sexual, and objectifiable ethnic category. It teaches Black church folk how to facilitate theo-psychological discussions on the unexamined cultural experiences of sexually traumatized African American persons, specifically of Black LGBTQIAP+ persons. It brings culture and society into dialogue with race and power. It creates Black religious "affirmatoriums" that exhibit at their core understandings of and sensitivity toward the experiences of Black sexual suppression and oppression. Black ecclesial queering demystifies the popular assumption that queering only derives from "an overarching queer subjectivity" that solely benefits and represents homosexual persons. It affirms and normalizes all gender performances while giving them the same access to God as their heterosexual counterparts. Queering produces a human enterprise of community-building that overturns and questions heterosexual Christianity for the sake of equity and social change. Finally, Black ecclesial queering creates nonseparatist homosocial safe spaces where LGBTQIAP+ Black eroticism and sexual expression are invited to flourish freely and sinlessly.

A Case of Congregational Queering: Union United Methodist Church of Boston

An Examination of Boston's Black Church Community(ies)/Culture

Although there is no monolithic or amalgamated Black church ideology or culture within the Boston metro area, the region's spectrum of Black church history is unquestionably steeped in prophetic social action and a racial reformation of New England Christianity. After Massachusetts abolished slavery in 1783, it became known as a sort of cradle for or example of abolitionism in the United States.[3] However, despite the fact that by 1790 the federal census recorded no slaves in Massachusetts, the racial difficulties that many freed people faced did not disappear. One example of Massachusetts's ongoing issue with racism after the American Revolution and the religious enthusiasm of the First and Second Great Awakenings can be seen in the inability of many white Christians to fully integrate their congregations. For instance, many of Boston's more historic Black congregations that were founded by freed slaves occurred because Blacks felt the need to worship God in their own traditions and with the freedom to sit in the front of the sanctuary as well as in the rear. For this reason, many of the freed slaves stopped attending the larger white churches "not with feelings of unkindness toward whites but simply for the best good of the Black soul."[4] Therefore, while Black Bostonians founded churches for varying reasons, religious particularities, and subcultures, their origins as spaces created to meet the spiritual and social needs of Black persons are identical.[5] In his book *Streets of Glory: Church and Community in a Black Urban Neighborhood*, Omar M. McRoberts shares a revisionist view of why and how Black churches in Boston were formed in the early 1800s. He asserts,

> The succession of Black communicants from White congregations in the early nineteenth century reflect a yearning among Black Bostonians for racially homogenous religious spaces free of the indignities, such as segregated seating and the denial of voting rights, that accompanied worship with Whites.... Churches had long been pivotal organizing centers for Black Bostonians. The nineteenth-century abolition struggle, which earned Boston its liberal reputation, was based in churches. Even after the arrival of the secular NAACP and Urban League in 1910 and 1919, respectively, churches and clergy continued to weigh in on race issues.[6]

By 1840, there were at least five Black churches on the northern slope of Boston's Beacon Hill neighborhood.[7] In the early 1800s Beacon Hill was home to one of the nation's first free African American communities.[8] In his historical account of Black churches in Boston and the Boston branch of the National Association for the Advancement of Colored People (NAACP), Robert C. Hayden argues that Black churches constitute "the only continuous cultural and self-controlled institution that Blacks in Boston and the nation have been able to maintain as their own from slavery to the present."[9] For the free slaves living in nineteenth-century Beacon Hill, these churches were not only spiritual spaces, but they also served as centers of discourse on race and Black oppression. They "were also central to the political and social lives of Black Bostonians. At these churches, faith directly informed action as men and women were sheltered from slave catchers, abolitionists fought to end slavery in America, and physical or material needs were satisfied."[10]

In his discussion of metro Boston's Black urban religious life, Omar McRoberts highlights two types of Black religious communities: the old churches of northern Blacks and the churches of migrant southern Blacks.[11] McRoberts contends that Black southern migrants and Caribbean immigrants may not have introduced religiosity to Black Boston, but they re-defined and refined the African diasporic and Caribbean particularism of Black religious expressivism in Boston in ways that should not be ignored ecclesiologically. One example of such is the regular occurrence of the Caribbean and African diasporic celebrations in Boston's Black congregations like Charles Street AME Church and Union Baptist Church of

Cambridge, Massachusetts. This ecclesial diversity proves that Boston's Black religious landscape must not be spoken of monolithically but rather pluralistically.[12] For instance, McRoberts describes Charles Street AME, People's Baptist, Twelfth Baptist, St. Mark's Congregational, Union United Methodist, North Russell AME Zion, and a few others as the old churches of northern Blacks that adapted their ecclesiologies to what McRoberts describes as "Northern patterns of worship."[13] He contends that these churches often found it difficult to appease southern Black migrants and charismatic Caribbean Christians with the types of intimate and more demonstrative modes of worship that often appealed to them.[14] Furthermore, the presence of Harvard and Boston University's young Black elite in Boston's oldest Black churches helped to "preserve the decorum of the church not only by their example but by giving Ransom (the pastor) a reason to continue in the cranial style of ministry favored by educated Northerners."[15] McRoberts describes this as the "Northern frozen chosen" stereotype.[16] In his history of Black Boston churches, Hayden recalls the following statement from John White, a third-generation member of Twelfth Baptist Church:

> You never clapped if there was ever any sort of good music.... You waved your handkerchief. Things were very reverent..... Young people had to follow rules and regulations. That was the church..... Very few people even said "Amen," except the deacons who had the "Amen corner" up front.[17]

What is most interesting about this passage and McRoberts's description of the northern frozen chosen is that while these churches were started in response to whiteness, they often subscribed to whiter modes of worship as a sort of subjective exercise of social class and upward mobility among Blacks in Boston. McRoberts goes on to share a detailed story about a recently installed pastor of St. Paul's Baptist Church in 1902, Rev. Simon P. W. Drew. According to a June 15, 1902, article in the *Boston Globe*, the deacons of St. Paul's ousted its pastor because of his practice of and appreciation for preaching in a southern revival style.[18] However, by 1900, the number of African Americans in Boston had increased to 11,591, nearly 2.1 percent of the city's population.[19] By 1930 Boston's population had grown exponentially, with Blacks concentrating in Ward 9 of the South End, then also known colloquially as Beacon Hill's "Nigger Hill."[20] The gentrification of Black families out of the South End and into Mattapan, Dorchester, and Roxbury took place in the 1950s.[21] However, with this growth came the establishment of Boston's Black elite, whose classism often manifested itself culturally and ecclesiologically. As Black southerners further diversified Boston's religious landscape, they often found themselves bored and alienated with the lack of demonstration in the Black northern frozen-chosen modes of Eurocentric worship. For this reason, many "migrants attended not only Black churches but also organized many of their own to invoke familiar modes of worship and facilitate mutual support."[22]

McRoberts also described what he calls the West Indian churches, which, like southern migrant churches, were also created for the sensibilities of Boston's West Indian community. But the northern frozen-chosen churches with more Eurocentric modes of worship often served as the spiritual homes of many of Boston's Black educated elite and notable religious leaders and prominent abolitionists like Frederick Douglass, David Walker, and later Martin Luther King Jr. Therefore, the influx of Black people into Boston's neighborhoods created new Black class structures and the development of what McRoberts calls the northern migrant and old churches of Boston. McRoberts suggests that Black religious life in Boston from 1916 until 1970, the years of the Great Migration, constitutes a mosaic of socio-religious pluralism, ethnic distinctiveness, and northern sociability that emerged from the religious expression of generic urban particularism.[23] The Black churches in Boston in the 1800s were created to provide free Blacks with stability and strength amid the tyranny of systemic racism. Like the history of Black churches discussed in chapters 1 and 2, the Black churches that were established in the 1800s centered on the faith, politics, arts, music, education, and survival of Black people. This was also the ecclesiological mission of these early Black churches in Boston. Likewise, when African, Caribbean, and Black southern migrants moved to Boston, they either joined preexisting Black churches to rebel against the principal institution of racism or started their own churches. Regardless of whether they joined churches or started their own, it is important to see the preservation of Blackness, Black theology, Black bodies, and Black survival. However, this collective Black theological trend within Boston's Black churches should not be seen as a means to aggregate all Black churches in Boston into a sort of homogeneous institution.

Black churches in Boston are also very diversified by the various communities of the African diaspora. Therefore, the inability to describe or categorize Boston's religious ideology with any sort of homogeneity is proof of how complex a conversation around Black sexuality could be in a Black metropolis like Boston. It is important to acknowledge that Boston's Black community comprises not only African Americans but also of members of the African diaspora from multiple continents. This matrix of complex Black multiculturalism in Boston creates conflicting framings of Black sexuality that make Black ecclesial queering an extremely complex endeavor upon which to embark.[24] One would think that Boston's rich Black church history of being both spiritually and socially engaged around issues of equality would cause its churches to become unquestionably affirming of Black Queer individuals. However, this was not the case. Most of Boston's Black pastors and religious leaders opposed LGBTQIAP+ civil rights because of their interpretations of scripture and biblical marriage.

How Boston's Black Religious Community Responded to Queer Rights

On May 17, 2004, attorney Mary Bonauto and Julie and Hillary Goodridge queered the historically heteronormative American institution of marriage in the landmark case of *Goodridge vs. The Massachusetts Department of Public Health*.[25] In March and April 2001, seven same-sex long-term parenting couples attempted to apply for marriage licenses in the state of Massachusetts and were denied. On April 11, 2001, the Gay and Lesbian Associate Defenders (GLAD) sued the Massachusetts Department of Health in the Superior Courts of the Commonwealth. The plaintiffs appealed directly to the Supreme Judicial Court. On April 18, 2003, the Supreme Judicial Court asked whether it was constitutionally valid for Massachusetts to "deny the protections, benefits, and obligations conferred by civil marriage to two individuals of the same sex who wish to marry."[26] They concluded in a 4-3 ruling "that it may not. The Massachusetts Constitution affirms the dignity and equality of all individuals. It forbids the creation of second-class citizens."[27] Massachusetts's legalization of same-sex marriage legally and publicly inserted same-gender love into the American family, marriage, and economic landscape.

Opposition to marriage equality in Massachusetts was not limited to members of the Republican Party, which was at that time a minority constituency of the Massachusetts legislature.[28] Despite votes from the Massachusetts judicial and legislative branches to redefine marriage, 53 percent of Massachusetts voters opposed gay marriage.[29] According to Gerry Chevrisky, president of KRC Communications of Newton, Massachusetts, which conducted the *Boston Globe*'s poll on gay marriage and civil unions, there was "a backlash against the court ruling.... People clearly want to take a step back and assess all of the available options."[30] Mitt Romney, the Republican and devout Mormon governor of Massachusetts, "reiterated his response to gay marriage, declaring he had '3,000 years of recorded history' on his side.... I disagree with the Supreme Judicial Court of Massachusetts."[31] House Speaker Tom Finneran proposed a constitutional amendment that would have essentially outlawed same-sex marriage as unconstitutional.[32] These and other forms of opposition reveal that the attempt to queer marriage in Massachusetts was not an easy task.

Additionally, the leaders of the African American Christian communities of Dorchester, Roxbury, Mattapan, Brockton, and other metropolitan Boston Black congregations overwhelmingly opposed the legalization of same-sex marriage. Right before its legalization, Rev. Dr. Gregory G. Groover Sr., senior pastor of one of the old churches of northern Blacks, The Historic Charles Street African Methodist Episcopal Church,[33] was quoted in a February 10, 2004, *Boston Globe* article, stating,

> As Black preachers, we are progressive in our social consciousness, and in our political ideology as an oppressed people, we will often be against the status quo, but our first call is to hear the voice of God in our Scriptures and where an issue clearly contradicts our understanding of Scripture, we have to apply that understanding.[34]

In addition to Reverend Groover's comments, the Reverend Dr. Ray Hammond, pastor and co-founder of Bethel, Boston's then fastest-growing AME church, was one of the more publicly vocal opponents of same-sex marriage in the Commonwealth's African American Christian community. A registered independent, Pastor Hammond supported gun control, opposed capital punishment, spoke out against same-sex marriage, and opposed most abortions.[35] He contended, "I'm not unlike what you tend to see in the African American church tradition which on a couple of these issues tends to be what people consider more conservative and on other issues tends to be what people consider more liberal or progressive."[36]

In February 2008 Pastor Hammond and over three thousand community leaders, religious communities, Black faith coalitions, ministerial alliances, the Boston Plan for Excellence, Jewish congregations, Roman Catholic dioceses of the state of Massachusetts, and twenty-five Islamic centers and mosques wrote a joint statement defining marriage as a union between one man and one woman.[37] And even after the official vote of the Supreme Court to legalize same-sex marriage in 2014, Rev. Arthur T. Gerald, pastor of the Twelfth Baptist Church, another one of the oldest churches of northern Blacks and the congregation where Martin Luther King Jr. was a member when he was a graduate student,[38] stated,

> The court's decision was constitutionally correct, but there is a difference between constitutional and spiritual law in America for Christians. I believe the decision is constitutionally correct.... but I have to stick with God. There's a biblical order to what we do, the Supreme Court decision goes against what we believe is the God-created purpose for marriage.[39]

These statements made by several of Boston's Black pastors in the early 2000s reveal that many of Boston's Black clergy believed their theological assumptions about biblical marriage—which, according to chapters 1 and 2 of this book, are the products of internalized heteronormativity within Black churches—were not only correct but divinely inspired. This dangerous and toxic mixture of Black heteronormativity and Evangelical Christian conservatism was the context in which Union United Methodist Church of Boston queered its ecclesiology.

Profile of Union United Methodist Church

The history of Union United Methodist Church of Boston predates its name. As early as 1796, African American believers began meeting for segregated study and worship on Boston's Commonwealth Hill. In 1818 these Blacks and other Black Methodists who were worshiping in the white Bromfield Street Methodist Episcopal Church petitioned the bishop to establish a separate Black Methodist church. At the behest of the Black Methodists, Rev. Samuel Snowden, a nineteenth-century formerly enslaved abolitionist and church planter, was appointed the church's first pastor.[40] Named after the location of its first edifice, the May Street Meeting House/Church grew so rapidly under Reverend Snowden's leadership that a second Revere Street location was soon established.

While pastoring the May and Revere Street churches, Reverend Snowden remained a man of "powerful personality and antislavery activism."[41] Under his leadership, the churches served as stops on the Underground Railroad, financially aided William Lloyd Garrison, and allowed Garrison to use church facilities for antislavery events, and their congregants welcomed fugitive slaves into their homes, offering temporary housing, food, and clothing.[42] David Walker, the famed publisher of one of the most influential nineteenth-century political and social documents, "The Appeal to the Colored Citizens of the World," was also a member of the May Street Meeting House.[43] In 1911 the churches merged and "became known as Fourth Methodist Episcopal when they moved to Shawmut Avenue."[44] Then, in 1949, Fourth Methodist Episcopal Church purchased the former Union Congregational Church and renamed itself Union United Methodist Church of Boston.[45]

Union's Context: The Historic South End

The history of Boston's beautiful urban "gayborhood" is laced with just as much racism and gentrification as any other inner-city neighborhood in America. Today, Boston's South End is filled with brick row-front townhouses separated with black iron gates, miniature French-style parks with black iron fountains, and manicured trees. The district is also home to several exclusive restaurants like the Bee Hive Restaurant and Lounge, Stephie's on Tremont, and the once famed gay citadel Stella Restaurant. While walking up and down the South End's various small streets and alleys, which are named after Massachusetts towns, it is not uncommon to see two persons of the same sex holding hands, caressing each other, or offering other public displays of affection. As Boston's main gay enclave, the South End is replete with gay-owned restaurants and bars, gay-friendly boutiques, and a lively after-hours scene with drag shows, go-go boys, cruising, and even weekly gay male sex parties.[46] However, the South End was not always home to thousands of upper-middle-class white Queer persons, exclusive lounges, and expensive restaurants. The extensive history of the South End began in the mid-nineteenth century. At that time, Boston and Commonwealth Hill had become so overcrowded that the state of Massachusetts hired Charles Bulfinch, a prominent nineteenth-century American architect, to construct a neighborhood on top of a tidal salt marsh between Beacon Hill and Roxbury.[47] Originally constructed on a landfill in the 1850s as a neighborhood of townhouses for the wealthy, the South End's layout follows "the English park model of residential squares."[48] Each street is equipped "with a large oval grass plot defining the center of the street."[49]

However, when Boston's elite citizens moved out of the South End into Back Bay, the neighborhood transitioned from being a wealthy residential district of townhouses into one of the most vibrant immigrant communities of the early twentieth century.[50] The legendary Panic of 1873 drove this transition.[51]

In hopes of surviving the Panic of 1873, several attractive buildings in the South End were repossessed by banks and sold at reduced rates.[52] This caused a racial divide that existed until the 1970s. Many of the large homes could not be sold as complete parcels, so homes were divided into smaller lodging units that were easier to sell and more affordable for Boston's growing immigrant and African American populations. The neighborhood remained low income and was filled with crime until the 1970s when Boston's white gay male population began buying property in the South End in large numbers. This was essentially the birth of the South End "gayborhood" and the beginning of a drastic season of gentrification that continues to haunt and ostracize the long-standing bearers of the South End's African American and immigrant history. While white gay males led the gentrification of the South End—reducing crime and increasing the median household income, property values, and socioeconomic values—it also created a huge problem for the historically African American churches that had been in the South End since the nineteenth century. For instance, with Black people now living in Dorchester, Roxbury, and Mattapan and parking being quite limited, Black churches in the South End, like New Hope Baptist Church and Concord Baptist Church, were forced to move out and into the suburbs because of gentrification.[53] To date, Union Church is one of the few Black churches still thriving in Boston's South End. I argue that Union Church's success is largely, if not solely, due to its decision to be the only Black church in the South End to queer its ecclesial mission to reflect the needs of the church's current Queer demographic.

Presently, Union Church worships and resides in a Gothic revival–style building built between 1872 and 1875 by Alexander R. Estey.[54] Much like Emmanuel Church that Etsey designed for Boston's Back Bay, Union Church was also built of Roxbury puddingstone. As a prominent landmark in Boston's Historic South End District, Union Church is known for its 170-foot stone steeple, bright red doors replete with large multicolored welcome flags, and its beautiful stained-glass windows framed with the same detailed wood as the nave, altar, pulpit, pews, and supporting columns. With distinctive decorative ornamentation at the apex of the nave's ceiling, pointed lancet arch windows, hood moulds, and label stops with lower ends that

Table 3.1. Union Church Regional Demographics Chart

Membership	451 persons 264 Female 187 Male 0 Nonbinary/NGC
Annual Budget	$600,000
Typical Sunday Attendance	150
Current Pastoral Educational Level	B.A., Harvard University M.Div., Union Theological Seminary Ph.D., Harvard University
Median Congregational Educational Level	Bachelor's or Master's (few doctorates)
Neighborhood Median Income	$62,850
Church Demographics	95.3 percent Black 3 percent Latinx 1.2 percent White 2 percent Other
Neighborhood Racial Demographics	47.2 percent White 17 percent Black 16.9 percent Latinx 15.5 percent Asian 1.7 percent Mixed 0.5 percent American and Alaskan Natives 1.2 percent Other
Neighborhood Population	Whites = 97,700 Asians = 58,100 Hispanics = 30,400 Blacks = 30,200
Neighborhood Median House Price	$1.2 million
Additional Neighborhood Information	89 percent of Black households on South End led by single Black women, 49.9 percent of the Black households are on food stamps

Data were collected during my doctoral qualitative research and from the Union local church membership and participation report to the General Council on Finance and Administration of the United Methodist Church 2017–2020 Quadrennium; http://cityofboston.gov/dnd/PDR/Maps_and_Neighborhood_Profiles.asp.

horizontally turn away from the windows. These Gothic decorations on Union's structure reveal the building's use and Eurocentric ownership before the 1949 merger of the Revere Street and Union Congregational churches. However, despite Union's imposing Gothic structure, which architecturally represents the gravitas of traditional mainline conservative Christianity, Union's ecclesiology differs greatly from its conventional building design.

Union Church not only stands out architecturally on the corner of Columbus Avenue and West Newton Street between Harriet Tubman Square and Titus Sparrow Park, but it also is distinguished socially as one of the most prominent and community-oriented Black congregations in the Boston metro area (see Table 3.1). Union Church is a great example of a ministry whose mission merges social action with spiritual formation. In the nineteenth century, Union's ecclesiology was rooted in Christian love, social justice, and radical hospitality. At that time, the church showed unconditional love to the battered Black souls of culturally and sexually objectified fugitive slaves.[55] Since its formation in 1796, Union Church has always struggled against the oppressive norms and systems of white supremacy, racism, and slavery. The first official pastor of Union Church, Samuel Snowden, was a former slave turned abolitionist. Upon moving into its current building on 485 Columbus Avenue, Mary McLeod Bethune was the opening speaker for the first worship service held in the Union nave on May 8, 1949.[56] In 1950 the church hosted the legendary National Association for the Advancement of Colored People's convention that decided to pursue *Brown v. Board of Education*. In the twenty-first century, Union's ecclesiology is still rooted in Christian love, social justice, and radical hospitality. Currently, the church performs acts of social justice by extending its urban Africana celebration-style spiritual home to the culturally and sexually objectified bodies of Queer persons.

A Tale of Quadrilateral Queering and Reimaging

In 2000 Union Church became the first affirming predominately and historically Black affirming congregation in the United Methodist denomination.[57] However, the story of Union's ecclesial inclusivity predates this official congregational vote to welcome Queer persons. During a regular Bible study in 1996 the eldest active member of Union fervently expressed the importance of Union's community engagement and global missions to its congregational identity. She shared, "in the 1970s, Union led the development of Meth-Union Manor, a four-building affordable housing cooperative in the South End. During the 1980s and 1990s, we fought against apartheid in South Africa and for economic equality for all at home."[58] Hence, at the core of Union's ecclesial history lay the tenets of inclusion and Black ecclesial queering. According to Ruby Blake, a member of Union for over thirty years, "I think it became easier because we always fought for justice, that's what we were about: justice, equality. That was one of the bedrocks of Union. It was almost an unsaid thing that gay rights were something we needed to take up. It's part of who we are."[59] The congregational call to establish justice and equality is the overarching backdrop and undergirding posture of Union's Black ecclesial queering.

In the late 1990s Rev. Theodore L. Lockhart pastored Union Church. As a group of three female parishioners stated, one of the highlights of his pastorate was a twenty-four-week discipleship Bible study class. According to parishioner Cynthia Moore, "The Bible studies were not regular Bible study classes because I felt I needed my theological degree when I was finished."[60] What Cynthia is describing here is the fact that these Bible studies were not just traditional lightweight engagements with sacred texts to gain a greater sense of personal piety. These classes were designed to stretch and push congregants to think more critically and deeply about the social implications and the multiple and often conflicting modern interpretations of ancient biblical texts. During a new member orientation class in the fall of 1996, Hilda Evans, a longtime member and then chair of Union membership and evangelism committee, asked Reverend Lockhart to consider the changes around the church in the South End. She said,

> Reverend Lockhart, I have a question to ask before you begin today's session. What is the official position of the United Methodist Church on homosexual persons? I don't mean to throw you off, but you know, this neighborhood has changed, and there are a lot of gay people living in the South End now. And it looks like we ought to be doing something, reaching out.[61]

As the chairwoman of the Evangelism Committee, Hilda wanted to know if the pastor and the church were going to value the intrinsic humanity of Black Queer persons or deny them access to Union because of their sexual identities. This important turn by one of Union's eldest members reveals that the demographics of the South End's gentrified neighborhood played a role in the transition of Union's Black ecclesiology becoming a queered Black ecclesiology. Hilda wanted to welcome Black Queer persons to Union because the South End had essentially become like Greenwich Village of New York and the Castro District in San Francisco. Hilda's question was merely a response to what was happening in the neighborhood. She essentially questioned whether Union's ecclesiology needed to be queered or left alone.

In the same meeting, Hilda also stated, "If we are going to be a church of the community in the neighborhood, we have to deal with the crisis of sexuality, the AIDS crisis, if we are actually going to be the church." Reverend Lockhart responded, "Okay, we need to do a study about what the United Methodist Church says and believes about gays."[62] This was a very important and wise move by Reverend Lockhart. Reverend Lockhart was aware of his limitations on the subject matter. And instead of avoiding the conversation due to ignorance, he instead leaned into the conversation exploratorily. The prophetic nature of Reverend Lockhart's willingness to facilitate such a conversation was a modern Black ecclesial miracle in and of itself, and as such, it should not go unacknowledged. Second, Reverend Lockhart should be respected for his willingness to consult writings on the matter of homosexuality that were outside of the sacred canon known to Christians as the Holy Bible. He was willing to consult extrabiblical information to make a sounder decision on sexuality in the twenty-first century. Additionally, as a registered nurse and well-respected African American woman, and a longtime senior member of Union Church, Hilda represented a huge shift in Union Church's ecclesial intentionality. According to Union member Ruby,

> It started with Hilda Evans, a longtime member. She was a member of the usher board. She was the chairperson of the Membership and Evangelism Committee for quite a few years. She was on this task force. And just a worker of the church. She asked Reverend Lockhart to look at the changes around us in the South End. Hilda was drawing attention to the growing gay population in the area and wanted to know what the pastor was going to do about outreach. Reverend Lockhart said, "Okay, we need to do a study about what the church [UMC] says about gays." Everyone knows that Hilda is the one that initiated this discussion.[63]

Hilda, a cisgendered heterosexual Black woman, began the process of Black ecclesial queering at Union. While it is unknown what exactly influenced her, Cynthia, June, and Ruby believe that newly formed friendships within the diverse and rapidly changing South End may have influenced her. Therefore, in the case of Union, Black ecclesial queering only needed the prophetic efforts and bold questioning of one person to begin. It began in the heart and mind of a layperson. However, it was not just any layperson. As stated earlier, Hilda was a well-respected church leader. At Union, which members supported and promoted Black ecclesial queering mattered. When Hilda raised the question about Union's stance on Black Queer persons to Reverend Lockhart, she faithfully served the congregation as a member of the usher board, chairperson of the Membership and the Evangelism Committees, church attendee, and regular financial giver. In other words, Hilda held a great deal of social and cultural capital in Union Church. Her willingness to ask the question about inclusivity was the first step toward a goal that would take three years to complete.

Here, Hilda was the pivotal personality in the queering of Union's ecclesiology. Before her questions and statements, the subject had never officially been addressed, and the pastor had never considered such a mission to be important. Any narrative about the queering of Union that fails to acknowledge the bold contributions of Hilda Evans is inaccurate. For Union, the initiation of Black ecclesial queering did not begin as a pastoral thought. In a pastoral confessional, Reverend Lockhart writes,

> Had anyone asked me to name "the issues" in the church or society that claimed my interest or attention, the matter of homosexuality would not have been on a list of "my issues." Among some Black friends, I might now and then have voiced the notion that the issue of homosexuality is but another trick of white folks to undermine the cause of racial justice in America or continuing proof that white folks enjoy tying themselves in knots about human sexual practice.[64]

As a result of Hilda asking such a difficult question, Reverend Lockhart appointed members to serve on a homosexuality task force within weeks. While Union was part of the United Methodist denomination, their process toward becoming open and affirming was congregationally initiated and executed. Reverend Lockhart describes the process:

> Friends and colleagues have asked me in recent years how I did it and how did Union, a predominantly African American congregation, get involved with the issue of homosexuality? The short answer is I was sent to Union

Church by a United Methodist bishop to perform ministry to and with the people of Union, and Union's church facility is located in a Boston neighborhood that includes a sizable homosexual community. That meant I was called and sent to serve them too.[65]

Reverend Lockhart's involvement with gay rights was not the result of a personal interest. The consideration never crossed his mind, but when it did, he responded with compassion. He was sent by a United Methodist bishop to serve the people of Union. The people of Union changed their ecclesiology to include Queer persons, and it was now Reverend Lockhart's responsibility to perform ministry to and with the people of Union.

Hilda's contribution to Union's inclusivity represents the prophetic power of dialogue and honest questioning to the process of Black ecclesial queering. Without the ability to ask questions or to question what already is, queering is just a thought. At least for Union, Black ecclesial queering began with questions—questions about the official United Methodist position on homosexual persons and inquiries about the implementation of these positions in a neighborhood where many gay people live. Union must be credited with creating a space during Bible study and new members' orientations where questions, like the ones raised by Hilda, were permitted to be raised and responded to with respect. This is a very important first step of Black ecclesial queering. It would have been nearly impossible to begin a process of Black ecclesial queering at Union if there had been no freedom for parishioners like Hilda to discern what Scriptures meant to them or others. Additionally, if Union had been assigned a biblical literalist pastor who said, "We follow the Bible, the Bible says this, this is what I think, and that is what it is," Hilda's statements would not have been as effective. When asked about the nature of asking questions about the Bible and life at Union, member Cynthia replied,

> I mean, we use the Bible, we're not Bible thumpers; we use Scripture, but I think we use it as a guide. Most of the pastors say the Bible is written by man; it was not written by Jesus Christ, you know? And part of what attracted me to Union is the social concerns and the justice issues. It's what drives the entire church. When we read Scripture, we see social concerns and justice, not oppressive laws.[66]

This is a very important point that chapter 4 examines further. One of the reasons that Union experienced so much success in its queering process is that it had already wrestled with the dynamics of biblical literalism, which often prohibits Black ecclesial queering from even initiating a process of subversion.[67] Union's communal tradition of reflecting on Scripture through the lenses of justice and equality created a safe space for Hilda to ask questions and make affirming inquiries and statements without fear of persecution. After she asked the questions, Reverend Lockhart shared that the official United Methodist position regarded homosexuality as contrary to Christian teachings and the Bible. This outraged the heterosexual parishioners attending the new members' orientation, and it sparked a heated two-hour discussion about the church's official position on homosexuality.

At the end of the discussion, Reverend Lockhart suggested that the persons present should participate in a special Bible study class to discern more about homosexuality and the position of the United Methodist Church. He proposed organizing a group to read a book titled *The Church Studies Homosexuality: A Study for United Methodist Groups Using the Report of the Committee to Study Homosexuality*, the only book of its kind during Union's initial queering phases.[68]

In January 1997 the church ordered several copies of the study guide and its accompanying workbooks and cassette tapes from the Reconciling Congregation program office of the United Methodist Church.[69] Then, on February 17, 1997, Reverend Lockhart and fourteen members of the Union congregation began a ten-session cultural and Bible study to explore homosexuality from the perspective of the *United Methodist Church's Committee Report on Homosexuality*.[70] According to Reverend Lockhart,

> At the conclusion of the study, the group wanted to do several things: (1) learn more about the African American homosexual community, (2) form a task force to study becoming a reconciling congregation under the Reconciling Congregation Program, and (3) arrange to have the course offered on a recurring basis for other interested members of the congregation. At the end of the latter study, the group chose to become members of a task force on Becoming a Reconciling Congregation. The task force decided to offer the course again for other interested persons to explore becoming a Reconciling Congregation. Bob Wyckoff and I shared in leading the course two or three additional times.[71]

After these sessions, Union United Methodist Church's welcome and affirming task force took the congregation through a two-year process of study, discussion, and discernment on the topic of homosexual inclusivity or exclusivity from June 1997 until June 1999.

An Overview of the Union Church Group Studies

Reverend Lockhart selected a particular book to guide all groups studying homosexuality in Union Church between 1997 and 1999. Therefore, it would be impossible to discern how Union queered its ecclesiology without first analyzing the contents of their study guide, which informed their localized process of Black ecclesial queering. *The Church Studies Homosexuality* begins by detailing the history of the United Methodist Church's struggle with homosexuality from 1972 until 1992. The first half of the book reports the UMC Homosexuality Committee's findings on the human reality of homosexuality by exploring the experiences and convictions of hundreds of gay or gay-affirming clergy and laypersons.[72] It carefully describes the terror and risk associated with United Methodist clergy having to come out of the closet. It says,

> A gay United Methodist minister stated: "I am called of God, I have all the gifts and graces for ministry, and I will happily stand on my record as to my work with local churches. . . . But, because I was honest enough to admit I am gay, I have been rejected, denied appointment."[73]

This is just one example of how Williams uses the committee's report to brilliantly capture real-life narratives that congregations could use to humanize homosexual persons and their many stories. The book does not just discuss homosexuality as a subject matter, but it also engages it as a lived reality for millions of human beings. After discussing eight queer narratives, the book uses the Wesleyan Quadrilateral to make queer meaning. The quadrilateral is a theological methodology of reflection crafted by John Wesley—the term was coined by Albert C. Outler—and focuses on Methodist beliefs concerning Scripture, tradition, reason, and experience.[74]

In *The Church Studies Homosexuality*, Williams gives careful attention to each of the four sources of theological reflection in United Methodism:[75]

The study of *biblical passages*, as well as attention to methods of *biblical* interpretation and approaches to the *Bible's* authority, have been at the forefront of our study. The insights and challenges presented by human *experience* have entered into our study through the informal mode of Christian witnessing to faith *experiences*, family narratives, individual and congregational testimony, and through the social, psychological, and biological sciences. Christian *tradition* conveys to us the wealth of positive and negative Christian experience over the centuries—affirming the centrality of love and the positive nature of the gift of creation, though sometimes degenerating sexual expression, or approving sexual activity only for the purpose of procreation. Most Christian *tradition* has rejected same-sex erotic relationships, sometimes to the point of brutal repression. The use of *reason* has been valued in our work through standards of critical study integral to the scientific disciplines as well as to the disciplines of *Biblical* study, theological reflection, and ethical analysis. Theological consultants drew our attention to diverse streams of *tradition* present within the United Methodist Church. Each of them emphasized that different viewpoints on human sexuality exist among Christians because of differences in how the sources and criteria for theological and ethical reflection are understood and interpreted. Thus, while The United Methodists hold in common to the primacy of *Scripture* and the relevance of *Reason, Tradition,* and *Experience* as sources and criteria for theological work, significant latitude remains. This has led, in turn, to different conclusions regarding homosexuality.[76]

Scripture, Experience, Reason, and Tradition: A Queer Usage of the Wesleyan Quadrilateral

Union United Methodist Church's ecclesiology is a queered version of the Wesleyan Quadrilateral. The Union Church demonstrates and defines its beliefs and ecclesiology in its approach to various aspects of its affirming praxis through its handling of Scripture, music/hymnody, the *Book of Discipline*, and the *Book of Worship*.[77] In an article titled "Understandings of Ecclesiology in United Methodism," Russell E. Richey argues that every United Methodist ecclesiology begins with the Wesleyan Quadrilateral. He contends,

> United Methodism defines itself and exhibits its ecclesial sensibilities with four books. Two of these, the Bible and *Hymnal*, one finds in the

pew and in the homes of the Methodist faithful. The other two, *The Book of Discipline* and *The Book of Worship,* some Methodists would have never seen. Nevertheless, each works for and works itself into the drama of the church's daily life. The *Discipline* and *Book of Worship* function off stage determining how the play unfolds, who acts, and what instructions to follow. Bible and *Hymnbook* script Methodist life together. For present life together, especially life in congregations, the four books orient Methodists toward the Word, mediate United Methodism's traditions, including particularly its Wesleyan heritage, offer experiential expressions of the faith once delivered, and order belief and practice accordingly. The books evidence United Methodism's actual use of quadrilateral ways of knowing Christ and being Christ-like. They also show, in their convergence, a convergence clearer, more so now, than in earlier days, how the four-fold epistemology or hermeneutic yields a common focus. In these four books, the catholic and missional, the high liturgical and fervid evangelical that Mr. Wesley held so curiously together come again into tension. The four books beckon United Methodists who press to one extreme or the other to reclaim balance and live our distinctive witness. Scripture, hymnbook, discipline, and book of worship define how United Methodists do church. Ecclesiology in its most familiar doctrinal form this may not be. But in structure and practice, in office and program, United Methodists nevertheless live faithfully into the ecumenical ecclesial consensus, adding thereunto what they affirm to be an apostolic commitment to mission. Methodists offer a *via salutis* to augment the tradition's *ordo salutis* and an ecclesiological via to augment the tradition's ecclesiological ordo.[78]

Here, Richey lays the foundation for the remainder of this chapter. Union's *experiences* with justice work and Black oppression obligated it to *reason* with the *traditional* Christian understandings of sexuality that were primarily based on interpretations of *Scripture*. Union essentially queered or used the Wesleyan Quadrilateral in a queer way.[79]

Black homophobic clergy have historically used biblical passages—or texts of terror, as Patrick Cheng describes them—to bastardize and other Black Queer persons.[80] For this and other cultural reasons, Scripture has been a primary point of contention for queer Christians across the ethnic spectrum. While the previous chapter sought to analyze and dissect the socio-historical aspects of Black homophobia, one should never forget that biblical language and imagery have often been the primary medium through which Black Americans have expressed their socio-historical meaning. Many African American Christians have never regarded the narrative of their enslavement, exile, and displacement in America as a sacred narrative or religious text by which to live as a sort of Black Bible of God's intervention on their behalf as did the children of Israel concerning the Exodus. Instead, Black Christians have normally expressed their socio-historical identity through the metaphor of the Exodus. Although African Americans are not Hebrews, they have traditionally used biblical concepts to make theological meaning out of their histories and challenges. I gave this example to show the importance of the Bible to Black Christians. For this reason, it is impossible to disassociate the socio-historical aspects of Black religious homophobia from biblical literature.[81] The Black heteronormative ministerial usage of biblical texts to terrorize Black queer folk is an example of how the letter that should give life can also kill at the same time (2 Cor. 3:6). The suicide rate of Black Queer persons alone is enough to illustrate how Black religious homophobia contributes to the killing of Black Queer bodies.[82]

If Black Queer persons are to be fully welcomed, included, and affirmed in a Black church, then the sociohistorical usage of Scripture is one of the first subjects that must be addressed. The cultural appreciation and historical reverence of the Bible is a major part of traditional Black Christianity. The Bible was one of the first books read by enslaved Africans in the Americas. Moreover, while the initial reason for restricting slaves from reading the Bible may have been laced with racist intentions, enslaved Africans brilliantly reimagined and reinterpreted the texts meant to enslave them as tools to set themselves free.

The Bible was not just a book of inspiration but also a safe space to preserve their family narratives. Before computers, Facebook, and other social networking sites, many Black Christian families also kept most of their family records, obituaries, pressed funeral flowers, special memorabilia, birthdates, and anniversary dates in the family Bible. Essentially, the Bible is a very important component of Black Christian life. Therefore, any attempt to queer a Black church that ignores or avoids wrestling with Scripture will ultimately fail. Lazy and unsuccessful queering begins with the avoidance of Scripture. Black ecclesial queering only works well when it is in direct conversation with Scripture; this is where Black ecclesial queering gains its footing. The reimagining and reclaiming of Scripture are the primary contributions that Black ecclesial queering makes to a Black church. Black ecclesial queering demands that Scripture be reclaimed as a tool of care for Black Queer persons.

Until now, the discussion has been about Black ecclesial queering from a theoretical and analytical context. However, theory alone cannot queer a Black context. To use a colloquialism, "The rubber must meet the road at some point"; eventually, anyone attempting to queer a Black church must confront and reimagine Scripture in a way that may be threatening or frightening to some. Black people have a strong cultural weddedness to the Bible that causes the process of rethinking Scripture to be extremely difficult.

After examining homosexuality through the lens of the Quadrilateral, the book then wrestles with important questions for United Methodists, such as, "Can homosexuality be an expression of life in grace or is it an expression of sin or sickness that impedes the work of grace?"[83] To respond to this and other questions, Williams argues that most contemporary ethicists contend that the practice of homosexuality is consistent with the ideals of Christian morality. In fact, "While a few ethicists regard homosexual practice as a gravely serious problem, our studies of the literature clearly show that they are an exception in the field of Christian ethics."[84] The book then moves from Christian ethics to scientifically informed perspectives on homosexuality. It concludes,

> We did find a consensus among scientists that no one knows how to create a human being's sexual orientation, whether homosexual or heterosexual. They pointed out that there is no evidence to suggest that deliberate role modeling by parents or teachers, or others who seek to exert influence over persons can be the significant cause of a person's sexual orientation, whether they are homosexual or heterosexual. Without real clarity on the question of causation, it is similarly difficult to conclude whether homosexual orientation can or cannot be changed.[85]

This quote is a perfect example of how the author not only leans on the varying fields of humanity to argue for the full inclusion of gays and lesbians into the Christian church, but she also carefully presents complex scientific, sociological, theological, and historical information very directly and simplistically, so it is accessible to nonacademic lay Christians. The book is intentionally simple and direct when making statements about language and identity because it is intentionally unearthing stereotypes that have traditionally been posited against Black Queer persons and their communities. For example, one section talks about life patterns and makes statements like,

"Monogamy exists among homosexual couples; research proves that there is no difference in parenting effectiveness that can be attributed to the sexual orientation of the parents, and there is no indication that homosexual men are more likely to commit sexual violence than heterosexual men."[86] The section concludes by arguing that the United Methodist Church must accept the reality that "homosexual persons are already active members of local congregations throughout the denomination."[87] Williams describes the UMC's ecclesial and denominational discrimination of homosexual persons as a moral dilemma.

The second half of *The Church Studies Homosexuality* teaches congregations what they can and cannot responsibly teach their parishioners about homosexuality. Williams rehearses the report's research from both sides of the aisle and carefully creates a practical but extensive list of dos and don'ts for UMC parishes connected to homosexual persons, like speaking with respect and using inclusive language.[88] Williams then creates a section with definitions, stories, quotes from Scripture, and ministry examples showing readers what inclusive ministry and pastoral care for Black Queer persons look like. These are the most valuable sections of the book relative to showing congregations how the enterprise of ecclesial queering could and has worked.

In the glossary section of the book, Williams shares understandings of terms and phrases like sex, homosexual, lesbian, coming out, transsexual, and others to facilitate discussion on homosexual language in UMC churches.[89] She then wrestles with the biblical passages that are most frequently used in anti-gay sermons and homophobic scriptural dialogue.[90] The book's final section, titled "A Sampler of Ministries," is what I describe as the *what to do and how to do it* section. She begins by suggesting that the primary way to educate the entire congregation about homosexual persons and homosexual rights is to identify members of the original study group who are willing to speak out during "Sunday school classes, United Methodist women circles, or other groups" without shame.[91]

Lastly, Williams recommends that churches open their doors for local gay and lesbian organizations to meet in their facilities. She also strongly suggests that the church should actively support legislation and other community actions that ensure the civil liberties of gay and lesbian persons. She concludes by saying that churches cannot discuss this topic just once, but there must also be an ongoing effort for continued learning. Williams recommends that churches supply their church libraries with books about homosexuality that are predominately geared toward young white adults and white adolescents.[92]

The book, which primarily reviews the UMC's report on homosexuality, was written to help UMC congregations "explore the controversial issues of homosexuality from a Christian perspective and to consider ways to be in ministry to and with persons who are homosexual."[93] Written during an era when the word "homosexuality" served as a blanket term for all nonheteronormative identities and orientations, *The Church Studies Homosexuality* specifically uses the term "homosexual" to describe Queer persons. However, the LGBTQIAP+ community has historically had a very difficult time with this term: "Because no universal agreement exists on terminology, and because language and culture continually change... problems occur in language concerning lesbians, gay men, and bisexual persons when the language is too vague, or the concepts are poorly defined."[94] Understanding the expansive identities of the LGBTQIAP+ community can be extremely difficult for heteronormative persons. Yet with the increased visibility of Black Queer persons in the United States after 1990, American language and culture have gradually shifted to be more attentive to the vagueness of the word "homosexual" when describing lesbians, gay men, bisexual persons, trans persons, Queer persons, and so on. According to George Chauncey, a Yale professor of history, gay, and lesbian culture,

> "Homosexual" has the ring of "colored" now, in the way your grandmother might have used that term, except that it hasn't been recuperated in the same way. Gay doesn't use the word sex," he said. "Lesbian doesn't use the word sex. Homosexual does. It also contains 'homo,' which is an old derogatory," he added. They want to have that idea there. They want to say this is not normal sex; this is not normal, family, it's going against God.[95]

What Chauncey is arguing for is a more culturally sensitive means of identifying gay or lesbian persons because the word "homosexual" is an old and derogatory word that centers on sex and decentralizes the person. However, the genuine efforts of the book's author should not be ignored because of Dorothy Williams's usage of the term "homosexual." Written in 1992, the book used the term "homosexual" not only to describe but also to humanize all Black Queer persons simultaneously.[96] While the term's use in 1992 inadvertently unearthed negative heteronormative stereotyping, Williams's original intent was to embrace and redefine the meaning of the word "homosexual" for the sake of maintaining or creating elements of ecclesial inclusivity. Homosexuality was once seen as a form of deviance, physiological illness, and illicit sexual behavior. Williams's book attempts to describe homosexual persons as "no less than heterosexual persons . . . individuals of sacred worth."[97] In the context of *The Church Studies Homosexuality*, the term "homosexual" should be interpreted as an outdated word that Williams originally used as an inclusive term for all nonheteronormative persons. Unfortunately, the church was acting in direct contradiction to what was happening at the General Conference level.

Union's Queering Rules of Engagement

Union used *The Church Studies Homosexuality* as an encyclopedia on nonheteronormative behavior and identity and as a guide for facilitating structured discussions on homosexuality. The leader's kit that accompanied the book included a leader's guide, six one-and-a-half-hour audio cassettes for audible learners, and alternative plans for an advanced ten-week retreat on understanding homosexual persons. One of the more practical contributions of the book was its rules for discussion. Williams recommended that pastors invite gay and lesbian persons to speak to church groups during the open and affirming process. After that, she contends that the church must begin a consistent and universal practice of using inclusive language. Williams suggests tackling the language issue by simply "developing an 'inclusive language' sheet for use in church bulletins, newsletters, announcements, and church life."[98] Williams presents the following rules for discussing homosexuality in UMC congregational settings:

Discussion Rules

1. We will speak with respect
   - *To* each other,
   - *Of* each other, and
   - *About* people outside our study group.
2. We will do our best to understand and express our own feelings on the subject of homosexuality.
3. When we speak, we will resist the natural desire to convince others that we are right. Instead, we will simply say what we ourselves have experienced, have read, or believe—and leave it at that.
4. We will be brief.

5. We will listen carefully to what others say.
6. We will keep confidential anything that a group member has said that might embarrass them if it were repeated outside the context of the study group.[99]

For Reverend Lockhart and the Union Church task force, speaking with respect about homosexuality meant recognizing the humanity in homosexual persons before discussing and bringing attention to their sexual practices. It meant using inclusive language and listening intently to ensure that persons understood what was said before speaking. Using inclusive language and speaking with respect is a form of social engagement where questions and statements are framed in a nonaccusatory, nondegrading, and nonoffensive manner and having the wisdom to know when silence is a better response to a point of contention than emotional confrontation.

However, speaking with respect and using inclusive language can also be quite complex. Heterosexuals' well-intended inquisitiveness sometimes borders on Black Queer objectification and toxic interrogation. For instance, when a heterosexual person is first introduced to Queer and nonbinary identities it is sinful to make assumptions about a person's possible sexual practices. It can also be difficult for heteronormative persons to be made aware of their linguistic privilege because their heteronormativity often precludes them from hearing the disrespectful tone of their questioning of and statements toward Queer persons. Furthermore, heterosexual privilege prevents many heterosexuals from being able to fathom worldviews outside of their own.

Black Queer congregants who courageously contribute to congregational queering by participating in conversations about gender and sexuality should be celebrated, but such would be a form of Black ecclesial scapegoating. By this, I mean that when heteronormative churches lean on their Queer members to be the face and driving forces behind the queering enterprise, this move in many ways puts the onus on Queer persons to do the work as opposed to the heterosexual individuals themselves. An example of this would be America expecting Black folk to fix the issues that concern racism and police brutality in the United States. Thankfully, this was not the case at Union. The push and driving forces behind Union's Black ecclesial queering came from cisgendered heterosexual women and the pastor.

The complexity of sex-talk in Black churches causes many Black church leaders to avoid these types of discussions. Consequently, most Black clergy belittle conversations about Black Queer persons to solely being about sex-talk. For this reason, many Black church leaders avoid talking about inclusivity and sexuality because of their pedagogical and socio-sexual ineptitude. This educational avoidance rooted in ignorance presents a problem because it inadvertently substantiates the problem. There is a unique pedagogical approach to discussing sexuality and gender in Black churches. Black churches like Union require a specific approach to Black ecclesial queering to effectively winnow white Western puritanicalism. The ignorance of the Puritans unearthed the brilliant denseness of American Indigenous-religious clay and replaced it with the toxic topsoil of radical puritanical Christianity. The avoidance of conversations around sexuality, homosexuality, and Queer life has been the breeding ground of Black homophobic sentimentality. Secrecy and silence have preserved and concretized Black homophobic practice and ideology; silence is one of the greatest hindrances to Black ecclesial queering. Considering these cultural factors, the rules for discussing homosexuality in *The Church Studies Homosexuality* are important because they give churches the language and tools for facilitating healthy conversations about Queer identity, gender, and sexuality. Nevertheless, the reality of the silence on the topic of homosexuality should not prohibit the encouragement of healthy dialogue about sex and sexuality in churches. Though speaking about sexuality was extremely risky because disrespectful engagement was always a possibility, Union used *The Church Studies Homosexuality* as a guide to monitor and create healthy discussion groups.

Black ecclesial queering is an enterprise that begins with listening and hearing multiple narratives and respecting those narratives as valid and real for the speaker. This level of respect creates common ground for narratives to be heard and spoken without the pressures of critique and scrutiny that often accompany persuasive conversations. A lack of the need to persuade others permits speakers to speak from their hearts instead of using debate tactics to win the discussion. At its core, Black ecclesial queering is an attempt to validate the voices and narratives of the silenced. Thus, listening and engagement are more effective tools for healthy sexual dialogue than debate and persuasiveness.

Further, whether one is interpreted as speaking respectfully or disrespectfully is solely based on the emotionality and life experiences of the interpreter or listener at the moment. Therefore, speaking with respect carries with it a responsibility that can only be assumed by the speaker. For Union, speaking with respect did not mean "saying things that everyone would agree with."[100] Rather, speaking with respect meant expressing your feelings about homosexuality and taking ownership of that expression. When Union Church's Homosexuality Study Group members took ownership of their own positions, they prohibited persons from creating hypothetical scenarios with which to distance themselves from the messiness of their statements. For example, during group sessions, Union member participants spoke in the first person, using *I, my, me, mine, for me, to me*, or *as I see it*. These pronouns forced persons speaking in the groups to take responsibility for what they were saying. Using first-person pronouns prevents persons from offering statements such as: "Someone said," "Someone told me," "I've been told," or other generalizations. When Union group participants took ownership of their words and used "I" statements, they were essentially expressing their ideas and feelings without appearing as projectionists. This one rule—speak with respect—prohibited Union parishioners from putting their words and opinions into the mouths of some other hypothetical person. In other words, this rule gave the group a real-life person with whom to interact in response to a question instead of a hypothetical person or situation.

The third rule of engagement at Union was the concept that one must resist the desire to convince others that they are right. The idea of right and wrong is undoubtedly a traditional dichotomy between "deontological and teleological theories of morality" upon which many humans thrive.[101] For many persons, the only goal in participating in group discussions about gender and sexuality is to convince everyone that *their* mode of scriptural interpretation and *their* sexual worldview is the only correct one. It can often be difficult for cisgendered African American heterosexual Christians to perceive a worldview that does not strictly fit into their biblically informed dichotomous and patriarchal notions of two genders and two categories: a right way (heteronormative—male/female) and a wrong way (nonheteronormative—nonbinary). If a heteronormative person enters a room to discuss nonheteronormative sexuality and they are only interested in proving their point, then the process of Black ecclesial queering can never begin. Black ecclesial queering only works when study group participants are willing to listen and grapple with the others' differing worldviews without convincing them to change. When group participants are allowed to speak, they must always speak about their *own* experiences, what *they* have read, what *they* believe, how *they* feel, but they must never force their opinions or beliefs on the entire group or others.

Union Church's task force also mandated that, during group discussions, all speakers be brief. Filibusters and long-winded monologues on sexuality tend to evolve into persuasive arguments that can quickly become obstructive, offensive, and communally polarizing beyond repair. Speaking briefly helps the conversation to flow evenly between participants without feeling like one person or like-minded persons are dominating the discussion space. Although there were no time limits or timekeepers, Union's task force asked participants to share their opinions caringly and to keep their comments concise and to the point.

Lastly, Union asked all participants to keep confidential what happened during group sessions. The confidentiality of church groups investigating sexuality is imperative. The entire goal of the task force was to create an inclusive space where persons could feel welcomed and affirmed. Confidentiality and trust are requirements for healthy group discussions on sex and sexuality. The only way to subvert heteronormativity is to introduce heteronormative persons to nonheteronormative persons and their narratives. Without such exposure, heterosexual empathy will never grow beyond mere pity. Interaction and awareness of others are the primary ways that empathy is produced. However, if group participants do not believe that their narratives will be held in confidence, they may be reluctant to share aspects of their stories. For this reason, vulnerability and confidentiality are undergirding principles through which Black ecclesial queering does its most transformative work.

Was Union's Black Ecclesial Queering "Black"?

One might argue that Union Church's queering was an entirely white enterprise because of the overarching ideals of American whiteness within United Methodism.[102] Regardless of the racial makeup of queerers like Hilda, it could be argued that the methodology as laid out in the UMC book was a white process. As a Black queer theorist I must admit that it would be within reason to interpret UMC's forms of ecclesial queering as an inherently white enterprise because white people wrote the book for a majority-white denomination. However, Reverend Lockhart understood that Black sexual discussions required special attention to the narratives of Black folk. Like Patricia Collins Hill, Reverend Lockhart believed that any interrogation of sexuality in a Black church had to begin with an investigation of the history of Blackness and Black sexuality in America. For this reason, Reverend Lockhart not only used white UMC materials to navigate Union's queering process, but he also intentionally invited Black clinicians to contextualize Union's queering process in Blackness. For this reason, Reverend Lockhart and the committee invited Rev. Wesley Williams, executive director of the United Methodist Urban Services of Boston, to serve as the clinician for one of the Union congregation's group discussions about the urban gay and lesbian community in the South End.

Reverend Williams, an African American, had served as a member of the United Methodist Church's General Committee on Homosexuality during the 1988 General United Methodist Church Conference. Since Union was already reading the study for United Methodist groups and using the *Report of the Committee to Study Homosexuality*, Reverend Lockhart and the task force decided to ask Reverend Williams to teach a six-week course on the history of gay African American communities and biblical texts on homosexuality. The course interrogated Black gay culture and the African American dynamics of homophobia that make it distinct from white American homophobia. Reverend Williams introduced the idea that Black homophobia was much more than a scriptural phenomenon or the result of incorrect scriptural interpretation. Instead, he argued that the history of homophobic practices in Black culture is a conglomeration of white socio-historical American-Christian values and Black weddedness to heteronormative ideals. Williams argued that Black and white religious leaders intentionally used these values to coerce African Americans into performing proper heterosexual habits.

Reverend Williams also taught the history of the United Methodist Church's homosexuality debate and shared how a church like Union might queer its Black ecclesiology. He encouraged Reverend Lockhart and the committee to use history, cultural studies, critical theory, literary criticism, rhetorical criticism, theology, and ethics to demonstrate how Christian disputes over homosexuality emerged in United Methodism. He suggested works like the books of James Cone, poets like Audre Lorde, and James Baldwin's lecture titled "Race, Racism, and the Gay Community" from a 1982 meeting of the New York chapter of Black and White Men Together. Reverend Lockhart also discussed how the UMC's inclusivity needed to be shaped in the future. This one action by Reverend Lockhart to Blacken the queering process at Union is what made its process a type of Black ecclesial queering.

Essentially, Union did not abandon its Blackness to queer its ecclesiology. Rather, Union's queering process included Black Queer voices as a part of the diverse chorus that constituted the cultural idea of Blackness and Black culture. During its queering process, Union invited Black gay and lesbian voices to "share information on the African American gay community's" history, cultural uniqueness, needs, challenges, and value to Blackness and overall Black culture because, at that time, very few of Union's members were both Black and openly gay.[103]

For Union, Black ecclesial queering started with an awareness of Queer persons due to a changing neighborhood and a desire to learn how to be in community with their new and evolving context. For Black churches, queering must include Black voices and cultural connections. The uniqueness of their geographical location combined with their desire to practice radical hospitality before the interrogation of anti-gay Scripture or traditional heteronormative Christian values of United Methodism is what drove their queering enterprise and guaranteed its success. This is an essential aspect of Black ecclesial queering. *Successful Black ecclesial queering necessitates engagement with Queer persons, Queer biographies, Queer stories, Queer histories, and present Queer realities over and above what the Bible or any other man-made materials have to say about Queer existence.*[104] Black ecclesial queering begins with Black Queer persons, not with an interrogation or apologetic articulation about Scripture, doctrine, or tradition divorced from reason, faith, and experience.

Additionally, Union's task force sought the assistance of three African American gay men: Matthew Florence, then executive director of MOCAA (Men of Color Against AIDS); Douglas Brooks, then a constituent member of Union; and Ed McClain of the PrideLights Foundation.[105] These different queer perspectives created the perfect platform for Union's task force to interrogate Black sexuality, Black homosexuality, Black homophobia, and Black ecclesiology. Such a move prohibited Union from creating offensive generalizations about Black Queer persons. These three gay Black men taught Union that the gay and lesbian community was a complex community of many identities and expressions.

In addition to their interrogation of Black queerness, the task force and Reverend Lockhart sought to build congregational consensus about being open and affirming by intentionally practicing transparency and openness throughout the discernment process. Nothing was done privately or without congregational feedback. Parishioners were allowed to ask direct and honest questions about passages like Hebrews 13, Leviticus 18:22, Romans 1, 1 Corinthians 6:17–20, and Leviticus 20:13, to name a few. While this may seem like an infinitesimal moment in Union's overall queering process, it is one of the major aspects of Union's queering process that secured its overall congregational success and consensus. Openness, transparency, and the willingness to hear all sides of the conversation are vital not only to the success of the discernment process but also for the benefit and success of Black ecclesial queering's commitment to the edification, betterment, and cohesion of the African American community at large.

According to Ruby, a twenty-year member of Union, the discussions about Scripture never really got out of hand during the discernment process because "Union and its pastors had always taught somewhat of a more liberal rather than literal usage of the Bible."[106] Even Reverend Lockhart stated that, at Union, the Bible was a book inspired by the Spirit of God but written by people, so most people understood the usage of a hermeneutics of suspicion even if they had never heard that academic phrase. However, to reduce any confusion, at the end of the studies, Reverend Lockhart wrote a statement to address many of the questions that had come up during the discernment process. His statement reads,

> I eventually wrote Union's Statement as A Reconciling and Inclusive Church, the original of which was prepared as a discussion paper for members of the task force. Once the task force agreed on the content of that statement, it was presented to the members of the congregation for their reaction and comments and, I believe, published on the church's website, and occasionally printed as a bulletin insert. After about eighteen months of discussion, the Statement was presented to Union's Administrative Council . . . which authorized at that time that steps be taken to register Union with the Reconciling Congregation Program. Union thereby became the first predominantly African American United Methodist congregation in all of United Methodism to officially identify itself as a "reconciling" and welcoming congregation to gays, lesbians, and all the rest of God's diverse people.[107]

On February 15, 2000, Union Church voted to become reconciling and inclusive, with the adoption of the following resolution: "We affirm the full participation in all aspects of our church life of all who confess Jesus

Christ as Lord and Savior, regardless of their race, color, physical challenge, sexual orientation and/or affectional orientation."[108] However, it should be noted that the queering of Union's ecclesiology was not without contest or challenges. According to Ruby, Cynthia, and June, all longtime senior members of Union:

Ruby: I mean, don't get us wrong. Members left, some members left, after we became reconciling. It was not that many. But we knew the ones who left; they did not say a word, they just stopped coming.[109]

Cynthia: We might have lost, but I don't think it was for that reason. As was stated earlier with Reverend Lockhart being humble and laid back or whatever—he was old school. People did not like the way he preached. It had nothing to do with the "gay and lesbian" issue; they did not like the way he preached.[110]

June: The little I know, I do not think there was any financial impact. People came and left. The people that stayed were still the givers.[111]

These statements are powerful testimonies of healthy queering. This might seem strange, because one might consider successful congregational queering to be restricted to the utopian ideal of an instance where a church was queered and no one left. Such a concept is a woefully unrealistic distraction that often causes Black ecclesial queering to fail. The truth is, everyone will not agree on the matter of inclusiveness in a historic African American church, and that is okay. Healthy queering is not measured by the quantity of a congregation's membership post-queering but rather by the quality of the queering process itself. Healthy congregational queering—which involves transparency, openness, respect, attention to Black history and Black culture, the narrative/history of the church, and a love for all—will help a congregation with the issue of retention of members if the queering resembles the essence of the church's cultural, social, and contextual identity. One of the reasons that the Union queering process appears to have had only a slightly negative effect on the overall well-being of the congregation was that it was done with a great amount of transparency, respect for the denominational polity, and pastoral care, which are all major features of healthy and quality congregational queering.

It would be incorrect to argue that Union's queering process ended on February 15, 2000. Such would suggest that the congregation's publication and adoption of a statement alone is the totality of Black ecclesial queering. Instead, Black ecclesial queering should be viewed as an ongoing process of making meaning from the margins. Throughout this ongoing process, Black ecclesial queering becomes more than just a subversion of norms and rituals; it becomes a new normal for the congregation and its parishioners. For Union, there is a living ecclesiology, a new normal that their Black ecclesial queering produced, and it redefined how they understood the church, evangelism, United Methodism, church missions, and Blackness.

The Present Queered Ecclesiology of Union Church

How does Union Church understand what it means to be a church, now that it has been and still is being queered? Union Church describes itself as "an urban, multicultural faith community committed to extending love and justice to all people."[112] While Union's two-hundred-year history is deeply rooted in the narratives of Black Bostonians, the church's current demographics span far beyond the traditional notions of what it means to be a member of a Black American church. Union's membership includes a spectrum of ethnicities, generations, economic brackets, and gender identities, as well as lifetime Christians, new converts, skeptics, and spectators.

Union is not considered to be some sort of exclusive social club or religious clique. Instead, Union views itself as an inclusive community of believers who support the church's work through prayer, weekly worship attendance, financial and spiritual contributions, community service, justice work, and being witnesses of love; this is what Union understands as *church*. For Union, the church has four real-life manifestations: worship, discipleship, service, and leadership. Under the direction of its present pastor, Reverend Dr. Gerald Williams Jr., Union has adopted a new local vision and mission that is both connected to the United Methodist tradition and contextualized to meet the needs of the church's present demographic. The project is called *UnionWorships, UnionDisciples, UnionServes, and UnionLeads*. It is the church's way of building and unifying the local assembly through corporate worship. The church's work may extend throughout the week, but Sunday is still the busiest day of the Union Church week because worship is one of the most primary reasons for a church community's existence.

During interviews with some of Union Church's members, it was always striking to me that while, in most cases, the interviewee was aware of and supported the social justice and radical activism that is so intricately woven into the DNA of Union's ecclesiology, there always seemed to be a strong reverence for and appreciation of the Union communal worship experience. Sometimes during interviews congregants may not have been able to explicitly explain their ecclesiology or theology using seminary terms or academic jargon, but it was evident that their exposure to and understanding of God was highly affected, if not solely informed, by the worship experiences and sermons from the Union sanctuary. If justice and activism are the work of Union Church, then communal worship, baptism, and celebration of the Eucharist constitute the Christian praxis that equips, energizes, and reenergizes the church for social engagement. This praxis alone deeply steeps Union's ecclesiology in the Black religious tradition. From the days of the brush-harbor churches where enslaved Africans worshiped to sustain themselves and amid the evils of slavery, throughout the civil rights era when Black churches held prayer meetings and hymn rallies to prepare marchers for dangerous protesting, Black churches have served as centers of therapeutic worship for weary Black souls; that is an essential part of their empathic potency.

On Sunday mornings, African American gospel music and the most current praise and worship songs fill Union's sacred nave with community and familial energy. In some strange and mystical way, the soundscapes of Black worship have a way of soothing Black souls that were either born into or exposed to Black religious traditions at some point in their lives. These aural experiences are so powerful and so important to the Black religious soul that they are often the only aspect of the Black worship experience that conjure up solemn or wholesome memories of Black church culture(s) for religiously exiled Black Queer persons. The sound and feel of Black Christians worshiping in the ecclesial community is a priceless and unduplicatable experience that white churches cannot authentically produce. Black church cultures are not just chords and harmonies; they are made up of a lived experiences of the people. The cultures of Black churches include the moans, coughs, infant cries, shouts of joy, quiet reflection, meditation, instrumentation, cracking sounds of pews, syncopated clapping, whispers and shouts, the hum of a Leslie cabinet, the flipping switches of the B3 organ, the soothing voices of Black pastors whose melodic speaking brings hope, and the sacred energy and felt sense of our ancestors. While these examples of the sounds of Black churches may not perfectly fit every Black ecclesial context, they do encapsulate one point: the experience of Black church is a communal production that echoes and reinforces a type of Blackness and Black religion.

However, what makes Union Church special is its conscious decision not to restrict the sound and feel of Black churches to Black heteronormative folk. Union realized that the soothing sounds and communal care of the Black worship experience were what many Black Queer persons were looking for, so they opened their hearts and welcomed the stones that the builders rejected. While many Black churches still seek to change Black Queer folk into Black heteronormative persons before fully welcoming them into their ecclesial contexts, Union Church queered the understanding of what it meant to be a part of the production and curation of Black ecclesial soundscapes and traditions. At Union, the worship leader did not have to "butch up" or be "more ladylike" to function in the service. The bifurcation of Queer identity is nonexistent in Union worship. Union is not just a *come-as-you-are church*, but it is also a *stay-as-you-are church*. Union does not equate spiritual transformation with sexual deprivation. For this reason, Union continues to be a dream come true for Black Queer Christians living in the Boston metro area who long for the sound and feel of Black worship without the shroud of heteronormativity.

Union believes that the church is the primary means through which disciples' faith formation is cultivated. Reverend Williams calls this *UnionDisciples*, which is about the practice of faith in the everyday life of a Christian. For Union, church is not just what happens on Sunday morning. It is also a community of spiritual support and spiritual growth through the practice of communal Bible study, age, and interest-specific prayer groups, fellowship, ministry groups, weekly Sunday school, and reoccurring midweek prayer calls. As a United Methodist church, the *UnionDisciples* strategy adheres to the UMC's *Book of Discipline*.[113] The *Book of Discipline* states in "The Ministry of All Christians":

> The mission of the Church is to make disciples of Jesus Christ. Local churches provide the most significant arena through which disciple-making occurs. . . . The mission of the Church is to make disciples of Jesus Christ by proclaiming the good news of God's grace and thus seeking the fulfillment of God's reign and realm in the world. The fulfillment of God's reign and realm in the world is the vision Scripture holds before us.[114]

While this ecclesial mission may be the same in all United Methodist churches, Union's queered interpretation and implementation of this mission make it distinct from its counterparts. At Union, disciple-making is more about creating an inclusive global community of Christian love than proselytization as a means of gender conformity and identity control. However, the church's respect for tradition remains intact past its queering process. The congregation is more focused on revitalizing and reenergizing the traditions of Christianity than discarding them. In other words, Union did not forget or discard its Christianity in the queering process, but rather, within their traditions, they analyzed the intrinsic queerness of the gospel message. Union revived and reinterpreted Christianity to be synonymous with Queer inclusivity. By extending membership, the journey of nonjudgmental Christian discipleship, and the soundscapes and feel of Black church worship, Union freed its Christian language and tradition to extend beyond the limited Western purview from which it was created. For Union, queering was not the process by which the congregation separated itself from the Christian practice of being the church. Rather, queering was an act of discipleship that Union saw as an extension and fulfillment of its mission and calling.

UnionServes is the official justice arm of Union Church. *UnionServes* aims to transform the neighboring communities of Boston through community service, political activism, social protest, Christian witness, bold international missions, and radical hospitality. Twice monthly, the Union food pantry feeds the homeless community of the South End. Many churches see this as a side responsibility of the church. The pressure to consistently create dynamic worship experiences to secure a congregation's sustainability and growth can make it easy to center a church's efforts solely around the production of a Sunday morning experience. However, Union maintains a healthy balance between worship and social responsibility. Union's ecclesial mission is to hold in health tension the theological traditions of justification, social justice, evangelism, and social transformation. The congregation makes room for each of the previously stated traditions to carry equal weight and value while using communal dialogue to promote faithful discipleship and Christian education.[115]

UnionLeads is the arm of Union Church that develops and mentors spiritual leaders through educational training to do the work of the ministry. Many times, when persons think about Black churches, the first thing that comes to mind is Black pastors. However, many Black churches could not and would not survive with the leadership of Black preachers alone. Since their beginnings, Black churches have been the product of the labor, finances, and resources of Black Christians living in the surrounding communities. In many Black Baptist traditions, local churches could not afford to pay a pastor a full-time salary. For this reason, many Black Baptist churches only worshiped on the first and third Sundays or second and fourth Sundays, permitting local churches to share pastors while maintaining their congregational distinctions. In Black Methodist churches like Union, pastors are constantly moved and elevated by district superintendents and bishops. Despite the denominational connectedness and episcopal structure of the Methodist tradition, local churches are still mostly supported by the resources and tithes of local members. It is also important to acknowledge that because of the itinerary of Methodist pastors, their base membership almost always outdates the pastor's tenure, creating an interesting dynamic within which an appointed pastor must work.[116]

At Union, however, Reverend Williams's primary challenge is securing long-term staff to assist in the overall church administration. Because Union serves as the flagship church for Black United Methodism in the state of Massachusetts and New England, when the church manages to bring gifted individuals to its staff, the episcopal district has had a tradition of scouting and assigning those persons to serve as acting or lay pastors of failing parishes. Thus, Reverend Williams has launched the *UnionLeads* project to cultivate lay leaders to carry on the tradition of Union inclusivity beyond the pulpit.[117]

Union Church is not an autonomous African American congregation. It is a local United Methodist church that is part of a connectional system, or interconnected network of churches, that enables United Methodist Christians "to carry out the mission of unity and strength."[118] However, despite the *Book of Discipline*'s explicit description of a universal understanding of United Methodist ecclesiology, the living ecclesiologies of United Methodism only exist in congregations on the local level. The local congregation is where members are forced to reason with Scripture, their own experiences, and tradition. This type of reasoning produces a type of local United Methodist ecclesiology that is meaningful for and specific to the local congregation.

Because of the varying contexts of United Methodism—the five geographic jurisdictions in the United States, and the seven geographical regions in Africa, Europe, and the Philippines—local United Methodist churches have identities, goals, missions, and ideals of their own that may or may not reflect the consensus of the entire UMC system. In researching Union Church, what I found most interesting were not the aspects of their local ecclesiology that perfectly aligned with its interconnected network of organizations and churches. Instead, I found myself most interested in the nuances and differences between Union and the other members of its connectional system. In these differences I discovered the most valued aspects of Union's queered ecclesiology.

A Final Statement on Union's Inclusive Ecclesiology and Process of Queering

The process of queering Union Church was a congregational initiative. Today, Union's inclusivity is so woven into the life of the church that it might seem difficult to imagine a gender-exclusive and sexually oppressive Union. However, the success of Union's queering did not come without difficulty. Union Church lost members, experienced a downward turn in giving, and even bore the burden of being labeled the "gay church" of Boston. Nevertheless, many of the members of Union stayed together, steadfast in their inclusivity, and in the end the congregation thrived.

Union Church's process of Black ecclesial queering involved eighteen steps:[119]

1. The bold gay- and lesbian-affirming inquisitiveness of a faithful heterosexual member in good standing. She was concerned with reaching out to that group. That was a part of her motive.
2. Pastoral support from Reverend Lockhart, the senior minister of the congregation.
3. As a response to the inquisitiveness of the faithful church member, the pastor invited interested persons to read *The Church Studies Homosexuality*, written and published by the UMC.
4. After that, persons decided that they wanted to become part of a task force to study becoming a reconciling congregation.
5. The pastor appointed them as an ad hoc committee without having to go through the normal procedure of having the church vote to approve the process for a new official standing committee of the church.

6. Direct congregational and small-group engagement with Black Queer persons, Black Queer biographies, and the needs of Black Queer persons. The group wanted that input from people within the group.
7. Prayer, Bible study, meditation, worship, and sermonic reflections.
8. Micro- and macro-level congregational studies of *The Church Studies Homosexuality*.
9. Reverend Lockhart wrote the first draft of Union's *Statement as a Reconciling and Inclusive Church* for the members of the task force.
10. Once the task force agreed on the content of that statement, it was presented to representatives of the Black and white gay and lesbian communities, who were asked to give feedback on the statement.
11. Eighteen months of one-to-one relational sharing with individual members of the worshiping congregation about inclusivity and homosexuality.
12. Reverend Lockhart preached a revival theme—Running the Business of Reconciliation—for the Rev. John Handson and the First Lutheran Church of Hamilton.
13. On the Sunday morning of Human Relations Day in 2000, instead of a sermon, there was a panel presentation by the task force members with each member sharing why they supported the statement and why the church as a whole should adopt it.
14. Following the panel presentation, the congregation took a nonbinding straw vote that was to be written on a piece of paper and given to the ushers. (On the day of the straw vote at Union, 75 percent supported the statement, 5 percent did not support the statement, and the remainder of the votes were split between undecided and invalid voters.) After this vote, the task force was convinced that 75 percent was enough to present the statement to the church council. Reverend Lockhart believed that they needed 85 percent to succeed. However, he trusted the intuition of the task force members.
15. On February 15, 2000, the statement was presented to Union's administrative council, and the church council voted to become a reconciling and inclusive congregation with the adoption of a Statement of Inclusivity.
16. The council authorized that steps be taken to register Union with the Reconciling Congregations Program;
17. Union reportedly became the first predominantly African American United Methodist congregation in all of United Methodism to

officially identify itself as a reconciling and welcoming congregation to gays, lesbians, and all the rest of God's diverse people.
18. A special service in celebration of this decision to become a Reconciling and Inclusive Church was held on Palm Sunday, April 16, 2000. Reverend Lockhart designed the service using resources from the Reconciling Congregation's Office and the UM Book of Worship, but some portions he wrote expressly for the Union Service itself.

Union Church is an institution steeped in notions of love, kinship, social justice, and community. Without fail, the church conceptualizes itself as a family. Both the head pastor and lay members emphasize the importance of implementing new church legislation through community engagement. The church did not queer its ecclesiology through executive decisions but rather through collective conversations and a majority vote. This is seen most clearly through Union Church's decision to become an open and affirming congregation. Instead of the head pastor deciding that the church would become queer affirming, a lay member's inquiry on Queer rights led Union Church's journey to Queer affirmation. From this inquiry, the church launched a full campaign during which they conducted Bible studies that, in turn, fostered deep and meaningful conversations about the sanctity of Queer persons.

Ultimately, Union Church chose to become affirming, a decision birthed out of the church's commitment to center kinship and its history as a justice-oriented church as the primary frameworks for its ecclesial connection. For Union, the church is a place where everyone matters, and they believe that the exclusion of Queer persons would undermine their self-proclaimed familial identity. Most importantly, the members of Union believed that they could never truly be a Christian community until they welcomed all persons into their community of kinship and love.

4
Models of Black Ecclesial Queering, Part II

A Pastoral Model—Mount Nebo Missionary Baptist Church

Congregational queering is not the only form of Black ecclesial queering. The ecclesiology of many Black Baptist and Holiness-Pentecostal churches is solely predicated on the theological and organizational preferences of the church's senior pastor. Many Black male pastors, especially Black Baptist pastors, possess excessive amounts of congregational trust, authority, and power.[1] According to ethicist Peter Paris, "American scholars have long been puzzled in their attempts to explain the amount of authority exercised by the typical African American pastor."[2] Paris contends that pastoral authority in African American churches is best understood as a type of African cultural retention.[3] For Paris, Black churches are American spaces where African American people re-create African tribal traditions, where chiefs and kings are imbued with a wide range of authoritative powers.[4]

In this chapter I analyze the authority and power of a Black pastor whose wide range of congregational trust and authoritative powers gave him the ability to queer his congregation single-handedly. I argue that his social and cultural capital enabled him to turn a traditional heteronormative Black church into a citywide haven for Queer persons. In this chapter I also describe and argue for a particular pastoral form of Black ecclesial queering. I focus on recounting and preserving the narrative of a man who was courageous enough to do what no one else would in his city.

Mount Nebo Missionary Baptist Church

Mount Nebo Missionary Baptist Church is one of the oldest Black churches in Trenton and one of the few Baptist safe spaces for Black Queer persons.[5]

124   QUEERING BLACK CHURCHES

Table 4.1. Mount Nebo Missionary Baptist Church Demographics Chart

Membership	250 persons 197 Female 53 Male 0 Nonbinary/NGC
Annual budget	$400,000
Typical Sunday attendance	100
Emeritus Pastor's Educational Level	B.A., Oxford College M.Div., Yale University
Median Congregational Educational Level	Associate or Bachelor's
Neighborhood Median Income	$55,000
Church Demographics	93 percent Black 4 percent Latinx 2 percent White 1 percent Other
Neighborhood Racial Demographics	45 percent Black 36 percent White 15.6 percent Latinx 2 percent Asian 0.4 percent American and Alaskan Natives 1 percent Other
Neighborhood Population	Whites = 97,700 Asians = 58,100 Hispanics = 30,400 Blacks = 30,200
Neighborhood Median House Price	$423,567
Additional Neighborhood Information	89 percent of Black households in the South End are led by single Black women, 49.9 percent of the Black households are on food stamps

Founded in July 1897 by five Black Trenton families and a handful of other Black Trenton residents, Mount Nebo grew for a period of time into a twenty-first-century intentionally diversified congregation with people of all races, ages, and sexual orientations, and from all walks of life (see Table 4.1). Throughout its 121-year history in Trenton, Mount Nebo Missionary Baptist Church has earned the reputation of being one of the most socially and communally active churches in the state. Historically, Mount Nebo's membership roster was filled with prominent white- and blue-collar African American citizens of Trenton.

Unlike the dense and well-documented history of Blacks in Boston's South End, the history of African Americans in Trenton is less documented. Many of Mount Nebo's more senior members were transplants to Trenton from the southern states of Alabama, Georgia, Mississippi, and Louisiana during the Second Great Migration in the early 1940s.[6] Other Mount Nebo members and Black Trenton residents came to the area from the Caribbean.[7] When Blacks arrived in Trenton from the South during the Great Migration to work in various factory positions in Trenton, Mount Nebo Missionary Baptist Church was the only church that prioritized faith and Blackness for minority migrants. Mount Nebo's warm and familial characteristics were reminiscent of the South for many Mount Nebo members like Charles Parker, who grew up picking cotton in Mississippi, during the civil rights movement, or Sarah Terrell, who was raised in Montgomery, Alabama. The fact that many of Mount Nebo's congregants are southern transplants is not a coincidence or a rarity. The Great Migration of African Americans from the racist southern states to the more integrated states of the North was a common occurrence during the 1900s.[8] The religious enculturation of many of these southern migrants caused them to seek spiritual homes in the Black churches of the North.[9] Since the church was the primary medium for meaning-making for some Black southern Christian migrants, it makes sense that migrant Christians like Charles and Sarah joined Black churches as a way of finding and creating community in a new place.[10]

According to Mount Nebo member Josephine Durnell, who grew up in an all-Black neighborhood in Louisiana, in the 1940s, "Trenton is definitely racist.... But this church brings me hope. It makes me feel like we're fighting against racism.... The outside community may be racist," she said, "but Mount Nebo Baptist fights for the community and equality."[11] While the formation of Mount Nebo Church predates the Great Migration, the stories of Durnell, Parker, and Terrell illustrate that Mount Nebo has long welcomed migrants and oppressed Black souls into its community of believers with open arms to help them feel more accepted. This was the drawing power of Mount Nebo Missionary Baptist Church from 1985 until 2008. Mount Nebo was the only Black church that was keenly aware of and responding to the needs of impoverished Black folks. However, the efficacy of Mount Nebo's social activism and prophetic witness was heightened and greatly expanded under the leadership of its most revered pastor, the Reverend Robert Williams Franklin. While the church's outreach initiatives may have always included social action and civil demonstration before his arrival, Reverend Franklin is solely responsible for the reputation that it developed in the early 2000s as a safe haven for substance abusers and Queer folk. Thus, in most of this chapter I examine the personality, vision, calling, and work of Robert William Franklin. Reverend Franklin intentionally and strategically introduced LGBTQIAP+ affirmation to Mount Nebo in a way that guaranteed its success during his pastorate. Simply put, Reverend Franklin used the power of the Black pulpit and preacher to change the church's views on sexuality and marriage equality.

The life and ministry of the Reverend Robert William Franklin offer an inspiring tale of prophetic preaching, social activism, and unique individuality.[12] His radically generous and gregarious personality was the foundation of his pastoral ministry, and it continues to be the energy that has sustained his ministerial itinerancy during retirement. Mount Nebo's ecclesiology, moreover, is a direct reflection of the life and ministry of Reverend Robert William Franklin. Reverend Franklin's interpretations of Black ecclesiology and Black theology coupled with his anti-literalist understanding of Scripture and commitment for social activism became the overarching characteristics of Mount Nebo's communal identity. They originally called upon him to be the pastor of the church because of his commitment to Black survival and social activism.

Throughout my years of qualitative research at Mount Nebo, I often attended Bible studies, Sunday school classes, diaconate meetings, and worship services. In moments of communal education congregants would quote what Reverend Franklin had previously said in a sermon more often than they quoted Scripture or outside theologians. Once, during their weekly Thursday night Bible study after Reverend Franklin's retirement, a member corrected a point made by the newly elected pastor using a statement that Reverend Franklin made several years ago. The majority of the comments I heard throughout my years of studying the congregation were, "Reverend Franklin used to say," "Reverend Franklin would say," or "like Reverend Franklin always used to say." I quickly realized that Reverend Franklin was the key to understanding Mount Nebo's queered ecclesiology.[13]

While the account of Mount Nebo's queering in this chapter may appear too biographical or too focused on a particular pastor, this should not be regarded as abnormal. Union Church, the subject of the previous chapter, is a connectional episcopacy where pastors are moved and appointed to congregations as senior pastors for various amounts of time. On the other hand, Black Baptist pastors have a long-standing history of pastoral tenures often lasting beyond thirty years. Because of the autonomous nature of Black Baptist churches, beloved and long-tenured pastors almost always possess cultural capital and trust from their congregations. In these contexts, parishioners will often grant their pastors the full authority and jurisdiction to change the church's polity, ecclesiology, or the theological ideals of the church without question. In other words, a well-respected and revered Black Baptist pastor who serves a congregation for ten years or more and substantially grows the church's membership or finances typically has the authority to operate the church as they wish. More importantly, such a person often leaves indelible marks and nostalgic effects on the spirituality, ecclesiology, theology, and overall faith traditions of the church and its members.

Many Black Baptist churches with long-tenured pastors also acquire the personalities of their pastors. It is common to see deacons and associate ministers mirroring the mannerisms and echoing the sentiments of their senior leaders. In most situations, Black Baptist and Holiness-Pentecostal churches are more likely to be personality-driven spiritual spaces than their Methodist counterparts. There is often so much pastoral transition in Methodist churches that congregants rarely have the time to develop deep relationships with their pastors, so they become more attached to the congregation and its members than they do to its changing ministers. However, in Black Baptist churches, pastors can serve for such long tenures that a pastorate can present itself as a small empire where the pastor is revered and respected as a patriarch or matriarch. Such was the case with Reverend Franklin and Mount Nebo Missionary Baptist Church.

The queering of Mount Nebo was not a congregational pursuit or undertaking; it was solely the result of Reverend Franklin hearing and heeding the voice of God to queer the church. Reverend Franklin had been there long enough. He had baptized the congregants' babies, married most of the couples, stood by the bedsides of dying members with their families, and even helped many of the congregants to pay their bills during moments of financial hardship. He had earned the cultural capital of the congregation and gained their trust. Therefore, by the time he heeded the call of God to queer his congregation, he did not fear massive opposition. Reverend Franklin essentially queered the church single-handedly. His pastoral queering was successful for a short time during Franklin's tenure.

Let me offer one final argument for focusing this entire section on one man. I have studied Mount Nebo Missionary Baptist Church closely for over five years. It started with a simple lunch with Reverend Franklin at Trenton's local country club. I discussed this book's topic with him and asked his permission to include Mount Nebo in the research collection. He was very excited and immediately agreed to give me all the support needed to complete this project. However, he also stated that he would be retiring in one year and that I should try to conduct my research within that timeframe. Reverend Franklin even helped set up most of the meetings. Despite many phone calls, lunch dates, and meetings with him before his retirement, I still needed more data. At first I was discouraged and nervous that the new pastor might not be interested in me continuing this type of research in their church. To my delight, the new pastor warmly welcomed me, and I was permitted to continue collecting data.

Upon Reverend Franklin's retirement, an unsettling truth emerged during a group interview. Twelve members began speaking openly about the fact that they honestly did not know what it meant to be open and affirming, nor did they realize that the church had such a huge reputation for being a haven for Trenton's Black Queer community. Frequently, they said: "Reverend Franklin said inclusion was what God told him to do, so we said okay. Some people got upset and left, but Reverend kept preaching about it, and we followed and stayed."[14] Even when I asked Reverend Franklin how he queered the church, he explained that he simply taught inclusivity in Bible study, through the preached Word, and in question-and-answer sessions after sermons. He essentially used Christian education as a tool to facilitate dialogues about affirming Queer folk, but he admitted that his queering was often vague and under the radar. He never told them that he was beginning a process of queering the church; he just proceeded to follow his own intuition without well-constructed strategies.

When asked, "When did the church agree to become open and affirming? And when did it officially become affirming?" he replied, "It didn't. It just naturally happened." This phrase "it just happened," while true, is also misleading. Nothing just happens in Black churches. Everything has a backstory with hidden roots. Queering never fully happened to Mount Nebo Church in a way that could be maintained. This complex connection between the Reverend's life and work and the transformation of Mount Nebo Church indicates that the only way to describe and depict the queered ecclesiology of Mount Nebo accurately is to interrogate the life story and spiritual journey of Reverend Franklin and his pastoral relationship with the church. The next section examines the pastoral style of Reverend Franklin.

Reverend Franklin: A Practitioner of Gospel Foolishness (1 Corinthians 1:18—"for the message of the cross is foolishness")

If two words could describe Reverend Franklin's pastorate, they would be *Queer* and *inclusive*. As a pastor, Reverend Franklin unconditionally embraced every person he encountered as a unique expression of God's Spirit.[15] As a life-giving spirit himself, Reverend Franklin embodied and modeled what it meant to be different, creative, surprising, and fresh in one's pastoral perspectives and actions. Reverend Franklin's pastoral presence was filled with an unlimited supply of spiritual energy empowered by love, faith, and imagination.

As a spiritual visionary, Reverend Franklin was a mover and shaker in every sense of the word. During my meetings with him, his prophetic genius was always apparent, and he was always thinking. The patterns of thought that swept through his mind were always offered as visions, hopes, and an analysis of life. Even when engaging with parishioners in casual conversation, he would always find a way to challenge them critically toward personal and structural transformation. Essentially, Reverend Franklin moved listeners toward spiritual transformation with his words and his life. Watching Reverend Franklin was also an engaging experience. While Reverend Franklin undoubtedly moved people with his words, he also moved when he preached and in normal conversations. He would physically accent his speech with sporadic movements and sways.

Reverend Franklin also frequently burst into random bouts of laughter as he explained the theological thoughts that ran through his mind. Whether in meetings, in the pulpit, or in his office, Reverend Franklin was always full of joy and smiling. Laughter and joy were spiritual practices of resistance for him. His joy often revealed itself in his hands and legs, which were always moving to a slight beat. His perpetual excitement also propelled him to change seats three or more times in a conversation and during worship services. Reverend Franklin was also known for only wearing sandals, even at the height of winter. While this last observation may seem somewhat superfluous, it is a great indicator of the type of freedom and out-of-the-box charisma that marked Reverend Franklin's pastorate. He was a free spirit, unbound and unrestricted. Reverend Franklin marched to the beat of his own drum.

Reverend Franklin's unique personality is exactly what made him such a radically inclusive leader. His differences, freedom, and wit naturally fostered mutually affirming relationships with a wide range of people, awakening their inner child. Reverend Franklin often took moments to laugh and playfully acknowledged the child within himself.[16] This uniqueness helped him see and celebrate the uniqueness of others. While Reverend Franklin is heterosexual and married to Mrs. Sally Jones-Franklin, with whom he raised a daughter, Samantha Franklin, and a son, James Du Bois, he was the quintessential example of a minister who lived and led queerly. He pastored from a queered worldview. I categorize Reverend Franklin's ministry as Queer, not just because he ministered to Queer people. Instead, I offer that his ministry was Queer because it made "the same different, the familiar strange, and the odd wonderful."[17] Reverend Franklin's ministry was a ministry of Christian insurrection and subversion; it was Queer. And by Queer, I mean that he did such in faithfulness to the diverse, unconventional, and marvelous aspects of the story of Jesus in the Gospels.[18] Next, I discuss how Reverend Franklin managed to gain enough social capital to pastorally queer his church singlehandedly without resistance from his flock. I argue that compassion, innate Christian hospitality, wit, brilliance, congregational trust, total pastoral authority, and unique prophetic sensibilities gave Reverend Franklin the freedom to pastorally queer the church he led and ultimately caused the church to be in a state of confusion upon his retirement.

How One Person Almost Queered an Entire Black Church

Once Reverend Franklin was asked to list his favorite things. He stated that his favorite day was Friday the thirteenth, his favorite book was *Oh the Places You'll Go* by Dr. Seuss, his favorite poem was "We Are the Young Musicians" by Ruth Forman, and his favorite sacred text was Ecclesiastes 10:19.[19] This list of Reverend Franklin's favorite things reveals keen aspects of him as a person and pastor and the revelation that pushed him to queer Mount Nebo. Reverend Franklin believed that it was his calling to "affirm the child within himself and within others."[20] He often found value in childlike openness and youthful practices. However, Reverend Franklin's affinity for Friday the thirteenth reveals his capacity to resist cultural and religious influences and embrace that which has been traditionally stereotyped as negative, demonic, and evil. For Reverend Franklin, the Christian call to ministry carries with it the responsibility to welcome and find value in the peculiar and unfamiliar with compassion and understanding. A product of Western superstition, Friday the thirteenth has traditionally been regarded as one of the most cursed days on the Gregorian calendar.[21] However, for Reverend Franklin, Friday the thirteenth represented an opportunity to encounter a stereotyped circumstance while simultaneously embracing its peculiarity.

Reverend Franklin was not afraid to embrace what others fear. He believed that triskaidekaphobia, a fear of Friday the thirteenth, was the product of religious indoctrination, superstition, and historical ignorance. As a pastor, Reverend Franklin was not afraid to embrace, affirm, and affiliate with the socially stigmatized and culturally demonized. This affiliation included the impoverished, the unhoused, the disabled, and Queer persons. While many Black churches have traditionally viewed nonheteronormative identities as sinful, Reverend Franklin saw his engagement with Queer persons as an opportunity to right a wrong. Pastorally queering his Black church represented a chance for him to encounter stereotyped people while simultaneously embracing and meeting their particular social and spiritual needs.

Surprisingly, it was his bold uniqueness and stark theological differences from other ministers in the area that created a slight craze around his pastorate. As a young pastor, Reverend Franklin was well loved and respected by the parishioners he served. According to Deacon Thomas, the seventy-one-year-old chair of the diaconate:

> What drew me, in the beginning, was that I heard that this young preacher was here, which was Reverend Franklin. Reverend Franklin was a very progressive young man, and he had a message that I had never really heard before. He was like, uh, he was a teacher. Most of his stuff was like current events and about how things were going in today's world. He worked from the Scripture, but he always talked about community and family and finance; that's the part that I really liked too, because when I first came, they had the start of the credit union, and that's the part I liked too. Okay, I'm seventy-one now, and I came here; I've been here now for thirty-four years, maybe thirty-three years. I loved every sermon that he preached, really.[22]

This is just one of the many statements I heard during my interviews with members about Reverend Franklin. This and other interviews reveal that there was very little that Reverend Franklin could not do while he was the pastor of Mount Nebo because they loved and respected him so much. He earned their trust and was in return endowed with an insurmountable amount of social and cultural capital.[23] His high level of social capital is best seen in the following fragment of an interview I conducted with one of Reverend Franklin's associate ministers:

> I think he was trying to bring about this message of inclusiveness of those people [LGBTQIA persons] from that community [LGBTQIA community], but it wasn't a lot of sit-down focus groups. It was always from the pulpit and the sermons; I've never seen any focus groups or anything of that nature come around. And I guess the other piece, I did not understand why the deacons did not have a conversation about it because they are part of the leadership. But looking back at it, he brought the church from the thirty people he had because it had split, and they got a new building, and they got a credit union. Everything was good. So I think some of the people who might have challenged him either died out or moved away during the split. So, who was left really wasn't going to challenge anything because they loved him; they just went along with it, with everything. Even if they might not agree with it, they just went along with it.[24]

Another example of Reverend Franklin's autonomy is captured in the following interview with Deacon Johnson. He recounted a very contentious moment in Franklin's pastorate that almost every member complained about. Because of their trust in him, I found great interest in the one moment when they all agreed that Reverend Franklin went too far. It was when Reverend Franklin hung a ten-foot photograph of a prostitute with cigarettes in her exposed G-string on the left side of the church's building facing city hall and the main street of the town.

> *Deacon*: They had made up different pictures, and they were putting them in different spots in the city, and no one would accept that particular picture. It was a picture of a woman with cigarettes in her pocket and with her G-string exposed. That was a very liberal, progressive thing for him, I guess. So Reverend Franklin said, "You can put it here." And he put it right out front, too, and he had another one, I think, on the other side or back. But he wanted that one out front to let everyone know that we accept . . . well, you know [waves hand and looks over glasses]. But, let me tell you, the deacons . . . we got a lot of chewing out on that one. The ladies were coming in, saying, "Why did you all let him do that? Why did you let him put that up there?" I mean, I got a little chewed out myself.
> *Brandon*: *What did you think about it when you saw it?*

Deacon: I said, "Well, that's Reverend Franklin." I think he got up one Sunday and explained it and preached on it, and then, after that, I think people either felt comfortable or grew to ignore it. No one was going to say anything.[25]

This event was an example of Reverend Franklin's extraordinarily Queer and revolutionary understanding of pastoral provocation as a strategy of change through confrontation. Since this chapter focuses on aspects of pastoral queering, we must consider whether Reverend Franklin was merely provoking his congregants for the comic relief of witnessing their displeasure and anger, or was there a deeper Queer meaning, theology, or theory within his actions? In speaking with Reverend Franklin about the portrait, he stated that he merely saw the mural hanging as an opportunity to market the church's inclusive ecclesiology. He thought the mural would show the community that prostitutes, drug addicts, and all of God's children were welcome to attend Mount Nebo regardless of their attire or recreational habits; this was what he wanted to achieve. He also found little value in reflecting on the fact that he never asked the church if hanging the portrait would be permissible. He stated that he knew that some persons would not like it, but their possible disdain held no merit in his decision-making process. He felt that it was his priestly right to hang the portrait if he wished. He also did not care if the attraction of prostitutes and drug addicts made parishioners feel uncomfortable because he believed that the church was for everyone. It is also important to note that his church was located in the middle of an urban area and the church regularly held Alcoholics Anonymous meetings and offered meals for the unhoused. He was more concerned about making those seeking recovery and sex workers feel welcomed by seeing their likeness on the side of the building than he was about his tithe-paying middles-class members living into the politics of respectability. Later on in this chapter, I discuss how Reverend Franklin "got away" not only with this instance but also with the enterprise of pastoral queering itself.

Reverend Franklin's Relational Model

Another example of Reverend Franklin's complete autonomy and pastoral authority can be seen in what he calls the *relational model*. Over the years I have had many public and private conversations with Reverend Franklin about his pastoral methodology. While the discussions were fruitful and filled with revelation, it was often difficult to grasp how he understood his pastoral theology or pastoral model. However, during his pastorate, he and the church's website carefully described a form of Christian discipleship that flowed from relationships instead of tasks and meetings.[26] Reverend Franklin described the outreach and inclusive aspects of his pastoral ministry as being based on a *relational model* for meetings and overall congregational engagement.

> The relational meeting is a thirty- to thirty-five-minute opportunity to set aside the daily pressures of family, work, and deadlines to focus deliberately upon another person, to seek out their talent, interest, energy, and vision. Through one-on-ones, our relational meetings, our LOM [Local Organizing Ministry] is teaching us that once we ask a probing question, then shut up and listen, and be alert for the next question. The LOM relational meeting is narrow in compass—one person face-to-face with another—but significant in intention. It is a small stage that lends itself to acts of memory, imagination, and reflection. It constitutes a public conversation on a scale that allows space for thoughts, interests, possibilities, and talent to mix. It is where a public newness begins. Imagine sitting face-to-face with all the people around 80 Legion Parkway for thirty- to thirty-five minutes, connecting in a way that transcends ordinary, everyday talk. And at that moment, a new public relationship may be born, through which both will gain the power to be truer to their wonderful, creative selves, to live more effectively and creatively in-between the world as it is and the world as it should.[27]

During the middle years of his pastorate, Reverend Franklin began using this model for meetings and community engagement. On the church's website, Reverend Franklin's personal written description of the relational meeting model is listed under the church's history ("Our Story") section, and the website contains no other information about the history of the church. I asked extensively why the church's history had been removed or what the history was, but none of the research participants could answer the question except to point out that "Reverend Franklin handled writing that type of information." At the height of my research at Mount Nebo, neither the recently appointed pastor,[28] deacons, church secretary, nor the more senior members of the congregation could produce a complete church history. Instead, I was given a very short history written as an ahistorical apology for a pastoral relational meeting model. For instance, the church's history now reads,

Today more than ever, many people are hungry for spirituality and community. But the most powerful and meaningful spirituality shows itself through action. Christian discipleship flows from relationships, not tasks or meetings. Relational meetings—connecting people in and around their interests—modeled by our Local Organizing Ministry (L.O.M.) today is the impetus behind Pastor Franklin's quest for us to reach Calvary Hill, Capitol Hill, and Wall Street. Our Nehemiah Programs for Academic Advancement, Choirs, Ushers, Molding Beautiful Caring Women's Ministry, Food Pantry, Summer Lunch Program, Senior Citizens Social Group, and Men's Fellowship, like our 22 July 1897 founders, are built around relational meetings. Our history demonstrates that intentional listening to another person is paramount. Fredrick Richardson said, "Great things can only be accomplished in a narrow compass." The relational meeting is a thirty . . . (the history then describes what a relational meeting is).[29]

While I cannot be certain, I presume that Reverend Franklin intentionally intertwined his new model with the church's history to bridge the tasks he set for himself as a senior pastor with the historical narrative of the congregation. Historians would describe Reverend Franklin's modifications of the church's narrative as a type of historical revisionism.[30] It is important to emphasize this action because nowhere in the church's actual history is there an account of the church's founders using the relational meeting model.[31] While the founders may have had relationships with each other before prayer meetings, it is not a proven fact that they utilized the relational meeting model to found Mount Nebo Baptist Church. Furthermore, the quotation that Reverend Franklin uses by James Madison reads and presents itself as antithetical to the revisionist history he is trying to depict. He does not use the democratic aspects of the relational model in his queering methods. However, he did believe that it was the relational connection that he developed from the model that increased the congregation's confidence in him. Reverend Franklin's reenvisioning of the church's history is another example of his absolute authority as the pastor of Mount Nebo Baptist Church. It is common for Baptist pastors to rewrite the histories of their churches for the sake of putting the focus on their achievements.

As a Yale-trained clergyman, Reverend Franklin was well read and well traveled. During his years in divinity school, he encountered and became friends with many lesbian and gay colleagues. It was at this time that he developed a deep appreciation for the inherent worth of LGBTQIAP+ persons. Interacting with Queer teachers and colleagues in seminary dismantled the heteronormativity within him by broadening his perspectives and helping him to build strong and genuine friendships. These bonds, not his studies, fractured his commitment to biblical literalist readings of clobber texts. Unlike Reverend Lockhart at Union, Reverend Franklin had a preexisting theology of inclusivity in his heart and spirit as a seminarian. When he began his pastorate at Mount Nebo, he had already reconciled the theological tenets of radical inclusivity with the tradition of Black Christianity. Mount Nebo became the organization upon which he practiced his radical theological sensibilities.

When Reverend Franklin arrived at Mount Nebo, he was fearless and full of radical theological ideas.[32] At the beginning of his pastorate, Reverend Franklin's natural spunk, mixed with the unstable organizational structure of Mount Nebo, offered a perfect opportunity for him to alter the church's ecclesiology when the church was in disarray. Therefore, queering for Reverend Franklin was risky and bold but not difficult. The people trusted him, believed in him, and their sense of congregational hope was intertwined with his personhood. They elected him because he was young and they saw him as a congregational savior. They believed that his youthful and expansive thinking would grow the church. He began pastoring them when they were in a vulnerable state as a congregation. Before Reverend Franklin's arrival, Mount Nebo had not only experienced a huge split but was also financially and organizationally unhealthy. For this reason, pastoral queering worked effectively for Reverend Franklin during the time of his pastorate because he was the organizational savior and rebuilder of the church. A pastor who has saved a church from closing acquires a great deal of pastoral autonomy, privilege, and power that the new pastor of a stronger congregation may never earn. Because of this pastoral privilege, Reverend Franklin mainly queered his church by simply pastoring it and loving the people enough to earn their unwavering respect. Every wedding, counseling session, hospital visitation, and other pastoral function earned him the social capital to tell the parishioners what they should believe without experiencing opposition or retaliation.

Additionally, his prophetic preaching and strong exegetical abilities enabled him to dismantle the traditional homophobic practice of Queer shaming that can occur in Black churches. In his words, "My organizational skills, teachings, and leadership are not genius. It is just my capacity to make common people achieve uncommon performance." For Reverend Franklin, the educational responsibilities of a pastor begin at the intersection of personhood, life's realities, and faith. As a religious leader, Reverend Franklin believed, preached, and taught that personal salvation and the attainment of personal piety were not the ultimate aims of the Christian faith. He endeavored to nurture the conditions for all people to thrive and flourish as human beings. Through Christian education, Reverend Franklin opened the minds and hearts of his congregants. The power of pastoral queering often rests in its capacity to educate. Teaching Bible studies and preaching sermons can change hearts, minds, and souls. Although it takes time, congregational trust coupled with a pastoral desire to educate a congregation should never be underestimated.

Lastly, it would be somewhat irresponsible to believe that pastoral queering hinges on quality pastoring alone. If that were the case, pastoral queering would happen more often because the liberal seminaries of the North have educated many clergypersons in prominent African American pulpits; however, very few of them were willing to start a pastoral queering process. Therefore, there must be more to the success of Reverend Franklin's pastoring and queering than congregational brokenness, preaching, teaching, pastoral authority, and good pastoral care habits. What made him different was pastoral courage. Franklin had the courage to queer. But where did his strength, bravery, and resilience come from? During an interview with one of Mount Nebo's deacons, the answer to this question became immediately apparent. One member recounted:

Member: When I first came to the church, they had started the credit union, and that's the part I liked too. It was just something that I really loved. It was about learning how to save, and it was also the spiritual part about savings too because he came up with this theory, what was it, ten, twenty, the spending, the savings, and the giving, you know. So he talked about that, and I mean just from all that, I really learned how to save in my work and retirement, and he taught me a lot just about how to put away money to have enough when you retire. And actually, when I retired, and me and my wife ... he actually took our 401Ks, and he told us exactly how to do those. Yeah, he has it set up in a good way. Several people in the church I talked to told me about how he set up their financial pieces, insurance, and savings. When I first came here, I loved it because he did classes on finance. And he also had a plan set up where we could invest through the stock market. We had a club that I was actually involved in different stocks that he gave us and how to, you know... We believed in him. We trusted him.[33]

Reverend Franklin's fearlessness was rooted in the fact that he knew everyone's business, and he used that pastoral privilege as a means to lead without concern for their opinions. He knew their business because of the relationships he formed with his members from the financial literacy classes and tax return seminars he held. He helped these persons to put their lives together. At the beginning stages of his pastorate, he served as a free financial analyst for all of his congregants. He saw this as an extension of his call to nurture the conditions for all people to flourish. The downfall of this type of pastoral queering is that its success hinges on the success of the pastor. If Reverend Franklin had not been successful in helping his congregants to attain more wealth, then his attempts at queering would have been less likely to succeed.

Three Characteristics of Reverend Franklin's Pastoral Queering at Mount Nebo

The queering of Mount Nebo Missionary Baptist Church is a quintessential case of what I call "pastoral queering." Without a doubt, Reverend Franklin's social capital empowered him to single-handedly queer Mount Nebo's ecclesiology. While researching Reverend Franklin's methods of pastoral queering at Mount Nebo, I discovered three important characteristics of his pastoral queering process: (1) the divine call and mandate characteristic, (2) the full pastoral authority coupled with congregational trust characteristic, and (3) the prophetic and socially conscious preaching and teaching characteristic. While they are distinct and individualized characteristics, they are interconnected and often overlap at different points. When describing the characteristics individually, there are similarities and repetitions, especially when the success of one is influenced by the existence of the other.

Characteristic One: The Call

Reverend Franklin was called by God to do the work of LGBTQIAP+ affirmation. According to his wife, he was initially reluctant to accept the call to pastor at Mount Nebo. A Texan at heart, he felt unsure about living in Trenton. A graduate of Yale, he had preexisting connections to continue what would be a lifelong professional career in finance that would require back-and-forth travel to Texas. He was also a brilliant preacher who frequently received requests to preach across the United States. However, there was something about Mount Nebo that he could not relinquish after visiting as a guest preacher, and they asked him to be their pastor. He had fallen in love with the people. He felt a calling to stay with them even though they could not pay him what he was worth. The magic that existed between Mount Nebo and Reverend Franklin was tangible during any visit to the church. Even now that Reverend Franklin has retired, you hear his name and stories about him repeated more than Bible stories or the church's historical narrative.

While attending a particular Thursday night Bible study, the pastor and I arrived at the church a few moments late. One of the associate ministers had started teaching due to the new pastor's lateness. The new pastor was welcomed and recognized when he entered, but the associate minister continued to teach the lesson. Curiously, during her presentation, she never referred to the Bible. Instead, she frequently used the following phrases: "like Reverend Franklin used to say," "When Reverend Franklin preached from this text," "Reverend Franklin always taught us to. . . ."[34] As uncomfortable as it was to sit through that exchange while watching the newly elected pastor from across the room, it revealed the enormous impact of Reverend Franklin's beliefs on their theological, biblical, and ecclesiological beliefs. God had called him to serve them, and they believed it! Whatever he taught, Queer theology or evolution theories, they listened deeply and trusted his prophetic intuition.

But what was most important was his commitment to a revelation he had in divinity school about homophobia being a sin that tarnishes Black churches. His concern grew into a calling. He felt called to address the sin of homophobia and to correct it at Mount Nebo. Pastoral queering always begins with a calling to queer from God in the heart of the pastor.

Characteristic Two: Congregational Trust

As a religious leader, Reverend Franklin transformed Mount Nebo into a loving and supportive community for all people. Before his arrival, Mount Nebo had experienced a terrible split that led to the establishment of the

Mount Tabor Baptist Church of Trenton, which is where most congregants went after the split. As a young Black Yale seminarian, Reverend Franklin had a huge task on his hands. With great hesitation and trepidation, Reverend Franklin felt called to transform a group of thirty people into a nurturing home for persons seeking to know more about God and Jesus Christ.[35]

Mount Nebo's queering story is a narrative of trust between a people and their pastor. The people of Mount Nebo trusted the prophetic voice of Reverend Franklin so passionately that they began accepting difference and different types of people in ways that they would have never imagined. In an interview with a member, I inquired, "Under Reverend Franklin, Mount Nebo became known as a church that accepted gay people. How did that happen?"

Member: Well, Reverend Franklin considered everybody a person. Reverend Franklin used to say, "We take you however you are" because we all are in a different place. He then married a gay couple one time, and we actually had this couple that left the church because of it.

Brandon: Was there a vote? Did the church vote to give him permission to do this stuff?

Member: I don't think they did. I think everyone just trusted him. And then I think, maybe, the leaders of the deacons did too because they never really questioned him. We always believe the same thoughts. I said, "Reverend Franklin, we have the same thoughts." I said, "What you do . . . I really love it kind of, no matter what."[36]

Essentially, Reverend Franklin's prophetic voice stimulated his congregation toward acceptance. The members of Mount Nebo Missionary Baptist Church trusted their congregationally elected pastor because they believed that he was a young prophet sent by God to them and for them.[37]

Thus, it could be argued that Reverend Franklin's pastoral queering in a Baptist context is affirmed through congregational acceptance. Baptist churches elect their pastors. Unlike the pastoral appointments by bishops in churches such as Union United Methodist Church of Boston's South End, Reverend Franklin was elected by the congregants to be the senior pastor of Mount Nebo Missionary Baptist Church. In other words, the people of Mount Nebo voted to follow the prophetic voice of one young man. However, while indeed the parishioners accepted the reverend's decisions, that does not mean his decisions would always be undisputed, because Baptist congregants can always disagree with a pastor. A Baptist pastor can be voted out of their position as senior minister with one majority vote. For this reason, I stand by my original statement that Mount Nebo was pastorally queered. A few congregants left the church who felt otherwise. They would reject the idea that the election of Reverend Franklin was a sort of democratic form of congregational queering because when the congregation elected him, they were not aware of everything that he would do after he was elected. Yes, they elected him, but it would be inaccurate to argue that they knew or agreed with all of the choices he would make in perpetuity.

An example of this would be when several church ladies became upset about the image displayed on the church's northern wall. The evidence offered earlier demonstrates that the case of Mount Nebo does not represent a type of congregational queering because that could be interpreted to mean that most of the congregation knew and accepted the varying directions in which the senior pastor would take the church from the start, a characterization that would be woefully inaccurate. Instead, Mount Nebo's queering is a type of pastoral queering that evolved out of congregational trust while manifested in the form of compliance. They felt that he was called to serve them (characteristic one), so they trusted him and complied with his decisions even when they disagreed with him. These characteristics gave way to the effectiveness of the most memorable characteristic among the three: preaching and teaching. They loved Reverend Franklin because they loved his preaching and teaching. His elocutionary skills were what originally attracted Mount Nebo to Reverend Franklin, and it became the conduit of his most audacious undertaking, pastoral queering.

Characteristic Three: The Power of Preaching and Teaching

Black pastoral ecclesial queering worked at Mount Nebo because Reverend Franklin had always taught his congregants how to blend unique and diverse perspectives into an integral and cohesive whole. Reverend Franklin's preaching and teaching were focused on matters of social justice instead of personal piety. Reverend Franklin always stood firm on his core value of love and caring for others. He had a way of presenting open-ended prophecies about the evils of American capitalism while concurrently creating educational spaces where new ideas and new voices could be heard and valued in the round, to use the words of Letty Russell.[38] Reverend Franklin taught the congregation about the universal and spiritual principles of love, abundance, wholeness, and happiness. While Mount Nebo remained a Black Baptist Christian community primarily dedicated to the principles as taught by Jesus Christ, Reverend Franklin's real vision was to transform Mount Nebo into

> an intentional, welcoming, affirming, and progressive Christian community. Embracing the First and Second Testaments and Howard Zinn's *A People's History of the United States*, offering prophetic preaching, teaching, and healing ministries to strategically fulfill our role as the major servant-leader institution in Trenton to synergize the total salvation—economic, social, political, and spiritual—of the community.[39]

Additionally, Reverend Franklin's preaching always remained true to the prophetic refuge traditions of Black churches. The lens through which he interpreted the world and the Word included a type of inclusive Black consciousness that made his Black theological teachings accessible to all kinds of persons. Herein lies the one aspect of Reverend Franklin's pastoral queering that made it a Black enterprise. He queered from a worldview charged by his experiences as a Black person living in America. During the numerous hours and weeks I spent researching, listening to his sermons, and talking with Reverend Franklin, it became apparent that his empathy for the LGBTQIAP+ community was directly informed by his keen awareness of the intersectionality of American racism, sexism, and homophobia. As a Black man, Reverend Franklin stated, "My Blackness calls upon me to recognize that Martin Luther King was right. "Injustice anywhere is a threat to justice everywhere."[40]

Mount Nebo Baptist Church is an interpersonally challenging and politically complex congregation. It is interpersonally challenging because the descendants of the original founding families are still active in the church. They often clashed over familial differences. This heritage also complexifies the political nature of Mount Nebo's ecclesial structures and chains of command. Though the church is Queer-affirming, its lack of social cohesion works against the church's ability to move forward as a unified body. Under Reverend Franklin, Mount Nebo was introduced to what it means to be Queer-affirming and essentially given no other option but to be Queer-affirming. Significantly, this decision was not brought about through congregational conversations but rather by hierarchical decision-making. In other words, Reverend Franklin subtly queered the church's ecclesiology by subverting small norms over time.

Interestingly, Mount Nebo did not push back against Reverend Franklin's declaration. This, in my opinion, was due to Mount Nebo Baptist's deep entanglement with the cult of personality. Many of the congregants loved Reverend Franklin and considered him to be a son or grandson and, as such, were willing to accept his decisions so long as that came with his continued presence in the church. Simply put, no one wanted to risk losing the cultural capital that came along with being on the pastor's good side for the sake of challenging his inclusive theology. This causes me to wonder if fear played a role in pastoral queering at Mount Nebo. Additionally, is this sort of fear a bad thing? Can fear be used in a divine sense, as it is with God in the Bible, where fear is a synonym for respect and the beginning of wisdom (Proverbs 9:10)? While I will not spend time answering these questions with speculations, it is important to consider the role and possibility of fear as a tool and method of pastoral queering. However, I do not support such usage. I question the integrity of any movement, whether its intentions are good or bad, that uses fear as a motivator or manipulative force to bring about a greater good. Moral good can never spawn from the motivations of fear. Forcing people into inclusivity is an unhealthy form of queering. Fear-based queering rarely thrives after the pastoral tenure of a senior minister. Sadly, this is true with Mount Nebo. The church's current organizational, membership, and financial dissipation demonstrate that a pastor's Queer affirmation without congregational buy-in can be risky and may fail in the long run. In the case of Mount Nebo, after Reverend Franklin retired, there was no process or protocol to ensure that the church would remain Queer-affirming—and sadly, it did not remain affirming.

The Challenges of Conducting Research at Mount Nebo

The study of Mount Nebo Missionary Baptist Church presented many challenges. First, it was difficult to fully understand Mount Nebo's theology of inclusivity because it was based solely on the ideas and beliefs of one person. The congregation was unable to articulate the intricacies of Mount Nebo's queering, its theology, or its ecclesiology. Furthermore, the generally inconsistent theologies of autonomous Baptist churches prevent us from attempting to situate Mount Nebo's queer theology within a broader denominational context. For example, while researching the United Methodist Church, I was able to incorporate the Wesleyan Quadrilateral as a theological lens for interpreting the process of queering. By contrast, Mount Nebo's theology was not as clearly defined or owned by its members. There was no central narrative of queering or congregational vote to validate a statement of Queer affirmation. Although Reverend Franklin was known for teaching substantive and theologically dense Bible study classes using cutting-edge Black theological resources to address specific social matters and injustices, he never allowed the congregation to think together about queering, thereby weaving affirmation into the hearts of the congregants. The people simply trusted him and followed his instructions to be nice to Queer folk. In an interview with the new pastor, I asked how he felt about Mount Nebo's inclusivity. The pastor responded,

> I think the church is still torn on that issue. I think they still believe that marriage is [really between a man and a woman]. On that issue, the former pastor, he was pretty much the one that was instituting that. From what I can understand from the time I have been here, the church never voted on the LGBTQIA matter. That was just being spoken from the pulpit, and anywhere he felt to say it, that was pretty much solely him. I didn't get that from the congregation, so that was basically him that was doing that. I get the sense they still believe it's between a man and a woman. And actually, it's interesting you said that because one member had said something to me about Leviticus 18 and all that. I mean, we have people that are in our community now that have been married and been partners and stuff like that. But as a whole, it's not.... I don't think it's accepted. And individuals that are that way, they try to keep it quiet as much as possible. Like I said, I don't think it's widely accepted. Mount Nebo is known for that because of the prior pastor.[41]

This answer proves that the congregational trust that Mount Nebo had in Reverend Franklin cannot be understood as general congregational support of his affirming stance. Neither should it be regarded as a congregational stance supporting LGBTQIAP+ persons or other social concerns that were important to Reverend Franklin. Instead, their trust in Reverend Franklin can only be interpreted as that: trust in him. They trusted him, but such blind trust did not translate into trust in Queer persons simply because they exist. Several members said: "I don't mind gay people being here but they can't work with the children's ministry." This statement reveals that the congregation trusted the pastor but still maintained a fear and a lack of trust in the innate goodness of all persons, especially LGBTQIAP+ folk. They were able to trust his prophetic voice and welcome Black Queer persons without fully comprehending and imbibing the radical actions of hospitality that they were performing. Further, many of the congregants were not educated on issues of sexuality and gender, rendering them unprepared to be allies to the Queer community and unable to fully understand the church's theological position.

Most importantly, although they knew their church was not hostile to LGBTQIAP+ folk, many congregants did not personally identify with notions of inclusion. In other words, many of the congregants never took on the identity of a Queer-affirming Christian for themselves. This caused them to ask harmful questions to many Queer members like: "Who is the man in your relationship?" or "How will you have children?" Therefore, though the church was Queer-welcoming, it was arguably not Queer-affirming. The pastor's impact on the personal theologies of the congregants was minimal because they did not actively and wholeheartedly embrace his message.

The second challenge in researching Mount Nebo Baptist Church resulted in part from Reverend Franklin's retirement. When I began conducting research, he was still serving as the church's senior minister. Being aware of the strong sense of authority with which he had queered the congregation, I spent a great deal of time studying him and getting to know him as a person.

When Reverend Franklin announced his retirement, I became immediately concerned that my research might be in jeopardy. If he was the primary queerer, the only person who understood the queering process, but he was no longer serving as the pastor of the church—would the church remain Queer after he retired? However, at that point, I realized that Reverend Franklin's retirement, instead of being a hindrance to the project, would present a rare opportunity to see if pastoral queering works. Will a pastorally queered church remain Queer when the original queerer is no longer the senior pastor?

In an interview with the new pastor, I inquired, "Where do you see the church going with Queer rights?" The new pastor responded,

> I think, first of all, we gotta get some training around it. But not right now, coming in as the new pastor. The thing is, I think many of them don't understand it, and since they don't understand it, it's a whole lot of confusion on

their part on what it is and what it means. So, there has been no education around it, and that's the part; it's the tough part because once there's been no education, it's just been thrown on them; they haven't been included. We say it should be inclusive language, but that wasn't an inclusive process at all. It was a one-way process. And so nobody ever voted on it, never had discussions around it, no focus groups, any of that stuff took place, just to say what it is. What are we dealing with? So right now, I think for me to try to do that in my first year, that's deadly.[42]

The dialogue above reveals that, at least in the case of Mount Nebo, a pastorally queered church may not remain Queer after the original queerer is no longer the senior pastor. While pastoral queering worked during Reverend Franklin's pastorate, the church did not remain Queer beyond his tenure. The church remains a welcoming space for Queer persons. However, the congregation offers no theological assistance for persons seeking to reconcile their faith and Queer sexuality. According to the search committee chair, during the search for a new pastor, the question of LGBTQIAP+ affirmation was a divisive factor among some congregants. Many persons who silently disagreed with Reverend Franklin's stance saw the search process as an opportunity to push a more conservative theological narrative. These divisions often manifested during the questioning of pastoral candidates, giving candidates the perception that their LGBTQIAP+ affirmation or rejection would affect large portions of the voting delegates in different ways. So, to avoid conflicts, the search committee chair stated that the candidates responded moderately and neither answered nor revealed their true sentiments about the question. This caused the majority of the Black Queer persons who once attended and served in leadership positions in the church to no longer attend services or tithe.

After being elected, Mount Nebo's new pastor was unsure about what affirming ministry means or requires. While he is not homophobic, he was uncertain about how to minister to Queer persons. He was also uncertain about his own theological beliefs regarding homosexuality and Scripture, and he was embarrassed that his own son was gay. For this reason, he began preaching against LGBTQIAP+ persons as a way of dealing with his own internal struggles with his gay son. These elements created an ecclesial environment that posed a great risk to Black Queer people. When Black Queer persons are welcomed into a space that is not ready for them or a space that changes because of a leadership transition, they can encounter questions and unconscious displays of heterosexism that could trigger memories of their past dealing with ecclesial homophobia. This alone could so traumatize Black Queer persons that avoiding church altogether could become the most viable option.

After studying and analyzing the history of more than fifty pastorally queered Black churches, it has become clear that pastorally queered congregations like Mount Nebo also become spaces where Black Queer persons often have to take on the inequitable responsibility of defending themselves or bifurcating their identities to fit in.[43] For instance, figuring out *Who knows I'm gay?* and *Who does not know?* is a constant struggle that Black Queer Christian persons have in heteronormative Black churches. Over time, this battle can become stressful, traumatizing, and tiring. Most times, this discomfort comes either from an inability to identify with the heteronormative conversations that take place or from the Black Queer persons wondering whether people around them are thinking about their sexuality. While one could interpret these emotions as insecurities, they are also symptoms of Black homophobia. For example, a prominent leader in the Mount Nebo church was a gay male who married his male lover. Reverend Franklin officiated the wedding. Although I did not personally know the couple at the time, I was invited to attend. I was shocked to find out that the wedding was being held at the couple's home because they felt uncomfortable celebrating their wedding in the nave of the Mount Nebo church for fear that it might make people uneasy. When this instance occurred, I had just been introduced to Mount Nebo as the liberal church in the Trenton community. However, it seemed a glaring contradiction that such a liberal place would not have allowed a same-sex wedding ceremony to be performed in its main sanctuary if a couple wanted to do so. At that moment I realized that Reverend Franklin's pastoral queering might have been the result of congregational trust, but it manifested itself in the form of toleration, not wholehearted acceptance. For this reason, the gay members who grew up in Mount Nebo felt affirmed by the theology preached from the pulpit but remained unsure of Mount Nebo's overall communal acceptance of themselves and other Queer persons.

Herein lies my final critique of pastorally queered spaces. At least for Mount Nebo, pastoral queering created an environment of tolerance. However, tolerance carries with it a great number of problems. Most importantly, tolerance does not require the tolerator to go through a qualitative process of exchange with that which is being tolerated. Toleration is merely the permission of something or someone to be present. Toleration does not require full acceptance or an appreciation of the differences that are associated with the person or thing that is being tolerated. According to Preston King,[44]

> Toleration is a problem of human relations. In this context, "to tolerate" generally means to endure, suffer, or put up with a person, activity, idea, or organization of which or whom one does not really approve. One can "put up with" an item both when one can and cannot do anything about it. For example, one can "put up with" the excesses of a ruler whose behavior one has no power to amend. Equally, one can "put up with" the excesses of a child even where one has no need to do so. In the second case, one has control; in the first, one does not. Both cases could be advanced as instances of "tolerance." But cases of the first sort (powerlessness) I shall label as instances of "acquiescence" or "sufferance" or "endurance" since it is obvious that acquiescence typically flows from powerlessness. I shall label cases of the second sort (powerfulness) as instances of tolerance. It is clear in any event that these two types of cases are distinct, and, for the purposes of this discussion, at least, differential labeling is essential. In this context, an agent will be said to "tolerate" an item where the item is disliked or disapproved and is yet voluntarily endured. On this definition, it is plain that tolerance requires some form of self-restraint by the tolerator.[45]

Herein lies a problem with Black ecclesial queering done only by a pastor. It produces tolerant churches—not affirming churches. Unless the church is inherited by a person who has the same queered theology as the original queerer, pastoral queering will disappear with the retirement, death, or termination of the original queerer's pastorate. Furthermore, the church must be willing to intentionally seek out pastoral candidates who will agree to their queered beliefs. For Mount Nebo, Reverend Franklin handpicked a successor for the church to agree upon. However, the person he selected was not sure about his theological stance on LGBTQIAP+ rights, and he knew nothing about ministering to Queer persons. For this reason, presently, there is nothing Queer about Mount Nebo except that no one is prevented from attending its services and participating in the church. Therefore, Mount Nebo's present nonqueerness could be regarded as the result of poor succession planning. Much like his queering process,

Reverend Franklin selected his own successor without any input from the congregation. He selected a cisgendered married Black male who believes homosexuality is a sin. One could argue that Mount Nebo's present state of being unqueered has occurred because Reverend Franklin should have better prepared his successor and his congregation for remaining Queer after his departure.

Analysis

A pastorally queered Black church comes into being when the pastor decides on behalf of the people that the church will be open and affirming without first obtaining congregational buy-in. As a methodology, pastoral queering is often inextricably linked to the tenure of a senior pastor or minister. It is an enterprise that is only successful when a pastor has gained enough social and cultural capital to change the church's ecclesiology without overwhelming backlash.

Pastoral queering begins and ends with a leader's decision to accept Black Queer persons into the life and ministry of the local congregation. It does not require a congregational vote or congregational consensus. It arises from preaching, teaching, demonstrating radical inclusivity, and offering nonheteronormative interpretations of Scripture and family. Many cases of this kind of queering start with pastoral awareness of Black Queer persons within the congregation. In most cases, pastors who initiate the process have previously practiced inclusivity in moments of counseling, care, and even in private ceremonies, like weddings and baby dedications. In the case of Mount Nebo Baptist Church, Reverend Franklin performed wedding ceremonies in the private residences of congregants and church affiliates before he queered the church.[46] Therefore, the Sunday morning sermonic articulation of his and Mount Nebo's implied inclusivity was more of a public performance than an articulation of a long-term praxis of inclusivity.

The leader-parish relationship is the undergirding power for pastoral queering, which leads to inevitable what-if questions. For example, what happens if the leader of a pastorally queered congregation leaves, retires, dies, loses congregational trust, or is no longer pastoring the congregation for other reasons? Can a church remain affirming after the pastoral queerer is no longer its leader? Reverend Franklin instructed Mount Nebo

Baptist to be Queer-affirming and gave it no other option. When he retired, the congregation's queered ecclesiology vanished. The new pastor did not understand Queer theology, nor did he desire to promote it. The congregation did not understand enough about the subject matter to retain its queered theology. They remembered the essence of inclusion in Reverend Franklin's preaching and teaching, but they could not explicitly take ownership of their Black Queer–affirming reputation. Hence, pastoral queering for them was influential in the short term but ineffective in the long term because they were not wedded to LGBTQIAP+ affirmation in their hearts and minds. Their queerness departed when Reverend Franklin retired.

Other scenarios could allow pastoral queering to thrive permanently. If a congregation idolizes the memory of a deceased pastoral queerer, it might be more difficult for a conservative minister to dismember it. Therefore, a pastorally queered context could remain affirming after the retirement of its pastoral queerer. This occurrence is just as rare as the occurrence of Black pastoral ecclesial queering itself.

The Preexisting Conditions of Union and Pastorally Queered Black Churches

Local Black congregations have distinct ecclesiologies. One of the most critical insights for a Black ecclesial queerer to understand is that Black ecclesial spaces have their own cultures. The culture of a Black congregation is its identity.[47] In Chapter 2 I argued that Black churches originated as nonracist citadels for battered Black souls. These eighteenth- and nineteenth-century institutions essentially queered the American civil religion of its white ecclesial progenitors.[48] Within these Black ecclesial spaces, Black people produced a Black religion that affirmed Blackness.[49] Peter Paris describes this as the fundamental distinction of Black churches. Paris argues that the original purpose and prophetic calling of Black ecclesiologies was and still is to affirm "the equality of all persons under God regardless of race or any other natural quality. This doctrine has been the essence of the Black Christian tradition and the most fundamental requirement of its churches."[50] This fundamental and common thread of Black ecclesiology is evident in Union United Methodist Church and Mount Nebo Baptist Church. Their ecclesial roots are steeped in prophetic teaching and preaching. Both Reverend Franklin and the various itinerant elders who served Union Church held that "liberation for all" is the essential component of the gospel message.

Union and Mount Nebo used resistance and education to combat the injustices committed against Black bodies.

Reverend Franklin responded to the call for justice in Trenton by establishing a credit union to make small loans accessible to the minority communities of the greater area. For Reverend Franklin, financial literacy and debt-free living were primary sociopolitical tactics to ensure freedom and wholeness for economically deprived Black folk. He created the credit union in response to racial inequality and economic disparities within Trenton's minority community leveling the field for Black financial survival and perhaps even prosperity. Furthermore, an interview with Mount Nebo's diaconate chair made it evident that Reverend Franklin's financial literacy was why many people trusted his ministry.

For Union's and Mount Nebo's congregations, the religious practice of radical hospitality was a way of making empowerment more practical and accessible. Both churches have long histories of providing African Americans with the space to make meaning and gain spiritual formation while strategically resisting racism through social action and intervention. They also value lived experiences and the individual journeys of Black religious persons just as much as personal devotion and the ordinances of the church.

Similarities of Union and Mount Nebo

Union, Mount Nebo, and 90 percent of the queered Black churches I studied had preexisting "Don't ask, don't tell" subcultures. This suggests that "Don't ask, don't tell" churches are the most amenable to forms of Black ecclesial queering. They offer contextual beginnings of a queered ecclesiology. They provide the trappings and fertile ground within which Black ecclesial queering may grow and has thrived. Before becoming queered, Union and Mount Nebo had previously dismantled aspects of Black ecclesial sexism by granting ordinations and licenses to women, thereby eliminating the traditional Black church model of single-gendered church leadership.

Union and Mount Nebo had a history of taking other social-justice stances before their queering processes. Both churches were formed and served as safe havens for Black folk. Union was founded to provide a spiritual home for formerly enslaved people, and Mount Nebo provided a place of belonging for

Black folks during the Great Migration. Both congregations had seminary-trained pastors and had previously employed Black Queer musicians and had Queer members at the time of queering.

The Differences between Union's and Mount Nebo's Processes of Queering

While both congregations conveyed deep notions of love, kinship, and community, their methods for queering their churches differed. On the one hand, Union Church did not queer its ecclesiology through the pastor's executive decision but rather through collective conversations and a majority vote. A lay member's inquiry into Queer rights became the first step of the journey to Queer affirmation. From this inquiry, the church launched an entire campaign, during which individuals conducted Bible studies that, in turn, fostered deep and meaningful conversations about the sanctity of Queer bodies. Ultimately, Union chose to become affirming, a choice birthed out of the church's commitment to centering kinship as the primary framework of interpersonal connection. Union Church's philosophy is that family is a structure where everyone matters; excluding Queer bodies would violate and undermine their self-proclaimed familial identity. Union Church adherents believe that they cannot truly be a Christian community until they welcome all bodies into their community of kinship and love.

On the other hand, Mount Nebo Missionary Baptist Church had a pastorally queered ecclesiology. Reverend Franklin was subtle in how he conducted the pastoral queering process. He gradually queered the church's ecclesiology by first teaching the congregation that women should not be discriminated against. He later made a connection between sexism, racism, and homophobia. Their willingness to follow him was due to Mount Nebo Baptist's deep entanglement with the politics of personality: many of the congregants loved Reverend Franklin. They were willing to accept his decision as long as it came with his continued presence in the church. There were, unfortunately, consequences. Ecclesially led Queer affirmation without congregational commitment to a sustained and expansive queering process is risky, and there is no guarantee that it will eventually last over time or throughout changes in pastoral leadership. For example, after Reverend Franklin retired, there was not a process or protocol established to ensure that the church remained Queer-affirming, and indeed, it did not.

Reverend Franklin did not educate or provide his successor or congregants with proper resources on sexual and gender identity, diversity, or transgender persons to sustain the church's newfound inclusivity upon his retirement. This type of negligent and haphazard queering rendered members unable to understand or articulate their congregation's theological position on inclusivity. While many congregants knew that their church was not hostile to Black Queer persons, they could not explain it theologically or biblically. This is often the long-term result of pastoral queering.

5
A More Excellent Way
A Black Ethogenic Report

An Introduction to the Black Ethogenic Report

Black churches are beginning to queer their contexts all over the United States. The queering methodologies of these Black churches vary greatly. This chapter reviews and reports on fifteen years of qualitative research on nearly two hundred congregations to create a method that Black churches can use to queer their congregations. Despite their differences, the data yielded four categories of queered Black churches, four common elements of Black ecclesial queering, and five preexisting conditions of queered Black congregations. Understanding these categories, elements, and conditions is essential for gaining a comprehensive knowledge of Black ecclesial queering. Unlike the preceding chapters, this chapter examines the more practical aspects of Black ecclesial queering by reviewing and analyzing the data for ecclesial trends, reoccurring theological themes, and social patterns of congregational queering.

There are four categories of queered Black churches: (1) a denominationally queered Black church; (2) a pastorally queered Black church; (3) a "Don't ask, don't tell" welcoming Black church; and (4) a congregationally queered Black church. This chapter explicates the concepts and categories of congregational, pastoral, and denominational queering as emergent methodologies that are nonlinear and nonsequential while describing congregational queering as a more excellent way of queering Black churches. In this chapter, the phrase "Black ecclesial queering" refers to and is used interchangeably with the phrase "congregational queering." I also organize these and other thoughts to convey the integrity and quality of Black ecclesial queering as a social and spiritual phenomenon.

Is It Possible to Queer a Black Church?

Is it possible to queer a Black congregation since Christianity, the Bible, and congregations themselves have been shaped within and formed by the iniquity of heteronormative ideals? As simplistic as it may appear, my response to this question is that it depends. The queerability of a Black congregation depends on the geographical and social context of the congregation, the amenability and adaptability of the church's congregants, and what one means when using the gerund or verb "queering."

The queerability of a Black congregation depends on if, by "queered," one means that a church has reached the pinnacle of perfection that exempts them from discriminatory bias, implicit hostility toward nonheteronormative identities, and gender variants. If this is what congregational queering is perceived to be, I do not believe a Black church can reach Queer perfection. The problems presented by Black heteronormativity are too complex and long-standing to dismantle Black ecclesial homophobia instantaneously with a brief series of sermons and workshops. Congregational queering is a continuous process that happens over time. While no one would love for queering to go quicker than I, hasty congregational queering is surface-level queering that is merely performative. The goal of queering a congregation is not to teach congregants how to perform inclusivity by checking off their "inclusivity box" for their achieved actions. Instead, congregational queering is a work of soul crafting wherein the humanity of a congregant is cultivated to see the humanity in those who have been othered.

The idea of queering as a virtuous Christian praxis of unconditional love and affirmation is not a congregational destination or goal that, upon achieving, deems a Black church as Queer. Instead, congregational queering is a lifelong congregational journey that puts a church in a perpetual state of subversion: reimagining, re-creating, and questioning itself over time to remain perpetually compassionate toward everyone, especially LGBTQIAP+ persons.

Second, the success or failure of a congregational queering process also depends on the congregation's context. For example, queering a heteronormative African American apostolic church in Alabama is an entirely different process than it would be to queer a Black United Church of Christ in New York City. When it comes to queering, a congregation's context matters. Moreover, congregational queering processes work most effectively in amenable and adaptive congregations. Black congregations with anti-racist, antisexist, and justice-oriented histories of being nimble and rarely, if ever, resting in the status quo are most conducive to Black ecclesial queering. On the other hand, nonadaptive congregations that are aggressively heteronormative and do not have a history of reflectively rethinking church in response to societal change and injustices are almost always unqueerable.

A Denominationally Queered Black Church

A denominationally queered Black church is entirely theoretical because, to date, none of the seven historic Black denominations have affirmed the presence of "out" Black Queer persons. I offer the description nevertheless as a suggestion of what a denominationally queered Black church could look like. It would take a historically Black denomination to vote to declare the denomination and all of its churches and constituencies as open and affirming to generate a denominationally queered Black church. If, for example, the African Methodist Episcopal (AME) Church were to vote to become an open and affirming denomination that ordained Black Queer persons openly as elders and bishops, allowed ordained AME elders to officiate same-sex ceremonies, and recognized same-sex marriage as nonsinful and respectable in the sight of God, then it would become denominationally queered. In the case of AMEs, this type of denominational queering would require just as much political strategizing as theological movement. By this, I mean that the AME Church cannot become an open and affirming denomination through the transition of the theological beliefs of its constituents alone; instead, it would require the vote and support of both the supreme legislative body of the AME General Conference as well as the local Episcopal districts. The process must begin with an Episcopal district, willing clergy, lay organizations of churches, or any other group or auxiliary that is willing to publicly push for the inclusion of Black Queer persons into the entire life of the AME Church.

Mobilizing any of the listed subgroups of the AME Church would in and of itself be a groundbreaking feat. The culturally indoctrinated aspects of Black homophobia often make it challenging to assemble various individuals within a historically Black denomination who are simultaneously willing to take a public stance as members of the Black Queer community or its allies. Queering the whole denomination would have to start formally from the General Conference, which is the supreme legislative body of the AME Church. The General Conference meets every four years in a different city. But prior to that, the queering of the whole international church would have to be initiated by a particular district, a group of Episcopal districts, or a group of clergies or the lay organization, which is a very powerful constituency in the AME denominational structure. Maybe two years before the next General Conference, these groups or the groups seeking to queer the AME Church would need to begin strategizing and drafting legislation to queer the church in their own connectional bodies and meetings, after which the legislation to queer would have to be submitted to the Revisions Committee. The Revisions Committee consists of forty people representing each of the twenty Episcopal districts—twenty clergy and twenty laypersons. The committee is brought together to consider, review, and receive all legislation (bills) submitted to the General Secretary of the AME Church. If a group wished to queer the AME Church, they would have to submit the legislative proposal to the Revisions Committee several weeks before the General Conference. The committee would then use a list of ten criteria to determine whether a bill was appropriate, ready, and presentable. One criterion is fiscal implications. For instance, if the bill requires that the AME Church has to spend more money, even one development project, that will first need to be vetted through the Finance Department before even going to the general floor. If a bill might have legal implications for the AME Church that could expose the AME Church to a lawsuit, we immediately refer that to our general counsel. Then the delegates wait to hear from the general counsel before they would even ask. And when the Revisions Committee feels that the bill is ready, they present the bills on the floor to be considered and voted on. The vote takes place after the third reading, and then, if approved, they become part of the discipline.[1]

After this process, then and only then could the AME church's Book of Discipline require all AME churches to be open and affirming. A more straightforward way to initiate a Queering process in the AME church could involve eliminating the sentence in the discipline that prohibits AME clergy from officiating same-sex weddings. However, merely removing this restriction is insufficient, as it might still leave room for loopholes and potential subliminal homophobic microaggressions similar to those found in forms of pastoral queering. It is only after Black denominations with an episcopal structure undergo a process of becoming open and affirming that they can then require all constituent members and districts to ordain Black Queer individuals as deacons and elders.

Denominational queering can be a very powerful instance of ecclesial engagement. For example, the AME Church established a panel on sexual ethics with the hopes of fully welcoming its own Black LGBTQIAP+ congregants without forcing them to bifurcate their identities. This initiative to formulate a sexual ethics discernment committee was submitted by the Reverend

Dr. Jennifer Leath and approved in a 985-371 vote, with 18 abstaining.[2] The AME Church's approval of Leath's resolution is a step in the right direction. However, the political aspects of denominational queering can be toxic for many Black Queer persons. Leath's stance should be interpreted as an exception and not as the rule.

One of the challenges of denominational queering is its potential to be performative and divisive. The persuasive nature of queering denominationally often includes passionate public speeches from inclusivists and exclusivists. The back-and-forth nature of Methodist conferencing presents opportune moments for prophetic speeches on behalf of and by Queer folk, but it also creates a platform for homophobic rhetoric to take the main stage. Denominational queering is almost always deeply rooted in toxic apologetics. Inclusivists and Exclusivists work hard to pull on the heartstrings and moral concerns of listeners. Such a tug of war prevents true substantive queering from happening at General Conferences. These moments are nothing more than political debates that can further divide the body of Christ. The split of the United Methodist Church is a prime example of this problem. Denominational queering is also problematic because it fails to trickle down to the local level. For example, when the United Church of Christ voted to become an open and affirming denomination, it still gave local congregations the ability to buy into or to opt out of the denomination's decision to be inclusive. This can lead to great confusion, and it places Queer persons in the denominations at risk of further harm. Successful denominational queering requires inclusivists to develop a comprehensive strategy to sustain the movement of queering in the face of political tactics and denominational loops that committees and legislative bodies can use to thwart the inclusive process.

Pastoral Queering and Other Examples of Pastorally Queered Congregations

To date, most existing queered Black churches in the United States were queered pastorally. The pastorally queered Black churches I studied varied on the spectrum of being "Don't ask, don't tell" churches to fully inclusive congregations. While the majority of the congregationally queered Black churches were in the northeastern and coastal regions, the majority of pastorally queered Black churches existed in the southern regions of the United States. One would think that a Black church located in a more politically and religiously conservative district would make pastoral queering extremely challenging. However, the data on pastoral queering contradicts the aforementioned assumption. For instance, the Victory for the World Church in Stone Mountain, Georgia, is a prime case of pastoral queering in a politically and religiously conservative state.[3] Although Victory was founded as an independent progressive Baptist congregation, the level of congregational trust coupled with Dr. Kenneth L. Samuel's pastoral influence permitted him to pastorally queer his church despite the local political conservatism. Dr. Samuel did so by making sermonic parallels between the social ills of Black Georgians and the injustices endured by LGBTQIAP+ persons. His congregation trusted his prophetic and sermonic utterances to the point of opening their hearts to the wounded souls of LGBTQIAP+ persons in the Atlanta metropolitan area. Congregational trust is an indisputable necessity if a pastor chooses to use pastoral queering as a methodology to queer the ecclesial context. The pastor-parish relationship is the undergirding power behind pastoral queering.

Another example of pastoral queering is pastoral advocacy for LGBTQIAP+ rights. Pastoral queering in the form of pastoral advocacy is when a Black pastor makes political stances in favor of LGBTQIAP+ rights in the public square. For example, the Reverend Dr. Amos Brown, the pastor of Third Baptist Church of San Francisco, displayed his allegiance with Queer persons in 1991 by supporting California's gay civil rights bill.[4] A moral principle of consistency drove Brown's decision and compelled him to confront bigoted acts and stand with the oppressed. Brown holds that homophobia in the American South results from "the White persons who set the climate and called the cadence."[5] Here, Brown affirms Horace Griffin's theory that a queered Black space destabilizes the white American–inspired judgment that Blackness is an inherently sinful, sexual, and objectifiable ethnic category.[6] Brown declares that Reverend Dr. Martin Luther King Jr. first oriented him to queering by "challenging the status quo of the order."[7]

Brown has a long career of battling racism. Still, he claims that the aim to queer a congregation's understanding of the Black family competes with the Black quest for civility. For many Black folks, queering counteracts the Black middle classes' pursuit to combat white caricatures of dysfunctional Black families with representational excellence.[8] In other words, for Brown, queering Black families challenges a traditional heteronormative quest for Black civility. Black individuals pursuing a "healthy" Black family believe that homosexual couples disrupt their pursuit of civility. Herein lies the limitation of pastoral queering in the form of pastoral advocacy; it is solely rooted in civil rights and restricted from expanding into the theological. Nevertheless, Brown did welcome LGBTQIAP+ folk into Third Baptist. He even swapped pulpits with Jim Mitulski, pastor of a Metropolitan Community church and hosted an HIV/AIDS testing day in his own church.[9] Brown argues that a congregation willing to accept difference will also naturally be available to Queer members.[10]

In this same vein, the Reverend Jeremiah Wright, the pastoral queerer of the Trinity United Church of Christ in Chicago, Illinois, preaches that LGBTQIAP+ folk are a part of the Body of Christ. For Wright, God's love is "greater than your love and my love, wider than our love could ever be, and deeper than what we could ever comprehend."[11] Therefore, access to God cannot be blocked for LGBTQIAP+ people, not even by heteronormative preachers. Dr. Wright claims that all humans are affirmed by God.[12]

A final example of courageous and well-intended Black pastoral queering is the Reverend Timothy McDonald III, founder of the African American Ministers Leadership Council and senior pastor of the First Iconium Baptist Church in Atlanta, Georgia. Reverend McDonald disrupted the idea of Black respectability and Black civility by helping his congregation see a clear distinction between having a love ethic and following a set of doctrines.[13] McDonald believes that it is essential for all Black churches to dismantle white supremacist theology from the enterprise of Black ecclesial meaning-making. His congregation started their queering process when a young member of the church died from complications of HIV/AIDS. McDonald's faith, which is based on the premise that all beings are God's creations, would not allow him to reject the legacy of the young man or his family. Pastor McDonald's pastoral heart compelled him to reimagine hospitality and inclusivity for himself and his congregations. McDonald began queering his congregation by first focusing on the health and identity crisis of LGBTQIAP+ folk in African American churches.[14] His actions reveal that a queered Black space must be attentive to the concerns of Black bodies while seeking the liberation and affirmation of their souls. For McDonald, theological conversation about gender and sexuality was important, but health care interventions were more important because of the large number of HIV/AIDS-related deaths connected to his congregation.[15] Pastors Brown, McDonald, and Wright prove that Black ecclesial queering is happening pastorally.

As discussed in chapter 4 and mentioned earlier here, pastoral queering is mainly contingent upon congregational trust. Pastors may only succeed in pastoral queering when they have earned the trust of a congregation.

Therefore, it is difficult, almost impossible, for a new pastor to earn the trust needed to queer pastorally. Nevertheless, longevity in leadership does not automatically lead to trust. Pastors may lose their congregations' trust over time while remaining in the position for political reasons. A pastor who gains the confidence of a congregation and serves for a lengthy period may succeed in queering their church.

The success of pastoral queering is also contingent upon the particular contexts of pastor and congregation; for example, perhaps Reverend Franklin succeeded because his church is located in a predominantly liberal Democratic region in the North. Reverend Franklin was even a member of the cohort of clergy who supported the law to legalize same-sex marriage in Trenton. Context therefore matters. It also matters because the efficacy of pastoral queering is contingent upon the social and religious context of the congregation.

Another example of pastoral queering can be seen in the story of Glide UMC, which was arguably queered by its former pastor Albert Cecil Williams. Reverend Williams became the pastor of Glide Memorial Church in San Francisco, California, in 1963. Immediately after becoming the pastor, he founded the Council on Religion and the Homosexual the following year. Williams hinged his ministry on the maxim "Come unto Me, All Ye, Weary, Heavy Laden, Doesn't Matter, Just Who You Are, All Are Welcome Here."[16] His first step in queering the ecclesiology was hosting a condom handout program at the end of worship services.[17]

When he became Glide's pastor, Williams had the full support of his Methodist regional conference to evangelize the queer community in the area. Pastoral queering is often a part of a church's evangelistic aim to grow and widen its demographics. This usually works best in pastoral queering because it doesn't push for a vote or deep theological conversations that can often cause churches to lose members during a congregational queering journey. While all of this was unique and groundbreaking work for its time, Reverend Williams was able to do this because he had total control and authority over the church and the support of his local United Methodist Church conference. Notably, his success in pastoral queering was not totally based on his personality but also highly contingent on the social location of his pastoral queering. Glide was, and still is, located in a predominantly liberal Democratic region; as I've said, context matters. The efficacy of pastoral queering is contingent upon the social and religious climate of the congregation.

"Don't Ask, Don't Tell" Black Churches

Most pastorally queered Black churches become "Don't ask, don't tell" Black churches. Most of the churches I studied were such churches. "Don't ask, don't tell" Black churches are ecclesial spaces that do not subject Queer persons to overt forms of homophobia and transphobia. These Black churches are welcoming but not affirming of Black Queer persons. While many Black churches still practice explicit homophobic and transphobic forms of biblical interpretation and social engagement, I discovered that many Black churches practice a sort of silent acceptance of Queer persons that avoids the hard discussion without affirmation. Many Black LGBTQIAP+ folk tolerate "Don't ask, don't tell" church culture as a way of avoiding religious exile. Chaney and Patrick offer,

> Overall, young African American men who have sex with men reported consistently high levels of involvement in African American churches. Very few mentioned that they or other MSM [men who have sex with men] averted religious affiliation. The data suggest that these men generally acknowledged no contradiction between being an African American MSM and being active in African American churches. . . . Some churchgoing Black men have sex with men who conform to masculine roles and are not easily detected. They "play the role," and their behavior is not distinguishable from heterosexual men: "Most of the men I know in church . . . even though they are married [and] they're sitting there with their wives . . . they have their [male] lovers probably sitting behind them or beside them."[18]

"Don't ask, don't tell" churches are unqueered ecclesial spaces that espouse heteronormative ideals while tolerating LGBTQIAP+ folk. Black Queer persons may receive spiritual nourishment without the fear of being identified, otherized, or rejected. These churches allow Black Queer souls to find spiritual nourishment while eschewing identity politics. This forces Black Queer folk in Black "Don't ask, don't tell" churches to bifurcate their identities when they are in worship. In "Let Us Go into the House of the Lord," however, Peterson, Woodyard, and Stoke noted, that gay congregants in "Don't ask, don't tell" churches sensed dubious hospitality in African American churches. Clergy and members are aware of the range of sexual behaviors practiced by male congregants and have established traditions of acceptance that include a welcoming posture without public acknowledgment."[19] As a result, some Christian gay Black men have detached from the church, either because they experience the space as unsafe or because they have internalized homophobia and oppression.[20]

"Don't ask, don't tell" churches should not be confused with a congregationally or denominationally queered church because "Don't ask, don't tell" churches intentionally avoid conversations about Black Queer identity and expression. They essentially remain silent on human sexuality to avoid sex-talk or discussions about sexuality in Black churches. "Don't ask, don't tell" churches do not directly minister to Black Queer persons as whole persons. The only service that "Don't ask, don't tell" churches provide for Black Queer persons is the ability to worship in a heteronormative ecclesial space without overt rejection.

"Don't ask, don't tell" churches often have Black Queer persons in some form of leadership. Whether as musicians, deacons, lay leaders, ministers, or pastors, every "Don't ask, don't tell" church that I researched allowed Black Queer persons to serve. Many LGBTQIAP+ individuals serving in leadership roles within "Don't ask, don't tell" churches have expressed a preference for serving in welcoming churches rather than churches founded by LGBTQIAP+ individuals themselves. This preference arises from the acknowledgment that the work involved in supporting an affirming ministry or LGBTQIAP+ church plant couple with their constant focus on sexuality and queerness can be emotionally and mentally draining for some Black Queer individuals. One anonymous ordained lesbian minister who was once a leading figure in the affirming ministry / church planting movement, described her time in affirming ministry as exhausting. After some time, she began attending her partner's theologically moderate heteronormative Black church. I asked her directly, why would you leave an affirming church started by queer folk to participate in a "Don't ask, don't tell" church that does not affirm you? She responded,

> I'm called to love those folks there. They're amazing people—like, you couldn't ask for a better spot in terms of people. I'm still getting to know them. It's a church that's heavily inundated with seniors but seniors of a particular status, so it is a highbrow early American Negro kind of church, you know. Kind of a "Don't ask, don't tell" church. I know personally that one of their directors and potentially one of their musicians are gay. Neither of them is "out," and I haven't seen any people in the congregation whom

I have pegged as such, so, you know, either they mask it well or don't come to church. It's my partner's church, and I started going with her because I was drained from inclusive church plant ministry. My partner is corporate, and because she's corporate, she's not as vocal about her identity. And so she has many people who revere and respect her. And so rather than, you know, muddy that for them, she's always up for the conversation if anyone asks, but no one dares ask. So we decided not to attend an affirming church but to go to her home church together, and her pastor peeped that I am a minister, and he wanted me to join his ministerial leadership team and, you know....

I wrestled with, should I disclose who I am? And I thought, you know, he's not sharing with me who the hell he's sleeping with. Why should I? And so as long as it doesn't infringe on any core values that I have around that—you know, I'm okay. And to be honest, I've had conversations, and I said, "Now you and I are probably different theologically." And he goes, "How so?" And so I started talking to him about it, and I said, "I would consider myself fairly liberal," and he said, "I would consider myself kind of moderate." I said, "Okay, I'll respect your pulpit in the way you call for, but if you want me to teach or lead in a particular way, I lead by example. And my example may bring forward some values that may not be normative, but they are so inherent to who I am, and that's who I will be." So we agreed that that works. What I meant by that is, if I hear you say something that's faulty about women or faulty about marginal folks or faulty about gay folks, I'm going to call you on it. That's what I've been doing with him, and he hasn't said anything about gays; they don't even touch that word in their church, but where he messes up a lot of times is he gives these really fucked-up examples, very hetero examples, where he privileges the male perspective.[21]

This Black Queer woman exists in a liminal space in this "Don't ask, don't tell" church. It is unclear if she is "out" in her church, but she staunchly advocates for an inclusive theology regarding sexuality and problematic gendered-religious concepts. She spoke candidly about challenging the theological assertions of her partner's pastor and was intentional about highlighting how he is receptive to critique. As a result, it is essential to emphasize that "Don't ask, don't tell" churches are not queered environments. They exist on a spectrum somewhere between affirming and nonaffirming. This in-between existence puts Black Queer persons at risk. "Don't ask, don't tell" churches are heteronormative spaces that also exist as spaces of possibility and hope. These ecclesial spaces are fertile ground for Black congregational queering. "Don't ask, don't tell" churches are the best places to begin a queering process because they are adaptive congregations. All of the Black churches that have been congregationally or pastorally queered were first "Don't ask, don't tell" churches.

Other Examples and Thoughts on Congregationally Queered Black Churches

Many of the oldest congregationally queered historically Black churches in America—Union United Methodist Church of Boston; St. James Episcopal Church of Austin, Texas; Covenant Baptist UCC in Washington, DC; St. Luke Missionary Baptist Church of Charlotte, North Carolina; and Myrtle Baptist Church of Newton, Massachusetts—have one thing in common: they became inclusive because they wanted to affirm the diverse identities within their existing congregations or contexts. Their queering processes began with an awareness of Black Queer persons and a desire to learn how to be more affirming. As former "Don't ask, don't tell" churches, queered Black congregations intentionally investigated cultural and scriptural misconceptions about gender and sexuality to substantiate their inclinations toward inclusivity. Queered Black churches interpreted their compassion for LGBTQIAP+ persons as divine mandates imparted through revelation. Queered Black churches believe that God called them to cultivate radical compassion and inclusivity as ecclesial characteristics.

Historically, Black congregational queering processes have also been strengthened, clarified, and sustained through prayer and discernment. Prayer is a spiritual procedure of transformation that lessens the precant's ability to be morally inconsistent and contradictory. Prayer also strengthens the precant's power to subvert the tyranny of heteronormativity with patience, wisdom, and love. Coupled with discernment, prayer was a deliberate form of communication with the Divine that helped queered congregations to recenter, recharge, and reclarify their commitments to be the Body of Christ. Prayer brought congregants closer to God, which changed their hearts and inspired them to abandon condemnation and fiercely embrace their love for the entire world. Discernment was the primary spiritual gift that queered Black churches used to mature and cultivate their congregations toward inclusivity. These spiritual practices helped congregations make Godly change with genuine compassion and empathy.

Ninety-five percent of all Black congregational queering processes began as forms of pastoral queering. Heterosexual pastors first queered their own theologies and worldviews. This process of self-queering constantly evolved out of a season of solitary prayer, deep reflection, and discernment. The pastors were initially ill equipped and anxious about discussing sexuality with their parishioners, so they resorted to personal prayer and inner wrestling. At some point, the pastor's internal wrestling grew into a form of prophetic courageousness that pushed them to teach Bible studies and preach sermons that affirmed LGBTQIAP+ persons. Their Bible lessons and sermons drew attention to the intersectional nature of sexism, racism, and homophobia and how their adverse repercussions are abusive to Black Queer persons. The pastors also exposed their congregants to the complexity of homophobia through careful planning and programming with the church's senior leadership. For example, programming included World AIDS observances, regular HIV testing, HIV/AIDS clinics, fundraising for HIV research, and actions such as establishing partnerships with local hospitals and health clinics to conduct gender- and sexuality-awareness workshops.

Next Steps for Black Ecclesial Queering: Build a Core Committee

Once the congregation has been exposed to the necessary foreknowledge needed for ecclesial queering, a committee appointed by the congregation should join the pastor in the discerning and learning process. These persons should include deacons, ministers, trustees, and many other church officials. This committee is essential as they will lead the church in becoming more knowledgeable about LGBTQIAP+ life and the origins and nature of heteronormativity. The committee should begin by cultivating strong relationships with congregants for the collection of appropriate information for the queering process. Committee members can cultivate and curate healthy dialogue through individual conversations and small-group and youth group conversations about LGBTQIAP+ theology, history, and life. Once the core committee has engaged in proficient research and presented a plan of education to the church, the body then engages in its own stages of queering. An education curriculum for church queering usually include an explanation of biblical interpretation and the history of heteronormativity. Those lessons are followed by churchwide training on engagement and affirmation. After the church has engaged in a study period, they move forward with making their church polity reflect a welcoming and affirming church. This process may include a members'-only business meeting and vote with a parliamentarian to assist. Although the church may vote to be open and affirming, much work still remains for the church and its leadership.

The Five Preexisting Conditions and Commonalities of Queered Black Churches

Despite Black denominationalism's lack of hospitality, a few historically Black churches have unashamedly provided unprejudiced pastoral care, spiritual formation, and radically affirmative ecclesial settings for Black Queer persons. Throughout my qualitative research on these congregations, I noticed several commonalities. First, all queered Black congregations began as "Don't ask, don't tell" churches. This proves that "Don't ask, don't tell" churches are spiritual spaces with inclusive possibilities. They are adaptable congregations where queering can occur.

The second preexisting condition was that all of the queered Black congregations I studied were already ordaining women to the diaconate and as clergy. During interviews, members and clergy from these congregations were incredibly proud about how they had previously confronted and wrestled with Black ecclesial sexism. Whether or not they dismantled ecclesial sexism is up for debate, but they all celebrated their granting of ordinations and licenses to women and eliminating the traditional Black church model of single-gendered church leadership. Many pastoral queerers, such as Kenneth L. Samuel during an interview for my master's thesis, spoke of eliminating sexism in the church as a precursor to queering because sexism and homophobia are similarly evil interlocutors. This form of pastoral queering hinges on the empathy of Black women. The thought here is that if Black women, who make up the majority of all Black congregations, are taught to interpret sexism and heteronormativity as a two-sided coin, then queering might become a more manageable feat. All congregationally queered Black churches also began their queering by condemning sexism.

For example, Covenant Baptist Church (CBUCC) was founded as an all-white congregation in 1945. Almost twenty-five years later they elected their first African American pastor, Rev. H. Wesley Wiley, to sustain the church community. Over the years of Wiley's leadership, the congregation assumed a predominately Black demographic. Later, his son—the Reverend Dr. Dennis Wiley—was called to lead the church in 1985. Following the election of Dr. Wiley, the church ordained its first woman clergy member, Rev. Dr. Christine Wiley, the wife of Rev. Dennis Wiley. During a harsh winter, the church loaned its space to the Max Robinson and Whitman Walker AIDS Clinic. Negative comments came from the congregation. Noticing the congregation's readiness to condemn those of different ideologies, Rev. Dr. Dennis Wiley swiftly took on the task of educating his congregation through a series of Bible studies and thought-provoking programming on homophobia. The Wileys also educated their congregation with guest lecturers such as Rev. Dr. Kelly Brown Douglas and Maha Silar. In 2004 the church voted to call the Wileys as coequal pastors and to become a welcoming congregation. The Wileys believed in a significant connection between the elevation of the church's first female pastor and its inclusion of all LGBTQIAP+ persons. They were addressing sexism and homophobia intersectionally. After such a substantial shift in the church's ecclesiology, the theme for the church became "A New Paradigm for a New Day." In 2017 the Wileys retired, and Rev. Dr. Alice B. Greene served as interim minister. In 2019, CBUCC called Rev. William T. Young IV to serve as its eighth pastor, and under his leadership, the church continues to strive toward perpetual queering to honor the legacies of Christine and Dennis Wiley.

Third, all of the queered Black congregations I have studied possessed what Peter Paris described as the fundamental and common thread of Black ecclesiology: the affirmation of the Black person. Paris argues that the original purpose and prophetic calling of Black ecclesiologies was and still is to affirm "the equality of all persons under God regardless of race or any other natural quality. This doctrine has been the essence of the Black Christian tradition and the most fundamental requirement of its churches."[22] This fundamental and common thread of Black ecclesiology was deeply woven into the ecclesiologies of all two hundred churches I studied. This essential and common thread of Black ecclesiology is evident in Union United Methodist Church and Mount Nebo Baptist Church. Their ecclesial roots are steeped in prophetic teaching and preaching. Both Reverend Franklin and the various pastors who served Union Church held that liberation for the oppressed, especially Black folk, is the essential component of the gospel message. Union and Mount Nebo viewed protests as important for Blacks. The equality of all persons under God, regardless of race or any other natural quality, is the most critical preexisting commonality among the queered Black ecclesiologies under study. This one preexisting commonality is one of the more salient characteristics that a congregation must have if it wishes to employ Black ecclesial queering as a tool of subversion and prophetic action. This standard prophetic dimension of racial liberation and social justice allows the Black ecclesial queerer to use the intersectional tenets of race and sexuality as an entryway for empathy and hospitality.

The fourth preexisting condition and commonality among all of the pastorally and congregationally queered Black churches and "Don't ask, don't tell" churches that I studied is that they were all committed to justice. Their fundamental and common thread of Black ecclesiology that was deeply woven into their churches manifested in the form of social action and an allegiance to the social gospel. The congregations had long histories of championing other social causes like women's rights, abortion rights, peace protests, and racial justice causes before queering. Some were founded by freed enslaved persons; some began as citadels for Black folk during the Great Migration. Some of the churches were significant figures during the civil rights movement of the 1960s, and others, like Martin Luther King Jr., took risks to oppose the Vietnam War. For example, Union and Mount Nebo viewed protests as acceptable modes of combating the injustices committed to and on Black bodies.

Ten Commonalities of the Interviewed Black Congregants

1. Most lay congregants and church leaders who participated in the study were familiar with popular scriptural verses, like Psalm 23 or John 3:16. However, their overall scriptural literacy, working knowledge of the history of the Bible, and biblical interpretive skills were relatively low.
2. There was very little understanding of the history of Black ecclesial homophobia among lay congregants and church leaders.
3. The majority of lay congregants and church leaders had difficulty explaining why being Queer is not a sin. Even when asked, none of them could frame their church's Queer inclusivity within the context of Scripture by, for instance, actually wrestling with the "texts of

terror."[23] Instead, they mostly resorted to the idea of God's love as the sole rationale for their church's queered ecclesiology. Love was their modus operandi.
4. The majority of the participants were female.
5. Queer congregants who were members at the time of the church's queering were longtime parishioners.
6. While all the interviewees were relatives, friends, or associates of Queer persons, none discussed their personal relationships with Black Queer family members during their interviews. Their explanations of their church's inclusivity and their own inclusivity revolved around discussions of Jesus's love for everyone and the inclusive nature of God's kingdom/kindom or family.
7. The reasons congregants offered for their church's queering were not rooted in an understanding of the sociopolitical complexities of the historical oppressiveness of Black homophobia. Instead, their knowledge of why their church became queered centered around personal aspects such as empathy, pastoral trust, and intimate association.
8. All of the key subjects were above the age of sixty because of the aging population of the churches. There were not many younger active members.
9. This study's key subjects served on core committee or were supporters throughout the queering process or agreed with the don't ask don't tell feel of the church.
10. This study's key subjects had served in highly respected lay offices before, during, and after their congregation's queering.

A More Excellent Way! The Four Basic Elements of Black Congregational Queering

While denominational queering is solely theoretical and pastoral queering is most prevalent, congregationally queered Black churches are scarce but offer the most effective form of queering. Only five percent of affirming Black churches have been queered congregationally. Unlike denominational queering, which is essentially a political methodology, and "Don't ask, don't tell" churches and pastorally queered churches whose queering methods are questionable. Black ecclesial queering is congregational. It is an intentionally communal and spiritual method of dismantling heteronormativity that the congregation conducts on itself. Although few churches have been congregationally queered, it remains the more excellent way. The congregationally queered congregations I studied approached the queering process as a spiritual, fluid, and unhurried contextual journey of postapologetic reeducation that wrestled with Scripture in response to a divine call. There are four essential elements of Black ecclesial queering: (1) Black ecclesial queering is congregational queering and it is an unhurried communal and spiritual journey that is contextual; (2) Black ecclesial queering is an intentional journey of postapologetic reeducation; (3) Black ecclesial queering is a challenging and rewarding process of dismantling hegemonic heteronormativity within the prose, narratives, and contexts of Scripture; and (4) Black ecclesial queering is a fluid and ever-evolving methodology of relationship building, listening, compassionate engagement, and love.

Black ecclesial queering is a spiritual journey based on the congregational queering model that subverts the heteronormative and Puritan-based envelopes that have shrouded Blackness over time. It takes time to destabilize the ideology of queerness as inherently bad. Black ecclesial queering is an unhurried method of theological subversiveness that brings culture and society into dialogue with race and power. It demystifies the widespread assumption that queering only derives from "an overarching queer subjectivity" that solely benefits and represents homosexual persons. Black ecclesial queering affirms and normalizes all gender identities and expressions through compassionate teaching and carefully curated engagement during Bible studies, Sunday school, and similar sessions. As a postapologetic methodology, Black ecclesial queering also unashamedly declares that Queer persons are already loved and affirmed by God while cultivating an atmosphere where heterosexual persons feel comfortable asking honest questions. Black ecclesial queering is an unhurried human enterprise of community-building. It is a congregational journey that overturns heteronormativity for the sake of the gospel, equity, and social change.

As stated, Black ecclesial queering is an intentional journey of postapologetic reeducation. Despite its need for improvement, Black ecclesial queering is the more excellent way of Queering Black churches. Black ecclesial queering teaches congregants that the hegemonic binaries of male and female are socially constructed categories that must be seen as fluid. Unlike Queer theory, Black ecclesial queering is also intentional about avoiding the white Queer mistake of seemingly making Black womanhood invisible for the sake of affirming nonbinary gender variants. Black ecclesial queering does not see Black womanhood or Womanism as antithetical but an essential characteristic of ecclesial Queering. In the case of Union, the Womanist sensibilities of their eldest and most respected member launched the church's queering process.

Black ecclesial queering also rethinks Christian apologetics. It practically uses Queer theology and the Black Queer Womanist theology of Pamela Lightsey as pedagogical resources of reeducation to dismantle heteronormativity in adaptive congregations. Black ecclesial queering is not an attempt to convince people that LGBTQIAP+ persons are a part of the *body of Christ*. Congregational queering is not combative queering that seeks to argue for the inclusion of LGBTQIAP+ persons into the church; however, it does not fear conflict. Instead, congregational queering teaches congregants that the intrinsic value and worth of LGBTQIAP+ lives must always be a given. In congregational queering, core committees use Queer theology as a reeducational resource to teach congregants that LGBTQIAP+ persons are already a part of the family of God. Congregational queering, to use the words of Linn Marie Tonstad, "should not be about toxic apologetics."[24]

As with Tonstad's argument, congregational queering is not a toxic form of apologetically convincing misogynistic, sexist, homophobic, transphobic, or xenophobic persons that they should extend grace toward Queer folk. Instead, congregational queering is a form of effectively educating congregations on how to queer their ecclesial contexts. A traditional Christian understanding of apologetics, as Tonstad argues, is toxic and antithetical to the aims of Queer theology and congregational queering. Indeed, many of the original gay and lesbian theologies of the 1970s were written in response to dominant Christian homophobia and heteronormative indoctrinations. Still, it would be wrong to view their works as solely apologetic in a toxic sense. I say this because Queer theologies were not written exclusively in response to homophobic rhetoric. Queer persons also wrote them for Queer persons who suffered from internalized heteronormativity to aid them in believing in their intrinsic worth using contextual religious language. Mark Jordan posits,

> Queer theology as it has been written exceeds the rhetoric of apology (in the old sense of that word). What looks like defense is often consolation or catechesis.... The "apologetic strategies" have not always been apologetic. They were also more than mere strategies or "arguments." If earlier writers of queer theology fell into the bad habits of dogmatic politics (remember

the manifestos!), they also returned to pastoral genres—to testimony and prophecy, to laments and litanies of holy predecessors.[25]

In this quote, Jordan calls out Queer theologians for pretending that our academic styles are perfectly transparent to every form of religious speech—that they offer a neutral medium in which to describe and judge everything. That is hardly true. Jordan is correct; if Queer theology has failed at anything, it is not always being transparent or applicable to many congregational contexts that Jordan describes as possessing varying forms of religious speech. Congregational queering attempts to do just that; to use Queer theology as a pedagogical resource of reeducation to dismantle heteronormativity in Black churches.

As I have said, core committees use Queer theology as a pedagogical resource of reeducation to teach congregations that LGBTQIAP+ persons are already a part of the family of God. This move is significant because it directly addresses a group erased from traditional Christian apologetics. It gives persons dismantling heteronormativity the ability to reclaim apologetics in a Queer form that says that even if we discover a verse from Scripture that appears to justify homophobia, we will engage it using a hermeneutic of suspicion and transgress it in the same way that Christianity has transgressed scriptural verses about slavery, eating shrimp, wearing mixed fabrics, and so on. True congregational queering is transgressive, even if the transgression is against Scripture. This means that a hermeneutic of suspicion authorizes congregational queerers to interpret clobber texts as literary works birthed out of heteronormative contexts to uphold and promote power, control, and traditional forms of Rabbinic Judaism and the traditions and institutions of Christianity that they influenced. Suppose a scriptural verse and the history of its interpretation are found guilty of being an alt-right form of personalized moral reductionism that pits one segment of the population against another by putting their identities in direct competition. In that case, the Scripture should be deemed a cautionable offense. A cautionary offensive scriptural verse is a human-written text that is found guilty of infringing on the intrinsic dignity of any human being in a dissenting manner. Reading texts with caution allows queerers to acknowledge and highlight the oppressive systems within a text, including ableism, misogyny, patriarchy, and heteronormativity, and the results of those systems, including economic inequality, maternal health disparities, and the reification of traditional family dynamics.

Although Black ecclesial queering avoids toxic apologetics, it performs its ecclesial queering by placing great value on wrestling with Scripture. While some Queer theologians may be able to ignore the importance of engaging clobber texts as a form of toxic apologetics, Black Queer theologians understand the importance of the Bible for Black diasporic peoples whose enslaved ancestors often secretly learned how to read as enslaved people using Bibles. Instead, Black Queer theology reads all Scripture using a hermeneutic of suspicion. Unlike approaching all texts as divine edicts, a hermeneutic of suspicion frees queerers to recognize, wrestle with, question, deconstruct, and dismantle hegemonic heteronormativity within texts.[26] When a congregational queerer uses a hermeneutic of suspicion to understand and deconstruct hegemonic heteronormativity in clobber texts, they interpret Scripture through the worldview of oppressed Queer persons and Queer theory instead of ideas that maintain heteronormativity. Queer Biblical hermeneutics approaches clobber texts with skepticism by interpreting texts through the quadrilateral of Judeo-Christian Scripture, acknowledging the toxicity of the heteronormative tradition, dismantling all heteronormative interpretations of texts by reasoning with Queer theory, and centering the experiences of Queer persons. When interpreting Scripture, the committee should look for the socio-historical elements of suppressed and oppressed persons and their intersectional manifestations, expressions, and performances within sacred texts.

The first move a congregation should make when operationalizing a Queer apologetic in a congregation is to avoid beginning the conversation with clobber texts. Always begin queering discussions in the affirmative. Never start the process of queering, with asking questions like, "Does the Bible condemn homosexuality?" "Do these scriptural verses prove that God opposes LGBTQIAP+ persons?" "Is it okay to be gay?" Instead, initiate the conversation with affirmative statements. Like Jacqueline Grant's tridimensional argument about racism, classism, and sexism as intersectional interlocutors of violence, congregational queering helps congregations explicate the social, political, and religious structures that pattern and impact all Black bodies.[27] Black ecclesial queering brings culture and society into dialogue with gender, sexuality, race, and power. Queered Black churches seek liberation and are attentive to the concerns of all persons. As a methodology, Black ecclesial queering is a new and ever-evolving phenomenon that has four stages of queering: relationship building, listening, compassionate engagement, and inclusion of LGBTQIAP+ interlocutors.

The Importance of Narratology

Emotional evidence through stories causes people to change. Storytelling is so important. People have to experience it and then process the emotional evidence that resonates with them. Queer biblical apologetics is not enough. All of the Queer Black churches that I studied used narratology as a primary tool in their queering process. When congregants told stories about their Queer children and the homophobic oppression that they have endured in churches and schools, such narratives tend to pull on the heartstrings of listeners to the point of causing them to question their preconceived notions about heteronormativity. In fact, even when churches are practicing Queer biblical apologetics, the exegesis of such texts is another form of narratology. Much as with the Wesleyan Quadrilateral, experience is a very important factor in our approach to Scripture and social transformation. Narratives have a way of informing, sharpening, and broadening our worldviews to make room for new forms of meaning-making. They inspire change and question social practices.

The materiality of shared stories about inclusivity or homophobia influenced the context and values of the churches I researched in ways that sermons or Bible studies could not. It chipped away at heteronormativity bit by bit and changed how people view themselves as individuals, their ecclesiology as a collective, and their interpretation of Queer identity. Notably, using narratives as a form of queering requires a certain element of persuasion. Successful queerers who use narratology to subvert heteronormativity in churches intentionally and unintentionally, because of the personal nature of their sharing, used specific language and the stylistic structure of lament to craft stories that would intentionally affect the souls of their audiences. Narratology is a powerful and useful tool of congregational queering. However, narratological reasoning can also be problematic and toxic.

Congregations who attempt to queer their ecclesial contexts should be careful to avoid forcing their Queer congregants to share personal stories of pain and hardship because of the possibility of retraumatization. This rule extends to the parents of LGBTQIAP+ persons. The painful evolution of accepting one's own Queer child coupled with the remembrance of cyberbullying and other homophobic darts that were thrown at their child and family at large can be overwhelming. Remember that the narratives of Queer persons and their family members should never be used as what sociologist Frank Furedi describes as the pornography of emotional hurt or an emotional striptease.[28] Stories about Queer suffering and marginalization should not be exploited for the sake of congregational queering. Equitable inclusivity in congregations cannot be achieved through trauma porn.

An equitable way to use narratology is to permit it to naturally evolve out of the process of compassionate conversations. While you should never force a Queer person or their family members to share their stories, such persons should be able to share their narratives if they desire to do so. It is also important that listeners learn how to empathize with compassion instead of responding to a person's Queer narrative with interrogated questioning laced with toxic presuppositions. Instead, congregants should place their attention on listening intently. When Queer persons tell their stories of pain and trauma, hearers should be sure to listen with love—with their minds, hearts, and soul—maintaining a pleasant disposition on one's face and making eye contact with the storyteller. Listeners should be interested and nonjudgmental, curious but not nosy, and captivated but not entertained. The storyteller should never feel pressed but rather comfortable and affirmed by listeners to share as little or as much as they wish.

Another form of narratology that I find more appropriate than public personal sharing is the reading of narratives. Austen Hartke's *Transforming: The Bible and the Lives of Transgender Christians* is an example of using narratives to create social change in congregations.[29] A great deal of his book's focuses on the narratives of transgender persons and their families. These narratives give inquiring parishioners the ability to think more deeply about lived realities. The distance that most congregations will have between themselves and the narratives in the book permit parishioners to ask honest questions without putting the narratives of their Queer church family members on the symbolic sacrificial altars of dialogue for the sake of congregational change. However, the distance between parishioners and the characters within narratives like Hartke's book should never cause parishioners to mishandle the sacred stories that they are reading through exploitation or entertainment. The secret stories of Queer persons should be regarded by Christian readers in the tradition of 2 Corinthians 3:2, as living epistles, written upon their hearts, to be read by humans.

Finally, and significantly, the sharing of one story need not always include aspects of pain and trauma. Some moments during my research revealed that the most effective narratives for many individuals were narratives that avoided the exploitive nature of trauma porn. Narratives about how Queer persons fell in love with their partners or their joys in parenting help heteronormative congregants perceive Queer living and thriving as embracing joy and tenacity. Additionally, churches must also be careful to avoid unrealistic, exceptionalist, stereotypical, and generalized stories about Queer life.

The Stages of Black Ecclesial Queering

Black ecclesial queering is a fresh and ever-evolving phenomenon that attempts to winnow Black congregations of their homophobic, transphobic, and heteronormative ideals. In chapter 3, I used the narrative of Union United Methodist Church to introduce Black congregational queering because it is the oldest congregationally queered Black church in the United States. Since Union's queering, many other Black congregations have queered their ecclesial contexts congregationally and even more have done so pastorally. This section of the chapter shares the commonalities between their Queering processes. As discussed, all congregationally queered Black churches center their queering strategies on relationship building, listening, compassionate engagement, and love.

Black ecclesial queering begins when God moves upon the pastor or one or more congregants' hearts to help their congregation be affirming of LGBTQIAP+ persons. After that, the persons to whom God revealed God's inclusive plan commence on a spiritual journey of prayer, discernment, and self-reeducation. While pastoral queering can lead to congregational queering, which was the case with Christine and Dennis Wiley at Covenant Baptist United Church of Christ in Washington, DC, most instances of congregational queering, like at St. James Episcopal Church of Austin, Texas, are birthed out of the hearts of compassionate congregants who desire to see their congregations evolve and grow into being inclusive over time. In most cases, congregants interested in helping their churches become affirming approach their pastors to seek ecclesial approval. These interested parties developed into a core committees or LGBTQIAP+ task forces upon gaining such support. The establishment of these official core committees is a critical moment in the process of Black ecclesial queering. Several of the churches I studied and have consulted used the Building an Inclusive Church: A Welcoming Toolkit 3.0 by Reconciling Works to construct their core committees. In this excellent resource for cultivating affirmation they describe core committees as core teams. This toolkit explains the concept of core committees in lay accessible terms.[30]

The most critical and vulnerable phase of Black ecclesial queering exists between the moment of divine impartation and the establishment of an official congregational core committee. The official process of congregational queering cannot commence until a church has voted to establish a standing committee to develop and guide the congregation through a process of queering. Before this moment, queering is not a fact but a hopeful intuition.

To avoid tie votes core committees should consist of an odd number of no more than nine persons to design, shepherd, and advocate for a welcome and affirming process. Because there are no one-size-fits-all templates for queering a church, the success of Black congregational core committees has primarily been the result of their willingness to educate themselves on the processes of other congregations to construct a contextually appropriate method for their churches. Creating a contextually relevant queering strategy for a congregation requires careful attention and a thick theological understanding of the congregation's history. Core committees typically spend about six months examining their church's history, analyzing how it has historically dealt with change and conflict, creating a detailed assessment of the church's power structures, and forming relationships with the congregants.[31] The findings from this period indicate how long the queering process will take or if queering is even possible.

In almost every instance of congregational queering, the reasoning and impetus behind the dismantling of heteronormativity are closely connected to some aspect of the church's history and original ecclesial mission. For instance, in my congregation, the theology of Myrtle's most prized stained-glass window depicting Phillip baptizing the Ethiopian eunuch became a central narratological part of our core committee's reasoning for queering. A core committee's ability or inability to connect the congregational queering process with the history and competing narratives of the congregation will determine its success or failure.

The core committee should also assess how the congregation has dealt with change and conflict in the past. If a congregation's core committee is attempting to go through a queering process and their church has successfully ordained women to the diaconate, ordained ministry, or a lay leadership position, it would be wise to consider the congregation's challenges when it began consecrating women as leaders. If a church could not transgress traditional notions of nonfemale leadership, such a congregation could never be queered. Recognizing the strengths and challenges that a church has experienced throughout seasons of change will inevitably help a core committee contextualize the queering process intentionally and accurately. It will also aid them in determining what LGBTQIAP+ persons they need at the table to educate them.

The core committee also examines and honestly reflects on the church's power structure.[32] They identify the well-respected families and individuals within a congregation and assess the senior pastor's power or lack thereof. Core committees also weigh the powers of formal lay boards against the informal lay leadership of church mothers, the pillars of the church, and the wider ecclesial web of members and their relatives and friends. The best way for a core committee to use the church's preexisting power structures and history to queer the church is through relationship building, information gathering, and critical listening. One pastor described this stage of the queering process as parallel to when Moses sent Joshua and Caleb to scope out the land of Canaan in Numbers 13. Core committee members are assigned to particular persons, families, and congregational ministries. Each core committee member's responsibility is to casually meet with their appointed parties over a meal to hear varying perspectives about the queering initiative to either discover or gain a queering ally or identify a common ground for compassionate educational engagement that intentionally regards disputatiousness as unproductive.[33]

Successful core committee do not regard their work as war or see themselves as soldiers. Instead, they see their work as a form of compassionate Christian education through communal engagement. This is one of the most critical components of congregational queering. Unlike Black pastoral queering, which is often conducted from the power of the pulpit, Black congregational queering is a form of recognizing the priesthood of all believers. During initial core committee engagement and Bible studies about gender and sexuality, congregational queering should never be force-fed to people; this type of dogmatic liberalism demonizes wrestling and growth over time. Congregational queering is patient and kind, holding no record of wrongs because it thrives on the possibility of individual evolution. Congregational queering is a praxis of compassion that is harmless as a dove and wise as a serpent. The compassion in congregational queering could be misinterpreted as an accommodationist ploy that appeals more to heteronormative sensibilities than to the painful cries of Black Queer vilification. This would be a mischaracterization of the impetus behind such qualities. The compassion within congregational queering mirrors the subversive nature with which Jesus loved the social outcasts, invalids, and despised persons within his society. Jesus's compassion not only led him to heal persons; it also led him to overturn tables in the temple. Jesus had empathy for people, but he also wanted them to obtain justice. Black ecclesial queering is birthed and manifested in subversive compassion.

On the other hand, in adaptive Black churches, Black ecclesial queering is regarded as a spiritual opportunity for congregational growth and intentional stewardship. Most adaptive congregations have preexisting "Don't ask, don't tell" characteristics that undergird their strong amenability. Congregationally queered Black churches have been guided by their core committees to understand the queering processes as a spiritual formation that deeply listens to what God is saying and doing in the congregation and the world. Such deep listening to God paired with a compassionate practice of critically and empathetically listening to each other through holy conversation, sharing one's own stories, hearing different perspectives, and stretching one's normative claims were the primary characteristics of every successfully queered Black congregation.

After gathering such meaningful information, all of the core committees worked to create a pedagogical approach to congregational queering that reflected the nuances of their context. For instance, the types of documentaries, public storytelling, Bible studies, sermons, panel discussions, and group reflections that were used varied in every church that I studied because the core committees sought to respond to the particular needs of their congregation. This guaranteed that any vote presented to the congregation to include LGBTQIAP+ persons would pass with a majority vote.

Strengthening Queering for Black Congregations

Congregational queering should center Queer voices, experiences, and all subversive discourses from the margins, such as Womanist theology, disabilities theology, and critical race theory—thus the need for LGBTQIAP+ interlocutors. However, as I stated earlier, this does not mean that Queer congregants should take the lead in dismantling heteronormativity within a Black church. Ecclesial Queer processes can be complicated for Queer members of a congregation. Queer parishioners may support the process but may not feel called to lead the process for fear of the spotlight being put on them or the possibility of a negative outcome; which could be a traumatizing reminder of familial disconnections and rejections. Core committees should regularly check in with known Queer members of their congregations to determine if the queering process is proceeding equitably.[34]

In almost every case of Black ecclesial queering I studied, the process lacked three fundamental phases: (1) lament, confession, and repentance; (2) comprehensive teaching on the affirmation of transgender parishioners; and (3) creation of affirming youth ministries. Black ecclesial queering needs strengthening in the area of LGBTQIAP+ pastoral care. Many queering processes have focused on heterosexual persuasion to the detriment of its Queer members. A church should never neglect the spiritual needs and formation of its Black Queer congregants because of a queering process. For instance, just as Black heterosexual congregants need queering, so do many Black Queer persons whose indoctrinated homophobia can prohibit self-acceptance.

Many Black Queer congregants in queered congregational contexts often criticize their congregations for the lack of lament and repentance in their queering processes. Most Black queer congregants have silently borne the harmful repercussions and aggressions of ecclesial heteronormativity. While heterosexual members need to hear the triumphant narratives of Black Queer persons, it is also crucial for churches to learn about the ways Black churches have harmed the Black Queer community. Churches must review the history of institutional harm that Black Queer folk have suffered in Black churches. For instance, in April 2004 the Church of God in Christ issued an official statement on gay rights titled "Marriage: A Proclamation to the Church of God in Christ Worldwide":

> Marriage between males and females provides the structure for conceiving and raising children. Compliance with this command of God is a physical and biological impossibility in same-sex unions. We, therefore, believe that only marriages between a male and female, as ordained by God, are essential for the procreation of humanity. We believe that the homosexual practices of same-sex couples are in violation of religious and social norms and are aberrant and deviant behavior. We believe that these unions are sinful and in direct violation of the law of God in that they are a deviation from the natural use and purpose of the body. Therefore, despite the progressive normalization of alternative lifestyles and the growing legal acceptance of same-sex unions, we declare our opposition to any deviation from traditional binary marriages of males and females. Notwithstanding

the rulings of the court systems of the land in support of same-sex unions, we resolve that the Church of God in Christ stands resolutely firm and never allows the sanctioning of same-sex marriages by its clergy, nor recognize [sic] the legitimacy of such unions.[35]

On Wednesday, July 7, 2004, the African Methodist Episcopal (AME) Church became the second historically Black denomination to make a statement and the first to vote officially to forbid ministers "from performing a marriage or civil union ceremonies for same-sex couples."[36] Furthermore, "the official position of the African Methodist Episcopal Church is not in favor of the ordination of openly gay persons to the ranks of clergy in our church. This position reaffirms our published position papers, public statements, and prior rulings, which indicate that we do not support the ordination of openly gay persons."[37] The National Baptist Convention, USA, Incorporated, allows full autonomy to its constituent churches to be welcoming and inclusive of LGBTQIAP+ congregants, yet in a statement released in January 2014,

> The National Baptist Convention gave specific instructions to its Military Chaplains, stating that "Endorsed Chaplains, although serving in a pluralistic environment, are not to participate in any activity that implies or condones same-sex marriage or same-sex union." Similarly, in June 2012, Julius Scruggs, then President of the Convention, responded to President Obama's statement of support for same-sex marriage with a letter stipulating, "The National Baptist Convention, USA, Incorporated does not dictate to its constituent churches what position to take on issues because we believe in the autonomy of the local church. However, the National Baptist Convention, USA, Inc. affirms that marriage is a sacred biblical covenant between a man and a woman.[38]

The official stance of the Christian Methodist Episcopal (CME) Church on same-sex marriage was adopted by the African American denomination's pre-2010 General Conference: "Marriage shall be defined as a union between a man and a woman, and under no circumstances shall the Christian Methodist Episcopal church either perform same-sex marriages or bless same-sex unions."[39] In 2015 the College of Bishops from the Christian Methodist Episcopal Church released a statement on the Supreme Court marriage decision stating,

The CME Book of Discipline in section 131.4g on Moral and Ethical Behavior explicitly discloses that some abortions and same-sex marriage are unacceptable.[40]

Specifically, we believe that same-sex marriages are contrary to biblical teaching and the CME Church's Discipline. Therefore, our clergy are not only admonished against performing or blessing same-sex unions, but a CME minister who performs a same-sex marriage or blesses a same-sex union violates the Discipline of the Church and is subject to disciplinary action. Furthermore, no property of the Christian Methodist Episcopal Church can be used for any same-sex marriage or celebration.[41]

Likewise, during a 2016 quadrennial episcopal address, Bishops Dennis Vernon Proctor and William Darin Moore of the African Methodist Episcopal (AME) Zion Church issued the following statement:

We continue to affirm as consistent with our scriptural and Christian tradition the understanding of marriage as being a sacred covenant between one man and one woman. While we acknowledge that each of us as Christians often fall short of that ideal and that even as norms and standards evolve over time; it is not for us to negotiate the teachings of Scripture to our proclivities but to aspire to the high values to which we believe Scripture invites us all.[42]

The Progressive National Baptist Convention and the National Baptist Convention of America Incorporated have remained silent on the issue and instead point to their autonomous polity. Each individual church congregation can do as it wishes. This silence, however, does not indicate denominational approval or affirmation of Black Queer persons. While the silence may present the option for constituents to welcome Queer persons, it also creates the opportunity for churches to reinforce their implicit leanings toward biased and puritanical notions of "normality" and patriarchy.

The previously reviewed treatments of LGBTQIAP+ persons by the seven historically Black denominations necessitate that Black Queer persons lament and Black denominations and congregations repent. During these moments, core committees should intentionally cultivate compassionate spaces where Queer persons are welcomed to lament and voice their disappointment with the Black ecclesial practice of homophobia. Also, during such moments, the core committee member assigned to facilitate such discussions should repent on behalf of the church. A more liturgical and corporate example of lament and repentance should acknowledge the countless Black Queer souls whose suffering was ignored by Black churches during the HIV/AIDS epidemic. Churches should repent liturgically and proactively work to reeducate their congregations on healthy sex practices that shun purity culture ideologies while simultaneously affirming sexual exploration under the auspices of consent. Cheng describes this in *Radical Love* as the fourth sacrament of reconciliation that involves the confession of sins.[43] However, there can never be absolution for transphobia, homophobia, and ecclesial heteronormativity. These interlocking systems are too complex for any sort of absolution.

Affirming Transgender Parishioners

Gender-based violence against transgender persons is a sin that Black churches needs to recognize, confront, and work to prevent because Christianity and Black churches bear its stain. For far too long, many of our inclusive Black churches and African American Queer theologians have solely centered their entire theological arguments for the full inclusion of LGBTQIAP+ persons on the gay male, lesbian, and occasional bisexual experience, eclipsing the transgender narrative and perspective. Additionally, most Black churches are unconcerned with the prevalence of transgender violence in America. In 2021, Black transgender persons including Tyianna Alexander, a twenty-eight-year-old Black transgender woman; Bianca "Muffin" Bankz, a Black transgender woman; Dominique Jackson, a thirty-year-old Black transgender woman; Fifty Bandz, a twenty-one-year-old Black transgender woman; and Diamond Kyree Sanders, a twenty-three-year-old Black transgender woman were murdered—and this is occurring with the same alarming frequency as Black men killed at the hands of the police.[44] But not once did Black churches, in any collective statement, come to the defense of transgender persons as they did the murders of Black men like George Floyd. It is as if Black Christian America has chosen to ignore the intersectional nature of American racism and transphobia that continuously lead to the tragic and senseless murders of countless Black transgender persons.

After the murder of Trayvon Martin at the hands of George Zimmerman, Black churches protested in overwhelming numbers by wearing hoodies and placing cans of Arizona Iced Tea and bags of Skittles on their communion tables as eucharistic reminders of the tragic deaths of young Black men like Trayvon and Emmitt Till. But for the deaths of Black transgender persons and Black women, the enthusiasm of Black churches seems to fade into a poor caricature of its prophetic tradition. The needless and senseless murders of Black men like George Floyd incites a type of outrage in Black churches that the murders of Black transgender persons do not. Why? What is it about Black churches that causes them to place tremendous and needed emphasis on the murders of Black cisgender male bodies while intentionally and unintentionally devaluing the lives of Black women and Black transgender persons by ignoring their narratives of trauma and senseless murders?

Historically, Black churches have valued Black cisgender male bodies over and above all other bodies. The preservation of the Black male body is a subconscious or professed aim of some Black churches. The Black ecclesial rejection of and lack of African American female senior pastors is a telltale sign of the Black ecclesial injustice of heteronormative masculinity. Black churches have historically taught very heterogeneous theologies. And while this section of my work is intended to speak to the issue of transphobia in Black churches, the intersectional nature of Black queering, which was birthed out of Pamela Lightsey's *Black Queer Womanism*, mandates all queerers to acknowledge the intersectional nature of sexism and transphobia.

One way to introduce Black churches to the transgender experience is through narratology. One of the most prophetic transgender theologians is Austin Hartke. His book, *Transforming: The Bible and the Lives of Transgender Christians*, is a groundbreaking text that all ministers should read.[45] Hartke's narratological form of queering purges Queer theology of its incestuous preoccupation with empirical apologetics. While I do not offer here the intricacies of Hartke's argument, I reflect on the precautionary measures he recommended—one being the need to understand that language matters. Several phrases are problematic and should never be used by Black congregants. Transgender persons should never be referred to as "a transgender," "transgendered," "persons who have had a sex change," "pre- and postoperative," "hermaphrodite," "he-she," "shemale," "tranny," or "drag queen." Cisgender persons should never inquire about the genitalia of transgender persons. It is inappropriate to refer to a transgender person's life narrative without their permission. A person should always use the pronouns that fit an individual's present identity when discussing their stories and backgrounds. Finally, it is essential to use the name that transgender persons use for themselves.

In addition to these practical suggestions, I share the following theological recommendations for Black churches and their pastors. Black churches should always initiate a contextual queering process to educate members on transgender theology. Second, Black churches should never restrict ministries to solely being populated by cisgender persons. For example, if a Black church has a mothers' board, transgender women should not be prohibited from membership in such ministries. Black churches should love and affirm transgender ushers, greeters, pulpit staff, senior pastors, trustees, finance committee members, stewards, deacons, and so on. The prohibition of transgender persons from such roles is a form of transphobia. Again, it is never appropriate to discuss the genitalia of transgender persons. When facilitated by nonintimate partners of transgender persons, such discussions are a form of oversexualizing transgender bodies. Such violent behaviors should be prohibited in Black churches and around Black Christian dinner tables.

I speak more about this later in this chapter, but the fluidity of transgender youths' identity should be normalized in affirming youth ministries. Transgender persons should not be required to maintain their present gender identities in perpetuity for heteronormative comprehension. Transgender persons are often forbidden from expressing the fluidity of their gender identities because "it will confuse straight folks." Forcing transgender persons to practice binary extremism for social acceptance is a heteronormative reinforcement of cultural toxicity that is highly transphobic. Instead of reinforcing transphobic ideas, our Black churches should teach their congregation's transformational theologies that subvert the heteronormative preoccupation with fixed gender identities. Just as the Genesis creation narratives indicate the transitory aspects of nature—darkness-dawn-morning-noon-afternoon-evening-dusk-night—and clownfish, slipper limpet, fish, snails, and coral animals exist as transgender creatures, so must Black churches respect transgender persons as individuals whom God made in God's image.

Practical Example

Not long after I shared my Queer identity with the congregation I was pastoring, countless numbers of parishioners began sharing and living into their truths. My sharing sparked a sort of revival within our congregation that liberally dispersed liberation, freedom, and joy throughout the networks of our congregation. During our congregational queering process, the greatest blessing was the opportunity to create an affirming, supportive, loving, brave space for a member of our youth ministry who was beginning their sacred journey of transition. After several months of mentoring and praying with the student, he exclaimed that he wanted to share his journey with the congregation during our weekly Sunday morning altar call and testimony period.

At first I was very concerned about allowing this teenager to put their vulnerability on display. I was worried because a congregational queering process should never use LGBTQIAP+ persons as sacrificial lambs. Additionally, it is highly problematic for churches to use young Queer persons as catalysts for congregational change. Black Queer persons should never be used as leverage, nor should they be forced to share their gender identities to create compassionate communal engagement. When the student asked me for permission to share his journey with the congregation, these previously stated precautions concerned me as a pastor. However, after speaking with the student's mother and his English teacher, it became evident that this process of sharing his journey had nothing to do with the church but with his desire to bring his whole self into the worship space. He informed me that his colleagues and teachers addressed him using male pronouns at school and that his gender expression was always male. However, on Sunday mornings, he found it necessary to identify as a lesbian while responding to female pronouns and the adorning of female garb. He no longer wanted the congregation that raised him to see him as a woman. He wanted the community to see him as he indeed was, a Black male.

After reflecting on his reasoning and meeting with his social and mental health workers and his mother, it became apparent that my pastoral concern was somewhat misplaced. I was so worried about preserving his safety that I failed to recognize his desire to share his journey with his congregation. For him, this was a way of reintroducing himself to the congregation. He expressed that he wanted to get it off his chest because he was exhausted from having to code-switch during Sunday morning worship services. He was essentially bifurcating his identity to fit into our hetero- and homonormative congregational system, which was sinful for the congregation. At this moment I realized that Myrtle's queering process, while effective, was lacking in areas of transgender theology and youth ministry. Furthermore, our queering process was book-ended by two coming-out narratives. Our congregational queering process began in response to *my* coming out. Upon its conclusion, God called us to commence a second phase of queering that included our youth ministry and our learning how to support our transgender members.

On a spring April Sunday morning, the young ministry member stood before our congregation and said,

> I understand LGBTQ issues are a sensitive subject, especially in a religious context, but comfortable silence is not an option. In the words of Desmond Tutu, "If you are neutral in situations of injustice, you have chosen the side of the oppressor." From time to time, I've asked my friends who are also members of the LGBTQ community to support me when I have an opportunity to speak or come to a concert or even a secular cookout, and the answer is always along the lines of, "Me? Church? Are you crazy?" And despite being raised in an environment of constant support and unconditional love, I was afraid of coming out publicly as a transgender male for years. I know this may be jarring for some. I've grown up here and walk through life as a girl named Angel. But I'm excited to open a new chapter as a boy named Achille.

As when I shared my truth, when our beloved member made his announcement, the church overwhelmingly supported him. He frequently shared updates with the congregation during altar calls. We had the honor of baptizing him. His baptism certificate bears his name.

Over the last few years, I have often reflected with great anguish on my church's congregational queering process. For a while, our intentions were virtuous. But because of our lack of resources, I have often feared that our naive queering was often more reactive than proactive.

At Myrtle I believe that we set ourselves up for success in many ways: devoting time in adult Sunday school to discuss inclusivity, setting up a core committee with a relatively horizontal power structure with LGBTQIAP+ persons at the table. We also fashioned our journey to the agape principle and benefited from the divine coincidence of the book of Acts' Ethiopian eunuch being baptized as our focal mural. Our core committee consisted of an appropriate blend of LGBTQIAP+ and non-LGBTQIAP+ facilitators and educators.

While the core committee could have benefited from meeting more frequently and having more specific and strategic journeying benchmarks, I also believe our self-initiated process reflected our limited knowledge of congregational queering.

The biggest mistake that we made was allowing our transgender youth ministry member to facilitate a discussion on gender and sexuality during an adult Sunday school session.

Another mistake that Myrtle made in our self-initiated queering process was allowing our transgender youth ministry member to facilitate a discussion on gender and sexuality during an adult Sunday school session. During the discussion, several members found it difficult to identify with the comparison between the Black pursuit for freedom in America and the Queer quest to be respected as the *imago Dei* within the dominant Black Christian society. The more divisive and argumentative part of the conversation centered on the question "Why does Myrtle need to declare itself affirming if our pastor is already out and Queer members are already accepted?" A teen should not have had to handle this discussion alone. This discussion should have been mediated and facilitated by an adult or cishet person. Queer persons, especially Queer youth, should never be allowed to explain or defend their identities. Such behavior is extremely toxic and reinforces an us-versus-them dichotomy. While it is essential to have LGBTQIAP+ persons at the table, ecclesial queering processes can be complex for Queer members of a congregation. Some Black Queer persons may support the process, and others may not. A lack of participation should never be regarded as a sign of disinterest but rather a matter of choice. Some Queer persons avoid congregational queering processes, fearing a negative outcome or an unaffirming congregational vote that might mean the loss of their spiritual community or spiritual exile or that could put a spotlight on them or their family members in harmful and useless ways. For this reason, Queer persons should not be called upon to lead a queering process. Instead, they should be welcomed to participate in the process in the ways that they feel are life-giving if they wish to contribute.

It is important to note that Myrtle was already a "Don't ask, don't tell" church before I came out. As a result, many heteronormatively minded members did not see the need to take the church through a congregational process to include LGBTQIAP+ persons more equitably. When the multilayered question

"Why does Myrtle need to declare itself affirming if our pastor is already out and Queer members are already accepted?" was asked, the chairs of the Myrtle core committee, Deacon Peter Goddard and Wanda Whitmore, responded that Myrtle needs to declare itself as open and affirming because it would signify to Queer persons that our congregation is a brave space where Queer persons can worship without the fear of homophobic rhetoric. From a Black historical perspective, the core committee used the imagery of lanterns being hung in front of specific white houses during the era of slavery to signify that they were stops along the Underground Railroad. Likewise, the demarcation of a church as open and affirming indicates that a church is truly inclusive. These statements created a moment of cognitive dissonance for many heteronormatively minded members because they were being encouraged to see the inextricable link between racism and homophobia. Sadly, one of the cofacilitators of this discussion was the transgender youth ministry member. As the facilitator of this discussion, the conversation left the student feeling particularly vulnerable.

In hindsight, we could have devoted more time to adult and children's Sunday school to educate the church on the queering process. Additionally, although the student and I were both volunteers called in Spirit to do the vulnerable work of coming out, "coming out" may be the impetus for queering, but it should not be a planned part of queering. Cishet congregants should be able to see the humanity of Queer parishioners without Queer tokenism or the drama of "coming out." To be honest, coming out can also be toxic. The politics of coming out does not always take into consideration situations where coming out is not possible. Necessitating that Queer people come out can also be problematic because it prioritizes the heteronormative as persons to whom coming out is owed. However, even with such critiques, the self-declarative parts of coming out should continue to be revered and respected as sacred when done for the sole purpose of freeing one's own self through declaration and confession. The aforementioned concerns are proof that more resources dedicated to intersectional education could have benefited our congregational process, particularly education about language. The Myrtle process and all congregational queering processes need access to their local health departments and local LGBTQIAP+ organizations like GLAD and others to educate them on the correct and incorrect phrases and concepts to use.

In this concluding chapter, I have focused on the need for Black ecclesial queering to expand to address the tragedy of transphobia within Black churches. Black affirming congregations also need to queer their youth ministries, which must include robust training and education on pronouns.

The Need for Open and Affirming Youth Ministries

During my research, the most disappointing discovery was that none of the affirming Black churches had queering phases that included specialized Christian education for children and youth. Most of the affirming Black churches completely ignored or avoided discussing topics of gender and sexuality with children for fear that it might create factions of discord among parents in the congregation. It became clear that congregational queering needs to extend to youth and children because, according to Beloved Arise, a fully affirming LGBTQIAP+ youth ministry whose mission is to celebrate and empower LGBTQIAP+ youth of faith, "As congregations and denominations continue to debate the biblical grounds for LGBTQIAP+ inclusion in the church, many young persons are coming out earlier. Recent studies estimate that 12 percent of church-going youth identify as something other than straight."[46] Additionally, affirming youth ministries reduce the likelihood of young LGBTQIAP+ suicides.[47]

In *Our Lives Matter,* Lightsey writes, "Because gender performance is so critical to the psychological well-being of children growing up within the Black community, by the time a Black queer female has reached adulthood, she has fought many battles—literally, figuratively, and emotionally—to survive gender oppression and be a healthy and whole individual. Add to this pain sexism and racism...."[48] In this passage, Lightsey brings Queer Womanist inquiry into conversation with the lived experiences of young Black queer females. She is concerned about Black Queer youth and what they often endure during adolescence.

Churches attempting to queer their youth ministries should begin by establishing four separate discussion and support groups. The first group should be a parents' support team. The presence of a supportive parent is an essential aspect of combating suicide among LGBTQIAP+ youth and children.[49] However, most Black Christian parents of Queer children are ill equipped to offer spiritual, social, and emotional support for their children because their churches have only taught them how to reinforce heteronormative ideals about normative adolescence expressions of gender and sexuality. These heteronormative Black ecclesial ideals almost always undergird the practice of homophobia and transphobia within Black Christian families. A welcoming and affirming youth ministry should provide two meaningful options of Christian education for the parents of Queer children and all parents. Churches must work hard to dismantle the unethically dichotomous nature of many queering processes. Many churches queer their contexts using us-versus-them (heteronormative church folks versus Black Queer person) approaches. To avoid this dichotomy, the initial class for parents must consist of the parents of Queer children and all parents. All parents must be reeducated on the complexity of human sexuality and gender. During these sessions, but not as the first lessons, parents should be taught to encourage safe sex practices, condom usage, contraceptives, sexually transmitted infection (STI) screenings, and the normalization of masturbation. Affirming youth ministries should also discourage parents from forcing upon their children toxic notions of abstinence and purity cultures. Parents should also be taught how to instruct their children on affirming all gender identities and expressions.

The second parents' group that affirming youth ministries should establish is a support group for the parents of Black Queer youth. This group should be a space for the parents of Queer youth to ask vulnerable questions without judgment. The responsibility of facilitating such a group should never fall upon the staff members of an affirming youth ministry alone. Instead, youth ministry leaders should establish cross-sector partnerships with national organizations like Parents, Families, and Friends of Lesbians and Gays (PFLAG). As the largest organization for LGBTQIAP+ persons, PFLAG's mission is to educate families on how to respect, value, and affirm their LGBTQIAP+ relatives.

The most important groups for affirming youth ministries are support groups for youth: one for Queer youth and another for all youth. Queering processes in church youth ministries often focus more on the parents of youth than the youth themselves. This is typically the case because core committees often work hard to mitigate any confusion among parents. The fear of parents feeling uninformed about what is being taught to their children often motivates congregational queering committees to appeal to parents more than youth. This is a major mistake because it puts the attention on parents and takes focus away from the Queer youth, the most vulnerable population in the United States. As with the parental divisions, the segregation of the two groups is not a reinforcement of an us-versus-them dichotomy. Instead, it provides more specific support for the most vulnerable youth within a ministry, LGBTQIAP+ children and youth. Affirming youth ministries should also normalize the fluidity of gender identity and expression among youth because many adolescents may be uncertain about their gender identities.

It is crucial that queering discussions not be relegated to assemblies of Queer youth. Because in-person bullying and cyberbullying are intersectional causes of Queer suicide, all youth should be taught how to love and respect all of God's children regardless of their gender identity or expression. Youth and children should be taught that all bullying—including homophobic and transphobic—is sinful, immoral, unethical, and inhumane. Black churches should cultivate redemptive environments where homophobic and transphobic remarks and behavior are not tolerated at youth activities. Teaching youth and children these practices early is a form of youth evangelism. The lack of affirming youth ministries in most cities, combined with the rising number of young people identifying as Queer, presents churches with an opportunity to offer ministry to a growing segment who may attend with at least one adult. However, church growth should not be the primary focus of establishing an affirming youth ministry. Youth ministries should be affirming because they can save lives.

Black youth ministries should also take several precautionary measures if they wish to be affirming. First, Black churches should ensure that all clergy, lay leaders, and staff members undergo a background check and training on gender identity, gender expression, pronouns, adolescent growth, development, sexuality, and caring for and supporting transgender youth. Second, youth leaders should ask their local health departments to assist them, with permission from parents, with providing age-appropriate sex education for all youth. The youth leader's responsibility is to ensure that the faith-based tenets of inclusivity are merged with the more biological and medical natures of a workshop led by a health department representative.

Second, Black churches should create reporting mandates for the abuse of Queer youth or any youth. I have received numerous gender-based violence and human trafficking reports during my pastorate. In every instance, I began by alerting the local chief of police, with whom I have a preexisting relationship, about the matters in question. In moments when it was reported or suspected that there was evidence of adolescent abuse in a home, the first thing I did was to investigate properly what was happening in that home. If I sensed that the house was a non-child-friendly environment, saw bruises, or discovered questionable behaviors from the parents and children after doing a random home check to see what the home environment was actually like, I would then alert the Department of Children and Families, the local police department, and the child (or children's) school officials. Finally, Black churches should establish a protocol for managing moments when youth or youth workers violate the inclusive policy.

Rethinking Pronouns in Black Churches

Congregational queering requires congregants to face their heteronormative assumptions and binary conceptions about gender and sexuality. Congregations should deeply reflect on how heteronormative ideas frame cultural expectations and social behavior. This discussion of pronouns exposes churches to divine truths about God's inclusivity. God created a world full of diversity. God created the day and night and the many light variations: dawn, midmorning sun, noonday sun, afternoon sun, and dusk. God also creates diversity in humanity through varying skin tones, heights, appearances, abilities, sexualities, genes, and genders, not just male and female, but also variations in identity and expression. Congregational queering teaches congregants how to recognize the image of God in every human being; queering guides congregants through a process of culling out the toxic social constructs of gender to prepare for the way of the Lord. However, such work produces numerous questions: Why do pronouns matter? What are gender-neutral / gender-inclusive pronouns? What does "nonbinary" mean? What do the phrases "gender nonconformity," "gender variance," "genderqueer," "nongender," "gender fluid," and "agender" mean? Why is it important to respect a person's pronouns? How can I improve my usage of nonbinary pronouns?

A pronoun serves as a substitute for a proper noun. In American linguistics, culture, and grammar, pronouns also identify individuals, express one's gender identity, and are used to refer to a person both in and out of their presence. Some people use nonbinary or multiple pronouns to express their gender. Other people forgo pronouns and gender categorizations altogether. Queer theory and Queer theology teach us that pronouns are not fixed and may themselves be fluid. Some persons may change their pronouns more than once. These forms of self-discovery and fluid expressions should be respected, encouraged, and celebrated as moves of the Spirit. Never refer to a person's pronouns as their "preferred pronouns." The word "preference" signifies a choice or a personal act of selecting one identity over another. The word "preference" is offensive because it reinforces the misconception of binary genders assigned at birth as natural and normative while simultaneously categorizing all gender variations as chosen deviant identities. Pronouns should never be referred to as "preferred," but as a way some persons present themselves to be referred to by others, just as a cisgender woman uses "she" and "her."

Gender-neutral pronouns are genderless—such as using "they" instead of assuming she or he. "They walked across the pulpit." Nonbinary persons live beyond the binary categories of male and female. Not all nonbinary people express themselves in nongendered ways.[50] Some may use "they/them," "she/they," "he/they," or any combination of the above and other pronouns. Also note that many cultures ascribe to three or more gender groups. The phrases and terms "gender nonconformity," "gender variance," "genderqueer," "nongender," "gender fluid," and "agender" represent persons whose gender expression transgresses the socially constructed gender binary. Persons who identify in these ways may use fluid pronouns. Some Queer persons forgo pronouns altogether. When a person does not use pronouns, say the person's name when you might be inclined to use a pronoun.

When Black churches use the pronouns with which a person identifies, it shows respect for the intrinsic dignity of all persons. It is essential to respect a person's pronouns because all persons deserve respect and are created in God's image. Cisgender persons possess privilege. Forcing someone into one's image of a gender binary disrespects the variety God created and forces people into a societal construct rather than recognizing differences in experiences. Intentional misgendering is a form of sexual harassment. Congregational compassion is personified in a parishioner's active and earnest attempts to use pronouns correctly and intentionally. Modeling correct usage of pronouns and creating an environment where congregants are free to assert, express, and change their pronouns comfortably is key to creating an inclusive environment for transgender and nonbinary congregants. The cultural effect of heteronormativity often warps the human psyche into only seeing human bodies within a male-female binary.

The best way to grow comfortable with using nonbinary pronouns is to practice. After a person introduces themselves to you, internally rehearse their pronouns to yourself while visualizing the person's face. When addressing a congregation, use phrases like "church family," "Christian siblings," "deacons," trustees," "New member Sam," "friends," "folks," "Saints," or "beloved," rather than "brothers and sisters."

But what if a person makes a mistake? First, mistakes are inevitable. If you misgender a person, immediately say, "I apologize," and move forward with the conversation. If the person or someone else corrects you, do not get offended or ask for an explanation; immediately say, "I apologize," and proceed. Performative apologies make misgendered persons feel uncomfortable, and they often solicit consolation from the offended. This can create a problematic situation where the misgendered is left to comfort the offender.

Essential Things for Clergy and Lay Leaders to Remember

Queering congregations should never forget that using a person's name is always an option. Parishioners always have the option to address a person by name when they cannot remember their pronouns. Congregants must also be open to learning more about nonbinary pronouns. Congregational leaders should practice using the forms of "they/them." Continue to educate yourself because gender is fluid, and language is ever-evolving. Congregants should also remember that traditional Black church honorifics—like Mr., Mrs., Miss, brother, sister, sis, ma'am, and sir—are often used in ways that misgender and alienate those who don't identify as male or female. Titles and phrases like "saints," "beloved," "Christian friends," "fam," and "friends" are more equitable ways to address parishioners. Church leaders should also make a habit of sharing their pronouns first to indicate that they are safe persons. Lastly, asking someone for their pronouns does not mean that they will feel safe sharing their pronouns. Sharing one's pronouns can feel manipulative if not done within a safe context.

What Are Some Commonly Used Pronouns, and How Can I Use Pronouns Correctly?

This list is not exhaustive but is meant to help one become accustomed to pronouns with which one may not be familiar.

She/her/hers

- Subject: She loves singing in the choir.
- Object: Those Bibles belong to her.
- Reflexive: She will do the altar call by herself.
- Possessive: That choir robe is hers.

They/them/theirs—These are gender-neutral / gender-inclusive pronouns:

- Subject: They love(s) singing in the choir. (They can be plural or singular, representing one person.)
- Object: Those Bibles belong to them.
- Reflexive: They will do the altar call by themselves.
- Possessive: That choir robe is theirs.

Ze/hir/hirs (pronounced *zee, here, heres*) or **Ze/zir/zirs**—These are gender-neutral / gender-inclusive pronouns:

- Subject: Ze loves singing in the choir.
- Object: Those Bibles belong to hir/zir.
- Reflexive: Ze will do the altar call by hirself/zirself.
- Possessive: That choir robe is hirs/zirs.

He/Him/His

- Subject: He loves singing in the choir.
- Object: Those Bibles belong to him.
- Reflexive: He will do the altar call by himself.
- Possessive: That choir robe is his.

Hu/hum/humes (pronounced *hyoo, hyoom, hyooms*)—These are gender-neutral / gender-inclusive pronouns:

- Subject: Hu loves singing in the choir.
- Object: Those Bibles belong to hum.
- Reflexive: Hu will do the altar call by humself.
- Possessive: That choir robe is hume's.

Fae/faer/faers (pronounced *fay, fair, fairs*)—These are gender-neutral / gender-inclusive pronouns:

- Subject: Fae loves singing in the choir.
- Object: Those Bibles belong to faer.
- Reflexive: FAE will do the altar call by faerself.
- Possessive: That choir robe is faer's.

Ey/em/eirs (pronounced ay/em/airs)- These are gender-neutral / gender-inclusive pronouns:

- Subject: Ey loves singing in the choir.
- Object: Those Bibles belong to em.
- Reflexive: Fae will do the altar call by eirself.
- Possessive: That choir robe is eirs.

Hir/hir/hirs (pronounced *here, heres*)—These are gender-neutral / gender-inclusive pronouns:

- Subject: Hir loves singing in the choir.
- Object: Those Bibles belong to hir.
- Reflexive: Hir will do the altar call by hirself.
- Possessive: That choir robe is hirs.

Tey/ter/tem/ters—These are gender-neutral / gender-inclusive pronouns:

- Subject: Tey loves singing in the choir.
- Object: Those Bibles belong to ter; those Bibles belong to tem.
- Reflexive: Tey will do the altar call by terself.
- Possessive: That choir robe is ters.

Wendy, Malik, Charlie, Paula—practice inserting names into sentences for people who forgo pronouns.

- Wendy loves singing in the choir.
- Those Bibles belong to Malik.
- Charlie will do the altar call by Charlie's self (or will do the altar call alone).
- That choir robe is Paula's.

Chapter Summary

All of the churches I studied deploy two forms of Black ecclesial queering: Black congregational queering and Black pastoral queering. Denominational queering does not presently exist in Black churches. Black congregational queering is rooted in congregational participation. While pastoral queering is courageous, it is not as effective as congregational queering. In congregational queering, a congregation studies, listens, and learns together. It is a spiritual journey of prayer, discernment, and discovery about honesty and openness, and is the most successful model of ecclesial queering. Black ecclesial queering is contextual and congregational queering that is the more excellent way to subvert heteronormativity in Black churches. The most promising news is that more and more Black ecclesial queering is occurring worldwide.

Conclusion

A Bright Side Somewhere

Introduction

This book's sole purpose has been to assist historically heteronormative Black churches with queering their ecclesial contexts, but this is only the beginning. Queering is not a onetime process that permits congregations to check off LGBTQIAP+ inclusivity from their long list of politically correct social awarenesses. Instead, queering is a fluid process of questioning and transitioning that never ends. For this reason, congregations must be careful to avoid vaguely evoking or loosely implementing queer strategies. Congregational queering requires that congregants face their heteronormative assumptions and preconceived ideas about gender and deeply reflect on how heteronormative ideas frame cultural expectations and social behavior. Noncontemplative queering is a type of performativity.

An example of this would be the supposition that displaying rainbow flags, hosting June Pride services, and saying that everyone is loved and welcomed is all there is to queering. Performative allyship is toxic. It is rooted in the self-gratifying aims of objective solidarity, which is merely performative association, as opposed to subjective solidarity, which is companionship and sociotheological affirmation through congregational consensus. Performative allyship is objective solidarity because it is not influenced or informed by personal belief or a truly queered perspective of human existence. The objective solidarity within performative allyship is what prevents it from being a reliable form of queering. Performative allyship is actually not queering at all. Rather, it is an act of staging or posturing that eventually retraumatizes LGBTQIAP+ persons because it covertly maintains the status quo by appearing to promote an ideal that it has yet to fully embrace theologically. As I explained in the previous chapter, there is a better way of queering a congregation than just doing it haphazardly.

Where Do We Go from Here?

Most, if not all, of the works in the first wave of Black Queer theology were written in protest and holy rage in response to Christian homophobia, but such prophetic works beg for a second wave of Black Queer theology by Black Queer persons and for Black Queer persons. Even this book is not enough because it only speaks about dismantling heteronormative spaces. This work does not talk about the rich examples of churches that Black Queer folks have started and the wealth of Black Queer theological knowledge that they yield. The second wave of Black Queer theology must work to help Black Queer persons celebrate the fact that many Black Queer persons do not need historically Black churches and are creating Black ecclesial tables and churches for themselves.

Queering Black Churches was written as a resource for historically heteronormative Black churches desiring to Queer their ecclesial contexts. I wrote to save the souls of Black churches and Black church folk, both Queer and non-Queer. But this is only the beginning. Black Queer Christians need a more robust construction of Black Queer spirituality, Black Queer hermeneutics, and practical theologies for Black Queer persons. Black Queer Christians need resources beyond the toxic matrix of Queer Christian apologetics to construct a tool to till the fallow ground of Black Christian heteronormativity. Black Queer Christianity does not need new Christian grounds because the pre-Reconstruction gardens of our foreparents are good enough. Black churches do not need a new faith. They need to embrace precolonial Afro-centric theologies and philosophies to till the fertile theological grounds of our forebearers. Black Queer theologies will be the topsoil for Black churches that will support growth and provide a healthy environment for all Black souls.

In my next monograph, I intend to write a Black Queer practical theological primer that brings attention to and gleans from the various existing Black Queer theologies of the world. Black Queer practical theologies are being practiced within many Black Queer communities in North America. These living Black Queer theologies are not monolithic, and many are still in the process of figuring out how to winnow away the anti-Black and anti-Queer conceptions of traditional Christian, Muslim, Buddhist, and humanist discourses and theologies. I feel called to write about them because I believe Black Queer theologies will lead to the revival of the church and Black theology in the next decade or so.

Examples of Preexisting Black Queer Ecclesial Spaces and Living Black Queer Theologies

The next wave of Black Queer theologies and Black Queer ecclesial research should focus on the lived experiences of Black Queer persons who left Black churches, Masjids, Hebrew Pentecostal churches, and other Black religious spaces to start their own affirming Black religious and spiritualist communities.

In the Christian context, Black Queer preachers and believers have founded over one thousand affirming Black church plants over the last thirty-five years. According to pastoral theologian Horace Griffin, increasing numbers of Black Queer folk are responding to Black church homophobia in a way that parallels the Black AME church's Richard Allen and the white gay Troy Deroy Perry.[1] Black gay and lesbian Christians are leaving Black congregations where they experienced denigration and are forming their own Black gay churches. Black queer historian Kevin Mumford writes in his book *Not Straight, Not White: Black Gay Men from the March on Washington to the AIDS Crisis* that even as early as the 1960s and 1970s, Black queer Christians like Brother Grant-Michael Fitzgerald worked, unsuccessfully, for the inclusion of gays and lesbians in the Catholic Church.[2] Reverend Elder Darlene Garner and Reverend Delores Berry, both influential Black lesbian women, played pivotal roles in the ministries and founding of Affirming Church Plants of color. Reverend Dr. Renee McCoy, a trailblazer in the Black Affirming Church Plant movement, established the Harlem Metropolitan Community Church in 1981—the first MCC church entirely governed by Black Queer individuals. Additionally, in 1989, she founded the Full Truth Fellowship of Christ Church in Detroit, and in 1978, she was a founding member of the National Coalition of Black Lesbians and Gays, which is dedicated to addressing the needs of the Black LGBTQIAP+ community.[3] There is also the work of gay men like the Reverend Dr. James Tinney, who was a prominent expert on Black Pentecostalism at Howard University, who was almost denied tenure and was excommunicated from the Church of God in Christ after coming out.

After Dr. Tinney revealed that he was a homosexual, his marriage with his wife, Darlene Woods, ended in divorce in 1969, and he fled to the academy. However, in 1982, after gaining tenure, he says that the Spirit of God led him to organize a lesbian-gay revival that resulted in him being excommunicated from the Church of God in Christ. A year later, he founded Faith Temple, a nondenominational church with a primarily Black gay and lesbian congregation meeting in New York Avenue Presbyterian Church in Washington, DC. Tinney was also the founder of the Pentecostal Coalition for Human Rights and a church publication, *Spirit: A Journal of Issues Incident in Black Pentecostalism*. He wrote articles titled, "Why a Gay Black Church?" and "Ministering in a Gay Church." These early articles are the beginnings of the work I wish to continue.

In his article "Why a Gay Black Church?" Dr. Tinney gave his reason for why affirming Black church plants are needed. Tinney wrote, "Black lesbians and gays have often found themselves caught in the middle (so to speak) in the 'twoness' of identity (to use a term of W. E. B. Du Bois)."[4] For Tinney, the Black gay or lesbian person did not fit into the landscape of Black churches, and they did not fit into the white gay and affirming church context because being both Black and gay was not wholly approved in either the Black heterosexual or white gay communities.[5] In other words, Black Queer people have to choose in moments of communal worship to either be Black or gay but never both. For this reason, Tinney and many other Black gay persons like Bishop Carl Bean started and planted affirming churches in the Black tradition. However, very little qualitative practical theological research has been conducted on the nearly fifteen affirming Black church plants that have evolved into strong Pentecostal traditions and full-fledged denominations in the shadow of Tinney's lifework.

The prophetic witness of the pre-Reconstruction Black churches is alive and well in the affirming Black church plant movement. The inclusive community-building of affirming Black church plants creates an opportunity for Black Queer persons to temporarily escape the heteronormative world that is unsupportive and violent toward them.[6] According to Ellen Lewin, professor of anthropology, and gender, women's, and sexuality studies, "This form of community building recapitulates the formation of African American churches such as the African Methodist Episcopal (AME) in the eighteenth and early nineteenth century, when Black worshippers responded to discrimination by their white co-religionists by forming their own denomination."[7] Additionally, the affirming Black church movement "transcends the quest for 'safe space.'"[8] Affirming Black churches are not just safe or brave spaces for Black Queer persons; they are also reimagined Black ecclesial spaces that force dying Black churches to rethink and question what it means to be and do church in the twenty-first century. Black churches need theologies focused on the lived experiences of Black Queer folk who left Black churches to start their own affirming Black church plants.

Affirming Black church plants are empirical communities of people called by God to exist outside of the fundamental, deep-seated Christian belief systems, doctrines, and theologies that have often characterized the church.[9] With millennials and generation Z increasingly identifying as the religious unaffiliated due to religion's failure to affirm LGBTQIAP+ folks, affirming Black church plants give us hope and a glimpse of what all churches can and should become if Black religions are to survive into the next millennia.[10] Affirming Black church plants are changing the American ecclesial landscape and showing Black churches and all churches how to do church differently. They offer churches a subverted understanding of what it means to be or do church that greatly challenges and critiques the heteronormative and Puritan-based ideologies that often shroud Christian communities of faith. They also show traditional Christian spaces that it is possible to subvert and destabilize the theologically heteronormative idea that a person's queerness is inherently sinful, sexual, and objectifiable. Affirming Black church plants show mainline churches the importance of having theo-historical and psychosocial discussions on the unexamined traumas and resilience of Queer persons. The existence of affirming Black church plants teaches the church universal about the importance of thinking about racism, poverty, health disparities such as HIV, sexism, and heteronormativity as intersectional issues, and affirming Black church plants show mainline churches how to reimagine and reclaim the idea of the church as a brave space instead of a space of harm and terror.

Towards Black Queer Theologies and the Sanctification of Black Queer Eroticism

Future works on Black Queer spirituality, Black Queer hermeneutics, and a practical theology of Black Queer persons must also think outside of the traditional Christian ecclesial framework. Black Queer Christians need a theology of intimacy, eroticism, and pleasure. The Christian concepts of fornication, two-person relationships or marriages, and the suppression of sexual exploration does not work for the lived experiences of many Black Queer persons, nor even most heterosexual persons. Sexual deprivation is unhealthy. Black Queer persons need to be taught that consensual Black

Queer eroticism, intimacy, and pleasure are good and spiritually healing experiences.

My focus on intimacy, pleasure, and eroticism could be interpreted by some scholars as a form of Black theological reductionism that reduces Blackness to bodies, thereby eclipsing the power and resilience of the Black soul. For too long, Black theology, in its pursuit to respond to the American legacy of chattel slavery, mass incarceration, and systemic racism, has too often maintained a toxic preoccupation with the body that reinforces and centers the same traditional white theological frameworks that have historically perpetuated the devaluation and enslavement of the Black body. But that is not what I am doing in this section of my work. Intimacy, pleasure, and eroticism have been theologically denied to Black Queer folks for so long that the only way to heal such terror is to respond to it with something that goes beyond critique and into the risky waters of theological construction. The forthcoming section contains Black Queer theological fragments that I envision as the beginnings of a much-needed conversation on the sacredness and creative aspects of Black Queer intimacy, pleasure, and eroticism. However, what is missing from this dialogue is a theology of asexuality, which I will reflect on in later works.

From the cascading feelings of vulnerability mixed with excitement to the pleasurable rush of dopamine-laced sensations of release, Black Queer sex is a Godly and a good thing that brings pleasure to the Black soul and its containing queer flesh.[11] While reckless, forced, manipulative, and unethical sex is evil, for far too long Black Queer Christians have been denied the theological freedom to unashamedly bask in the goodness and human fulfillment that consensual sex and intimacy bring. The liberating practice of Black Queer sex has also been tamed by the understandable pursuits of the medical community to eradicate the HIV/AIDS pandemic. Sadly, the moral medicalization of Black Queer sex also created an element of sexual fear-mongering and pleasure trepidation that has stunted the evolution of Black pansexual freedom in America and bruised the Black Queer capacity for pleasure and joy. For centuries, many Black Queer souls living in America have denied their bodies, minds, and sensoriums entry into the spiritual portals of erotic ecstasy in exchange for a destructively toxic type of puritanical spirituality that leaves many Black souls empty after worship, longing for a human touch or the freedom to embrace one's own Black body with self-pleasure through masturbation.[12] Even some married Black heterosexual partners avoid normalizing and exploring their passions by keeping their erotic desires in the shadows of mental fantasy without actualization, preventing themselves from seeing their evolving sexual urges as undefiled. This complex Black sexual reality makes the idea of reclaiming intimacy, pleasure, and eroticism for both heteronormative and nonheteronormative Black bodies complex and challenging.[13]

There is also the question of reclamation. Can intimacy, pleasure, and eroticism be reclaimed if they were never afforded us in the shadows of chattel slavery? Can a body that has always been policed reclaim what it has never had? The response to such pondering is dependent on what one means by reclamation. In this context, I use the word as a reclaiming of one's most authentic self that was born unblemished and as an empty canvas with no preconceived notions about sexual normality or sexual deviance. This original nature before nurture is the reclamation I seek. It is a type of reclamation that mirrors the question that God spoke to Adam and Eve: who told you that you were naked? Such questioning reveals the divine nature and sacredness of nudity, which we have perverted beyond its original erotic intent. I will explain what I mean by erotic later in this chapter.

From our youth, we are taught to regard the nonheteronormative pleasure-seeking cries of our genitals as demonic urges to be ignored or put down through prayer and abstinence. However, these religious gimmicks and psychosocial bio-hacks have never worked because abstinence-only programs harm children, teenagers, women, and especially young girls.[14] They are also based on maintaining patriarchal dominance and puritanical norms. Furthermore, silencing one's Queer sexual needs creates a shadow of secrecy where risky behavior, disease, and gender-based violence thrive. Prayer is an ineffective mechanism for suppressing queer and erotic urges because, within Black religious traditions, and in any Christian tradition for that matter, prayer, and worship are inherently erotic, queer, and intimate modes of connecting with God. Prayer and worship are inherently erotic as they can be viewed as expressions of spiritual or divine eros, facilitating self-discovery and a profound understanding of our nature at its deepest levels. These practices reflect a profound longing for an intimate union with the Sacred.[15] Audre Lorde's theory of the erotic teaches us that eroticism and intimacy are spiritual planes of deep joy, peace, prayer, worship, and play, all wrapped up in one.[16] They coexist and intersect in ways that are beyond the limited human enculturation that has brainwashed us into thinking about said categories as innately nonanalogous. Prayer, worship, eroticism, and intimacy are also intrinsically related because they all use bodies as conduits of otherworldliness through stimulation. However, this type of intermixing of pleasure, eroticism, and religious thinking is foreign to many Black Christians and Black Queer persons who have been trained to restrict spiritual ecstasy to praise breaks or what W. E. B. Du Bois described as the Black soul's frenzy of shouting.[17]

One of the most widely read and cited Queer theorists and sexuality specialists is the white Queer French philosopher, historian, political activist, and poststructuralist Michel Foucault. However, Foucault's theories in his *History of Sexuality*, as great as they are, fall short when it comes to the discussion of dismantling Black heteronormativity. As Queer as they are, Foucault's theories are still embedded in Eurocentric gay male privilege that is rarely extended to Black Queer persons, Black women, and Black transgender persons. For instance, when Cornel West was interviewing bell hooks, he asked her if it was possible to fuse African American sensibilities and the European critical discourses of Adorno, Marcuse, Derrida, and Foucault to assess the political realities of "Afro-Americans." bell hooks responded,

> To be intellectual, no matter what the color, is to be deeply influenced by other intellectuals of various colors. When it comes to Black intellectuals, we have to, on the one hand, be very open to insights from wherever they come. On the other hand, we must filter it so that we never lose sight of what some of the silences are in the work of White theorists, especially as those silences relate to issues of class, gender, race, and empire. Why? Because class, gender, race, and empire are fundamental categories that Black intellectuals must use to understand Black people's predicament.[18]

Here, hooks argues that the Black intellectual's responsibility is to make noise in the silence. By this, I mean that hooks is compelling Black prophetic pragmatists, poets, and scholars to critique and fill in the gaps of white theorists by writing our own Black theories that are widely influenced but solely birthed out of the experiences of Black folks. hooks prophetically reminds Black intellectuals to be leery of writing theories that are too intoxicated with responding to theories that are spawned from the experiences of the privileged white elite. For this reason, instead of using Foucault's *History of Sexuality* to describe and theologize on the sacredness of Black Queer eroticism, I have chosen to evoke the sacred worth of the Black lesbian mother-warrior-poet Audre Lorde, who herself said that "the master's tools will never dismantle the master's house. They may allow us temporarily to beat him at his own game, but they will never enable us to bring about genuine change."[19]

In *The Uses of the Erotic: The Erotic as Power*, Lorde describes eroticism as an intentional assertion of the creative energy of women that empowers them to reclaim their own bodies, with their own language and their own histories for the survival and perseverance of the female self.[20] She begins by dispelling the myth that the erotic is innately perverse by contrasting it with the legalized sex trafficking of the pornography industry. Lorde states that the erotic and the pornographic are not the same. One could argue that her psychoanalytic framework is flawed because it borders on a form of utopian biological essentialism regarding female eroticism. This reductionist perspective implies that womanhood is solely defined by the physical aspects of sex. However, such an interpretation would be a misreading of her work. For her, the inherently creative sexual nature of the erotic and the profoundly spiritual dimension of female identity are not only inextricably linked but also codependent on each other. For Lorde, the most self-responsible source of a woman's power is only found within her acknowledgment of the unanimity of her erotic power and the deep planes of her spiritual power. The integration of such "offers a well of replenishing and provocative force to the woman who does not fear its revelation, nor succumb to the belief that sensation is enough."[21] Here Lorde proves that the female sense of self begins with her integration of the erotic into the everyday.[22] In a Lordean sense, Black Queer eroticism, regardless of its various forms and identities, is sacred, spiritual, salvific, and erotic and must be integrated into the everyday.

The integration that I refer too does not reinforce the oversexualization and infantilization of Black Queer persons. As an evil social concept, the sexualizing of Queer folk is a strategic heteronormative procedure of domination and reductionism. The theo-cultural perverting of Queer folk is a mode of heteronormative social control that reduces Queer persons to the act of sex alone. This type of evil reductionism radicalizes the stereotype of the oversexualized Queer person with fabricated indictments and allegations. For example, Christian societies have historically stereotyped Queer sexualities as the deviant and promiscuous progenitors of HIV in the Black community.

Gay men are always depicted as sexual predators seeking to hook up or "turn out" younger males and married men. Heterosexual men often objectify lesbians as mythical pornographic creatures of entertainment and fantasy. The most sexualized members of the LGBTQIAP+ community are transgender persons whose bodies are often so oversexualized that the simple human function of restroom usage is politicized. This type of villain stamping is highly toxic and problematic. In response to such dangerous fear-mongering, many Queer persons have worked hard to prove that sex is only a tiny portion of who we are as humans. These Queer quests for civility are understandable and well intentioned. However, such quests can also represent an unconscious reactions to internalized homophobia. This quest for civility is especially problematic because it borders on trying to prove one's Queer civility to their heteronormative oppressors by reducing one's sexuality as unimportant and irrelevant to who they are. When Queer persons minimize or suppress their sexualities and sensuality to appear civil to the heteronormative gaze, they inadvertently reinforce the idea that traditional heteronormative purity codes are the moral standard. For this reason, conversations about the reclaiming of Black Queer sexuality can be precarious because it is true that LGBTQIAP+ persons should not be oversexualized. It is also true that it is unhealthy for Black Queer persons to deny or suppress their need and right to experience pleasure.

The future trajectory of Black ecclesial queering ought to focus on dismantling the heteronormative sexualization and infantilization of Black Queer bodies. Simultaneously, it should equip Black Queer Christians with theological tools to unreservedly embrace pleasure and intimacy platonically and erotically. A reclaiming of Black Queer sexuality is not a reductionist reinforcement of unfounded rumors about LGBTQIAP+ oversexualization. The reclaiming of Black Queer eroticism as good and sacred bolsters the Black Queer right to pleasure, joy, and sexual fulfillment without puritanical guilt. Like the Song of Solomon in the Bible, a rethinking of Black Queer sexuality celebrates intimacy, kissing, touching, foreplay, and pleasure as empowering human interactions. Without a celebration and reclaiming of intimacy and eroticism, Black ecclesial queering edges toward toxic puritanical homonormativity.

Consensual Black Queer eroticism is sacred. Particularly when experienced for the first time, it serves as a life-giving and self-affirming resource, revitalizing the deepest recesses of the Black Queer soul. This liberation allows individuals to express feelings once unspoken and to recognize passions that were once ignored.[23] The inherent sacred worth of Black Queer persons is rooted in their boldness to courageously choose satisfaction and integrative completion over the toxicity of sexual suppression and denial. By integrative completion, I mean the Lordean concept of the unanimity of erotic power and its inextricable linkage to the sacredness of human worth and existence itself. In a Lordean sense, the Black Queer sense of self begins with the willingness to integrate with openness and fearlessness the erotic into the everyday. The Lordean premise of the daily integration of the erotic stretches far beyond the mere interpretations of sexual contact as self-empowering and healing, and it aids us to see the erotic in music and the overall pleasures of life. Lorde encourages her readers to think beyond the medieval and puritanical assumptions about a platonic relationship between humans and music to recognize the innate eroticism within the art form itself. Lorde invites us to notice how the syncopated beats and rhythms of music open up the human soul in "response, hearkening to its deepest rhythms, so every level upon which I sense also opens to the erotically satisfying experience, whether it is dancing, building a bookcase, writing a poem, or examining an idea."[24]

The Sacred Eroticism of Black Lesbianism

The future of Black Queer theologies necessitates a more robust practical theological explication of pleasure and intimacy among Black women who love Black women. Black Queer theologies must evolve into full-bodied celebrations of the spiritual power of Black lesbian friendships, marriages, group vacations, organizations, and the power of the varying expressions of gender among the lesbian community. Additionally, Black Queer theologies must wholeheartedly embrace Black lesbian eroticism as spiritual, salvific, and sacred. In its future iterations, Black Queer theologies should construct a sacred theological appreciation for pleasure and sensuality that centers on the sensual and platonic joys of Black same-gender-loving women. Because the theological complexity of Black Womanist eroticism has never mattered to Black churches, Black communities, or the Black gay community, the sacredness of Black female pleasure must become a salient motif in Black Queer theologies. In her book *Our Lives Matter*, Pamela R. Lightsey argues that the writings of avant-garde scholars on Black Queer persons often ignore the experiences of Black same-gender-loving women.[25] She states, "The absence of Black lesbian, bisexual, transgender, and queer voices in representing their unique perspective is not good for the academy or our churches, especially black churches. Unfortunately, most of these conversations talk about us and not with us."[26] In this statement, Lightsey exposes the patriarchal condescension that often pervades Black ecclesial thought. In response to these sexist delinquencies, Audre Lorde presents a model for acknowledging the sacred eroticism of women. A thicker and more equitable form of Black ecclesial queering and Black Queer theologies should detail the sacred eroticism of Black women using a Lordean approach.

In *Uses of the Erotic: The Erotic as Power,* Lorde condemns heteronormativity for misconstruing the eroticism of women as trivial, psychotic, and pornographic.[27] Her queer analysis intersectionally envisioned the sacred erotic worth of a woman's sensual and platonic pleasures as good. Without regard to expression or identity, Lorde calls upon all women to take control of their bodies and claim their innate right to be erotic and pleasured. Lorde encourages women to erase the "erotic differences between straight, bisexual, and lesbian desire to promote such desire as a creative force for revolutionary change."[28] Lorde regards female eroticism as a revolutionary, creative, sacred, sinless, and pleasurable source of empowerment and information for women. Like Lorde, more sophisticated expressions of Black Queer theologies and Black ecclesial queering should work to challenge traditional interpretations of Scripture and cultural norms to incite, celebrate, and rejuvenate Black pleasure. Black ecclesial queering must make room for new theologies where Black women have agency of their own romantic, sensorial, and clitoral pleasure with other women without deprivation or guilt. It also necessitates a thicker practical theological description of eroticism that respects the aptitude of pleasure outside the varying patriarchal obsessions with phallicity.

The Sacred Eroticism of Black Transgender Persons

Parallel to Black Queer theologies' and Black ecclesial queering's requisite to embrace Black womanist eroticism is their pursuit to espouse transgender eroticism as sacred and salvific. Just as the power of the erotic is an important human need for many cisgender persons, eroticism is also an essential facet of life for many transgender persons. While it may be easy for well-meaning cisgender persons to avoid discourse on transgender sexuality under the guise of not oversexualizing the transgender community, such avoidance can also be harmful because it ignores the human need for touch, affection, love, intimacy, platonic eroticism, and sex for transgender persons. Black ecclesial queering and Black Queer theologies view society's cisgender normativity as an inherently problematic social construction. They accord equal theological significance to the lives of transgender individuals as they do to the lives of cisgender lesbians and gay men. These perspectives not only acknowledge but also honor the capacities for joy, pleasure, and eroticism in the experiences of transgender persons, deeming these aspects as sacred and holy. When

Black transgender persons experience the eroticism they have initiated or to which they have given their consent, it is life-giving, freeing, empowering, and delightful. Even when eroticism is stimulated through masturbation and self-pleasure, it can deepen the person's awareness of self and their creative ability to conspire with their own soul to experience erotic joy and touch. Transgender eroticism extends beyond the notion of providing pleasure exclusively to another individual. This perspective rejects the idea of sexual objectification, challenging the assumption that transgender bodies exist solely for the purpose of bringing sensual and platonic pleasure to others. Instead, transgender eroticism centers on the pursuit of pleasure for oneself and the mutual enjoyment shared with an intimate partner. The embrace of sacred transgender eroticism is life-giving as it subverts the fear associated with transgender embodiment, transforming it into a sacred celebration.

The Sacred Eroticism of Black Queer Men and Other Black Queer Spaces

The future of Black Queer theologies also necessitates a practical theological explication of Black gay male eroticism. The sacred eroticism of Black Queer men transgresses Black Christian puritanicalism. Before the existence of affirming Black churches, scholars like Marlon M. Bailey describe Black Queer persons as having boldly established their own brave spaces like the extravagant masquerades, drag competitions, the House and Ballroom culture, galas, nightclubs, bathhouses, gender-exclusive platonic home gatherings, intentional moments of erotic spirituality during sex parties, and orgies.[29] Predating the existence of affirming Black churches, these social interactions and institutions fulfilled the need for community and spirituality in what Lorde would describe as empowering and life-affirming erotic engagements. Black Queer theologies must consistently prioritize initiating and centering their theological reflections on the lived experiences and perspectives of Black Queer individuals, including the distinctive experiences of Black gay men. Aligned with the theological focus I dedicated to Black transgender, lesbian, and non-binary Queer experiences, it is crucial to acknowledge the experiences of Black Queer/gay men. As a Black Queer male, I feel called by God to advocate for the well-being of my brothers and to address our needs, desires, and capacity for pleasure. We need a theological exploration of Black gay male eroticism from a Lordean, E. Patrick Johnson, and Baldwin perspective that delves into the nuanced aspects of Black gay male culture.

Black Queer theologies must acknowledge and explore the theological implications of the closet from a non-judgmental perspective, recognizing that being "out" has not always been and is not currently a viable option for many Black Queer individuals. These secret spaces allowed Black Queer persons to be themselves in physical spaces without judgment or ridicule. They created opportunities for Black Queer persons to interact with one another without the pretense of nonattraction or the risk of violence. These moments, when experienced with consent, are healing. For example, among undetectable persons or persons on preexposure prophylaxis and the oral antibiotic doxycycline, "Barebacking and gay sex . . . is the work of taking an active role in creating one's freedom, in continuing to live one's own life, and in experiencing and giving pleasure even when the 'truths and modes of behavior that provide a measure of comfort to the multitude provide barebackers with none.'"[30] According to recently conducted research on gay barebacking,

> It was found that individuals often engage in bareback sex for specific reasons such as connectedness, the abandonment of responsibilities, feelings of completion regarding sexual intercourse, and finally, the naturalness of the sex act. Moreover, research conducted by Crossley demonstrates that expressing freedom, rebellion, or empowerment may figure significantly in a predisposition toward barebacking.[31]

Black Queer locations of sociopolitical resistance are like the hush harbors and subversive ecclesial worlds of enslaved Africans. Like their enslaved Black forebears who founded churches in brush harbors and established Negro associations, many Black Queer individuals create or find alternative nations, realms, or subcultures within the heteronormative American nation. These communities take shape in the form of gay clubs, LGBTQIAP+ fraternities and sororities, bathhouses, and annual destination trips. When the enslaved Africans reached the sacred spaces of refuge and identity formation that the pre-Reconstruction Black church represented, they could see each other as humans and console each other through fellowship. Likewise, LGBTQIAP+ persons of color have often snuck away in secret to hush harbors for intimate moments of consolation and meaning-making with other likeminded humans. In his seminal research, Anthony P. Natale interviews an African American male who has sex with men and is also heavily involved in the church. The interviewee notes that illicit sex with other men is a sort of outlet or opportunity to be his "other true self," terminology often reserved for the numinous experience:

> I started going to the baths because it evolved from separating out my sex life from the church. I did all that I had to do, did my duties, talked the religious talk. When I had the first available time, I would go. I would also make up excuses. It was in the parks, online, and in bathhouses. The park is the scariest because then the police can catch you. There is that chance, in a bookstore or a park. Actually, it was a rarity to be with someone I knew.[32]

What is important here is not that the male had sex with other men. What is essential is that the spaces he found for those experiences functioned like a refuge. They brought him closer to a unique community space (sacred or psycho-socially and erotically) with like others. Additionally, platonic house parties; game nights; and yearly group trips to places like Martha's Vineyard, Provincetown (P-town), The Castro in San Francisco, Greenwich Village in New York City, Martin Luther King Jr. weekend in Atlanta, Miami sizzle, Pride festivities in many cities, the San Juan brothers excursion in Puerto Rico; and many other events have also been sacred spaces and moments of African American LGBTQIAP+ meaning-making.

In his groundbreaking work on Black Homosex-Normativity, Marlon M. Bailey says that "I do not suggest that Black gay men do not think about or fear seroconversion and that HIV never plays a role in their sexual decision-making. Instead, I argue that other needs and priorities such as sexual pleasure, intimacy, connection, and satisfaction are also key factors, and in some cases, more important ones."[33] These sexual encounters create opportunities for Black LGBTQIAP+ persons to authentically commune with bodies in a way that the general public would not accept in broad daylight. In "Raw Sex as Limit Experience," Holmes, O'Byrne, and Gastaldo argue that "Sperm has a very powerful symbolic function for men who have sex with men; it is the odor of masculinity, the 'fluid' that tastes like a gift."[34] The swallowing and touch involved in many gay male cumplay scenes and sets is a powerful moment of erotic resistance and, most of all, pleasure. It is important to see queer sex, in all of its forms, as pleasure. Black Queer eroticism should never be reduced to resistance. Such reductionism centers what bell hooks called white supremacist capitalist patriarchy or oppression, which should never be the focus of Black Queer sex or Black Queer eroticism. However, the ways in which Queer eroticism unavoidably critiques and subverts heteronormative puritanicalism should not be ignored. Safe unprotected gay male penetrative sex is an example of pleasure and resistance in Black Queer male sex. It is a resistance because socially, anal sex has been viewed as sodomy. It is spiritual pleasure because barebacking among undetectable persons or persons on preexposure prophylaxis and the oral antibiotic doxycycline "represents a 'way in' for developing ethics and subjectivity appropriate to a non-disciplinary society, an act of courage associated with the ethics of the self rather than as an act of insanity or despair."[35] The sexual exploration of LGBTQIAP+ individuals should be acknowledged as courageous and sacred engagements, fostering spaces for Queer spiritual connection and healing. Nevertheless, there is a need for further exploration to address the issue of LGBTQIAP+ loneliness—a genuinely experienced reality for many Black Queer individuals. For some queer individuals, the quest for a life partner or genuine friendship can devolve into an unjust game of chance, entangled with toxic elements such as body shaming, the expectation to conform to extreme gender norms for likeability, and pervasive judgments. These assessments, which are particularly exacerbated on modern dating websites and applications, evaluate a person's intrinsic worth through the lens of America's pernicious beauty standards. Future works in Black Queer theologies must wrestle with and think more intimately about Black Queer eroticism.

Conclusion

On April 26, 2010, Eddie S. Glaude Jr., the then William S. Todd Professor of Religion and chair of the Center for African American Studies at Princeton University, wrote a provocative editorial in the *Huffington Post* titled "The Black Church Is Dead." In the article, Glaude argued that "the idea of this venerable institution as central to Black life and as a repository for the social and moral conscience of the nation had all but disappeared."[36] Glaude posited that the concept of socially conscious, morally prophetic, and culturally relevant Black churches is a phenomenon of the past because Black churches have grown silent concerning matters of Black human suffering. Glaude sees Black churches as a dying or dead ecclesial breed that only exists in the nostalgic memories of Black religious historians and middle-class African American Protestants.

Glaude assesses that twenty-first-century Black churches are complicated spaces often viewed as progressively prophetic institutions. In reality, they are mostly quite conservative, apolitical, and silent about important matters of cultural, political, and evangelical correctness rooted in biblical literalism.

While most of Glaude's argument was based in social criticism and analytical provocation, the latter half of his ecclesial assessment was deliberately prescriptive. He tells Black churches how to resurrect and reenliven themselves with breaths of new life. According to Glaude, these breaths will enable Black churches to reimagine and rethink their meaning to be simultaneously Black and Christian. However dead they may be, he argues that Black churches can be resurrected and brought back to life by breathing something new into their ecclesial structures. Glaude interprets this revitalizing breath of new ecclesial life as a resurgence of the prophetic voices and social progressiveness observed in some Black churches from before the Reconstruction era through the 1960s. Through such rekindling, Black churches can regain life and reclaim their original mission to work on behalf of those who suffer most. Queering is the rekindling that Black churches need. Queering is also the refreshing that many Black Queer Christian folks need. There is no greater feeling for the souls of Black Queer Christian persons than unconditional love and affirmation, for God is love. Even self-affirming Black Queer Christian souls, who have diligently nurtured robust self-acceptance, often do so in response to the severe forms of hatred and rejection they have faced. In the face of such adversity, they turn inward, relying solely on their own strength and resilience as a shielding mechanism to protect themselves from external negativity or hostility. However, because of the inextricable links that bind us together as human, the self-acceptance of one's queer self is not enough to heal the traumas of Black homophobia. Just as America must right her wrongs for African Americans to be granted the liberties they were promised during Reconstruction, Christianity at large and Black churches must also do the work to queer their congregations to right the wrongs that Black Queer Christian folk have endured in the churches they love and support.

Sadly, for most Black Queer Christian persons, Black churches and the broader white heteronormative American culture is still the cause of much grief and weariness. The grief of being exiled from the Black religious center and marginalized to the fringes of society often creates insurmountable amounts of mental tiredness and soul fatigue in the spirits of Black Queer Christians. The burden of code-switching to appear passable or hiding one's identity to the point of an identity crisis is enough to destroy the psyche and soul of any human being. Sadly, most Black churches are unaware of this tremendous burden. The heterosexual's lack of awareness of such burdens is a manifestation of heteronormativity Heteronormativity is a way of being in the world that emerges from ignorance. Black heteronormativity, transphobia, and homophobia, like racism, are not solely fears of the other.

They are also toxic cultures of behavior and microaggressions rooted in normative ignorances that prohibit Black Queer persons and overall human flourishing. Therefore, Black churches must do more than allow Black Queer persons to exist among them. Being welcoming, accepting, and inclusive is not enough. Black churches must also do the intricate and challenging work of subverting every oppressive norm and element of white Christianity within their ecclesial ranks. If Black churches are to remain true to their original missions to liberate and care for all Black folks, they must become ecclesial spaces where Black Queer pleasure, eroticism, and sexual expression are invited to roam freely and sinlessly with wholistic affirmation. If this never happens, then Black Queer persons must continue to enflesh their own freedom in a Shawn Copeland sense and create their own Black Queer hermeneutics to construct innovative, fresh, and practical ways of thinking about Black Queer life that will enlighten and educate Black Queer persons.[37]

In the introduction, I described queering as a type of spiritual gardening of the Black religious landscape. Unlike Glaude, I do not believe that all Black churches are dead. Many Black churches are heteronormative, but there is a growing number of affirming congregations, and they represent the type of love-induced life that is thriving in Black Christendom.

America legalized same-sex marriage on June 26, 2015. About a year later, on June 12, 2016, a mass shooting occurred at Pulse, a gay nightclub in Orlando, Florida. Within this context of growth and loss, life and death, increase and decrease, Black Christians have been challenged to bring to light discussions on gender and sexuality that have traditionally been secluded in silence and secrecy. Additionally, more and more Black religious leaders have come out as LGBTQIAP+ themselves, giving cause for hope. Pastors like Gerald Jay Williams; Tonex, aka Antony Williams; and a member of the Grammy-nominated Gospel group the Pace Sisters' DeJuaii Pace have all come out as Black Queer persons. Moreover, several clergypersons have become public allies of the Black Queer community, like the Reverend Delmon Coates, Ph.D., the pastor of the Mount Ennon Baptist Church in Clinton, Maryland; the Reverend Jacqui Lewis, Ph.D., the pastor for Public Theology and Transformation at the Middle Collegiate Church in New York; and the Reverend Senator Raphael Warnock, Ph.D., the pastor of the Ebenezer Baptist Church in Atlanta, where the Reverend Dr. Martin Luther King Jr. once served as co-pastor. Even though the African Methodist Episcopal Church has chosen to offer no official policy on homosexuality outside of the inability of their clergypersons to officiate LGBTQIAP+ wedding ceremonies, at a meeting in Orlando, Florida, on July 8, 2021, the church passed a resolution with a vote of 985-371 and 18 abstaining to appoint an ad hoc Sexual Ethics Discernment Committee to make a recommendation to the general body about LGBTQIAP+ matters. The Reverend Dr. Jennifer Leath, Ph.D., an ordained Black lesbian elder in the AME Church and assistant professor of Black religions at Queen's University, Canada, drafted and submitted the resolution to the general body to form the committee.

Pastoral, denominational, and congregational queering are also happening beyond the American border and around the globe. In his article "Globalizing Queer? AIDS, Homophobia, and the Politics of Sexual Identity in India," Subir K. Kole states, "Queerness, and queering, is now global. Many emerging economies of the global South are experiencing queer mobilization and sexual identity politics, raising fundamental questions of citizenship, religion, and human rights on the one hand and discourses of nationalism, cultural identity, imperialism, tradition, and family values on the other."[38] Congregational queering is also budding on the continent of Africa; "intersections of queer studies and religion in contemporary African contexts are examining how queer studies can contribute to a deeper understanding of the politics and dynamics around same-sex sexualities, LGBT identities, and rights in Africa."[39] Over the last twenty years, nearly 150 Christian denominations, church associations, fellowships, emerging church groups, and individual congregations worldwide have attempted to welcome or welcome and affirm.

This number of 150 Christian groups worldwide comprises the following types of organizations: Historically heteronormative churches affiliated with large national denominations embarking on intentional queering journeys to welcome or welcome and affirm LGBTQIAP+ persons; denominations, church associations, fellowships, emerging church groups, or individual congregations founded by LGBTQIAP+ persons; unofficial and unsanctioned denominational groups founded by LGBTQIAP+ persons; and LGBTQIAP+ religious unaffiliated grassroots and community outreach initiatives that are funded by grants that facilitate training or congregational dialogues. These organizations are often focused on addressing the HIV/AIDS crisis.

To paraphrase S. K. Kole, "Queering is now global."[40] Kole uses the word now to suggest that Western images of queer sexualities and cultures in advertising, film, performing arts, the internet, or the political discourses of human rights are presently causing queering and queerness to circumnavigate the globe. Kole states that "the phrase 'now' in the above sentence indicates that it was not global earlier." While I understand the point that Kole is attempting to make here, his adverb usage is misleading.

CONCLUSION 219

Kole's notion that queerness was not global earlier is problematic because it ignores the innately queer histories of many Indigenous cultures disrupted by the terrorism of colonialism, also known as the Christianization of communities and nations worldwide. For example, the Native American "two-spirits," the "third gender" in Hindu holy texts such as the Mahabharata and the Ramayana, the five genders of the Java Island Tribes in Indonesia, the Egyptian tomb of Niankhkhnum and Khnumhotep where two male lovers from the fifth dynasty of Egypt are depicted in a tomb like a heterosexual couple, the "mudoko Dako" of the Ugandan Langi, and the ancient paintings of the San people in Zimbabwe depicting men practicing in ritual sex are all examples of the existence of queerness before the Christianization and Muslim occupation of the world's territories.

There is an often-heard critique that Queer theory is "white" and "Western." Therefore, Queer theoretical approaches cannot be meaningfully employed in African contexts. However, according to Queer African scholars like Adriaan van Klinken, African Christian traditions harbor a strong potential for countering conservative anti-LGBTQIAP+ dynamics. "Prior to European colonisation, throughout the African continent, we see far different, more relaxed attitudes towards sexual orientation and gender identity."[41] Hence, queerness is not a new phenomenon in the African context. The African pursuit to queer Christianity on the continent of Africa is a mere return to or retrieval of what was the case before colonizers forced their ideals upon the African peoples. The African pursuit to queer Christianity on the continent of Africa can be argued to be a reversion or returning to the precolonial African spiritualities and understandings about gender fluidity that once thrived on the continent. Queer African academics such as Zethu Matebeni and Stella Nyanzi argue that they "use queer to underscore a perspective that embraces the history of gender and sexual plurality in African history and seeks to transform, overhaul and revolutionize the presently colonialized African order rather than seek to assimilate into oppressive hetero-patriarchal-capitalist frameworks."[42] Klinken argues that "there is also evidence of emerging LGBT-affirming African Christian counter-mobilizations and narratives. LGBT Christians in several African countries have begun organizing themselves in grassroots communities and movements."[43] Although the previously stated progressions pale in comparison to the complexity and severity of Black ecclesial homophobia in the United States and worldwide, the progressions are promising indications that Black ecclesial queering can and is happening in varying forms around the globe.

I wrote this manuscript to inspire adaptative and "Don't ask, don't tell" Black churches to courageously queer their ecclesial contexts. The queering narratives shared throughout these pages prove that although it is impossible to do queering without making mistakes, Black ecclesial queering is nonetheless possible. There is no such thing as a perfect case of ecclesial queering, but a Black congregation can increase its opportunities for equitable queering by gleaning from the strategies within this book.

APPENDIX 1

Another Example of Congregational Queering by the Covenant Baptist-United Church of Christ

Brief History of Covenant Baptist UCC (CBUCC) and Summary of Narrative
Covenant Baptist Church was founded as an all-white congregation in 1945. Almost twenty-five years later, the congregation elected its first African American pastor, Rev. H. Wesley Wiley, with the intentions of sustainin g the church in the community. During the years of his leadership, the congregation assumed a predominately Black demographic. Later, in 1985, his son Rev. Dr. Dennis Wiley was called to lead the church. Following the election of Dr. Wiley, the church ordained its first woman member of the clergy, his wife, Rev. Dr. Christine Wiley. Noticing the congregation's readiness to condemn those of different ideologies, Rev. Dr. Dennis swiftly took on the task of educating his congregations through a series of Bible studies and thought-provoking programming on homophobia. In 2017 the Wileys retired, and Rev. Dr. Alice B. Greene served as interim minister. In 2019 CBUCC called Rev. William T. Young IV to serve as its eighth pastor, and the church continues to thrive through educational programming.

<u>1969</u>—CBUCC elects its first Black pastor
    Rev. Dennis Wiley starts the church's first gospel choir

<u>1985</u>—Rev. Dr. Dennis Wiley is elected as the church's pastor
    Dr. Wiley teaches a Bible study on "Money, Sex, and Religion"
    Dr. Wiley ordains women clergy and deacons
    Dr. Wiley baptizes a woman with AIDS
    Max Robinson HIV/AIDS Clinic moves into CBUCC

<u>1990s</u>—Dr. Wiley teaches "Struggling with Scripture"
    Dr. Wiley hosts a churchwide meeting and retreat

<u>1994</u>—Community Institute and Revival "Breaking Down the Barriers that Divide Us" begins
    Founding of the Christ-African Theological Institute

<u>2004</u>—CBUCC becomes an inclusive congregation with Rev. Dr. Dennis and Christine Wiley as co-pastors (April)
    CBUCC has LGBTQ ministers and deacons, although some are closeted
    CBUCC hosts a conversation: "What It Means to Be Transgender"

<u>2007</u>—Two students from Wesleyan Seminary seek ecclesial endorsement. Those individuals and their partners seek to hold a Holy Union ceremony at the church.
    Co-pastors form an Advisory Council
    Co-pastors meet with minsters, deacons, and trustees separately
    Co-pastors meet with the congregation to gather consensus (April 25)

Holding of first LGBTQIAP+ Union ceremonies

Co-pastors hold another meeting, pause same-sex marriage ceremonies, and form a task force to develop a process for the congregation to engage in further study to achieve a well-informed vote

2008—Vote is held to add same-sex marriage to the church's ministry (July)

2009—DC Clergy United for Marriage Equality begins

APPENDIX 2

The Eight Phases of Black Ecclesial Queering

1. The awareness of heteronormativity
2. Prayer and discernment
3. Pastoral queering, part I
   a. Ordination of women as clergy and deacons
   b. Bible studies
      i. Starts with affirming texts
      ii. The study of clobber texts
   c. Sermons
      i. Often begin with LGBTQIAP+ affirming statements woven into sermons
         1. Litanies begin addressing racism, sexism, and then homophobia. These sermons and litanies are meant to prove that oppressive measures are intersectional.
      ii. Full sermons to affirm LGBTQIAP+ persons
   d. HIV community information and outreach programming
      i. World AIDS Day observance
      ii. HIV testing
      iii. HIV/AIDS Clinics (donations and referrals to)
      iv. Fundraising for HIV research
      v. Partnerships with local hospitals and health clinics
   e. Institutes or workshops on gender and sexuality
   f. Ordination of Black Queer persons as clergy and deacons

Black ecclesial queering begins with discernment or prayer, which may be done by a senior pastor. The senior pastor then begins with Bible study and Sunday worship services that include affirming lessons and sermons. These lessons may start by noting sexism, racism, and homophobia and their negative repercussions. Most of the work requires the careful planning and programming of the church's senior leadership. For example, programming may include World AIDS observance, HIV Testing, HIV/AIDS Clinics, fundraising for HIV Research, partnerships with local hospitals and health clinics, and gender and sexuality awareness workshops.

4. Development of a congregational core committee:
   a. Meet separately with ministers, deacons, and trustees
   b. Create a list of potential core committee members
   c. Introduce the idea of queering to the congregation with a slate of names of the potential core committee
   d. Orientation and training for the core committee
   e. Compassionate educational engagement
   f. Critical and empathic listening
   g. Developing collective mission, goals, benchmarks, and whys

APPENDIX 2

    h. LGBTQIAP+ competency training
    i. Developing a clear communications plan
    j. Congregational assessment

Once the congregation has been exposed to the necessary foreknowledge needed for ecclesial queering, a committee appointed by the congregation joins the pastor in the discerning and learning process. These persons may include deacons, ministers, trustees, and many other church officials. This committee is essential as it leads the church in becoming more knowledgeable about LGBTQIAP+ life and the origins of heteronormativity. The team starts with building relationships for appropriate information gathering. This includes family and individual conversations along with small groups and youth group meetings that include LGBTQIAP+ interlocutors.

5. Relationship-building and information gathering
    a. Develop contextually appropriate relationship-building and information gathering
    b. Family engagement meetings
    c. Individual engagement meetings
    d. Church ministry meetings
    e. Youth meetings
    f. Inclusion of LGBTQIAP+ interlocutors

Once the core committee has engaged in sufficient research and presented a plan of education to the church, the body then engages in its own stages of queering. Education curricula for church queering usually begin with biblical interpretation and the history of heteronormativity. Those lessons are followed by churchwide training on engagement and affirmation. After engaging in a period of study, the church moves forward with making their church polity reflect a welcoming and affirming church. This process may include a members-only business meeting and vote with a parliamentarian to assist. Although the church may vote to be open and affirming, much work remains for the church and its leadership.

6. The ten stages of Black congregational queering
    a. Prayer
    b. Exposure
    c. Teaching the history of heteronormativity
        i. Kelly Brown Douglas
        ii. Horace Griffin
        iii. Reading the book *The Color Purple*
        iv. The faults of the church
    d. Bible studies
    e. Congregational education on gender and sexuality
        i. Panels
        ii. Community dinner discussions
        iii. Family engagement meetings
        iv. Individual engagement meetings
        v. Church ministry meetings
        vi. Youth meetings
        vii. Parents' meetings

    f. Pastoral queering, part II
    g. Test vote and final information gathering
        i. Gaining consensus on the purpose and goals of the test vote
        ii. The decision to move to an official vote or return to phase four
6. The vote
7. Postvote queering

Four Essential Elements of Black Ecclesial Queering

1. Black ecclesial queering is an unhurried communal journey that is contextual.
2. Black ecclesial queering is an intentional journey of reeducation.
3. Black ecclesial queering is a fluid and ever-evolving methodology.
4. Black ecclesial queering is a challenging and rewarding process.

Notes

Preface

1. I do not capitalize the letter *W* in the term *white* to linguistically decenter whiteness as a normative cultural identity.
2. I capitalize the letter *W* in the term *Womanist* and *Womanism* and *Q* in the term *Queer* in its noun and adjectival forms to linguistically center these cultural identities.
3. E. Patrick Johnson, "'Queer' Studies, or (Almost) Everything I Know about Queer Studies I Learned from My Grandmother," *Text and Performance Quarterly* 21, no. 1 (2001): 1–25.

Introduction

1. James H. Cone, "General Introduction," in *Black Theology: A Documentary History*, Vol. 2, *1980–1992*, ed. James H. Cone and Gayraud S. Wilmore (Maryknoll, NY: Orbis Books, 1993), 1–11.
2. Pamela Lightsey, *Our Lives Matter: A Womanist Queer Theology* (Eugene, OR: Pickwick Publications, 2015).
3. At times I use "African American" and "Black" interchangeably.
4. Joseph Drexler-Dreis, "Theological Thinking and Eurocentric Epistemologies: A Challenge to Theologians from within Africana Religious Studies," *Journal of Africana Religions* 6, no. 1 (2018): 27–49.
5. This argument is quite similar to that of Edward Farley. He argues that the direction of theology has been distorted by the requirements of what he described as a sort of professional pastoral competence. Farley believed that practical theology was obligated to provide an understanding of how faith guides human behavior in living contemporary circumstances.
6. R. Ruard Ganzevoort and Johan Roeland, "Lived Religion: The Praxis of Practical Theology," *International Journal of Practical Theology* 18, no. 1 (2014): 91–101.
7. Victor Anderson, *Beyond Ontological Blackness: An Essay on African American Religious and Cultural Criticism* (New York: Continuum, 2016).
8. By this I mean that all of them were open but only a few were publicly affirming!

Chapter 1

1. Robert K. Gnuse, "Seven Gay Texts: Biblical Passages Used to Condemn Homosexuality," *Biblical Theology Bulletin* 45, no. 2 (2015): 68–87.

2. Molefi Kete Asante, *Afrocentricity and Knowledge* (Trenton, NJ: Africa World Press, 1990); Molefi Kete Asante, *Afrocentricity* (Trenton, NJ: Africa World Press, 1988); Molefi Kete Asante, *The Afrocentric Idea* (Philadelphia: Temple University Press, 1998).
3. Asante, *Afrocentricity*, 57.
4. Aliyyah I. Abdur-Rahman, "'The Strangest Freaks of Despotism': Queer Sexuality in Antebellum African American Slave Narratives," *African American Review* 40, no. 2 (2006): 223–37.
5. James H. Sweet, "Male Homosexuality and Spiritism in the African Diaspora: The Legacies of a Link," *Journal of the History of Sexuality* 7, no. 2 (1996): 184–202.
6. Ibid., 191–92.
7. Amar Wahab, "'Homosexuality/Homophobia Is Un-African'?: Un-Mapping Transnational Discourses in the Context of Uganda's Anti-Homosexuality Bill/Act," *Journal of Homosexuality* 63, no. 5 (2016): 685–718.
8. Greg Reeder, "Same-Sex Desire, Conjugal Constructs, and the Tomb of Niankhkhnum and Khnumhotep," *World Archaeology* 32, no. 2 (2000): 193–208.
9. Marc Epprecht, "The 'Unsaying' of Indigenous Homosexualities in Zimbabwe: Mapping a Blindspot in an African Masculinity," *Journal of Southern African Studies* 24, no. 4 (1998): 631–51.
10. Netisha Currie, "William Dorsey Swann, the Queen of Drag," *National Archives: Rediscovering Black History* [blog], June 29, 2020, https://rediscovering-black-history.blogs.archives.gov/2020/06/29/william-dorsey-swann-the-queen-of-drag/.
11. Robert R. Ellis, "Reading through the Veil of Juan Francisco Manzano: From Homoerotic Violence to the Dream of a Homoracial Bond," *PMLA* 113, no. 3 (1998): 422–35.
12. Vincent Woodard, *The Delectable Negro: Human Consumption and Homoeroticism within U.S. Slave Culture*, ed. James Joyce and Dwight A. McBride (New York: New York University Press, 2014).
13. Devon W. Carbado, Dwight A. McBride, Donald Weise, and Evelyn C. White, *Black Like Us: A Century of Lesbian, Gay, and Bisexual African American Fiction* (Berkeley, CA: Cleis Press, 2011).
14. Charmaine L. Wijeyesinghe, ed., *The Complexities of Race: Identity, Power, and Justice in an Evolving America* (New York: NYU Press, 2021), 24.
15. Todd Wooten, *White Men Can't Hump (as Good as Black Men)*, Vol. 1: *Race and Sex in America* (Bloomington, IN: Anchor House, 2006).
16. 1863 American Freedmen's Inquiry Commission Papers, MS Am 702, Houghton Library, Harvard University, Cambridge, MA; Matthew Furrow and Samuel G. Howe, "The Black Population of Canada West, and the Racial Ideology of the 'Blueprint for Radical Reconstruction,'" *Journal of American History* 97, no. 2 (2010): 344–70.
17. Richard Godbeer and Douglas L. Winiarski, "The Sodomy Trial of Nicholas Sension, 1677: Documents and Teaching Guide," *Early American Studies* 12, no. 2 (Spring 2014): 402–43.
18. Ibid., 427.

19. Woodard, *Delectable Negro*, 7. Woodard describes an underlying culture of consumption that included cannibalism and homoeroticism. The practice of homoeroticism was an exercise of power that delved into the latent homosexual interests of white slave masters. The degradation of African male bodies was connected to the honor of white slave masters. White men were governed by a set of cultural mores surrounding power that allowed them to engage in homosexual relationships with Black men while maintaining the hegemonic order of southern society. Woodard displays how the matrix of sex, brutality, and hunger was fully displayed in the seasoning of an enslaved African named James L. Smith. See James Lindsay Smith, *Autobiography of James L. Smith* (Norwich, CT: Norwich Press of the Bulletin Company, 1881), 79–80. Woodard writes, "Smith's narrative offers a closer look into the sexual dimensions of white male rage, obsession, and desire for Black men during slavery. As a youth, Smith works on the Mitchell plantation. One sunny morning, a ship captain comes to the Mitchell plantation to purchase grain. This man sees young Smith and admires his countenance. He wants to make the youth into a sailor, initiate him into the rigors and challenges of manhood at sea. . . . Smith will soon learn, though, that his culinary responsibilities involve much more than food preparation. In addition to choosing the young slave to feed his physical hunger, the captain has also chosen Smith to fulfill other despotic hungers."

20. Linda Brent (Harriet Ann Jacobs), "Incidents in the Life of a Slave Girl. Written by Herself," *Documenting the American South*, 288–89, accessed June 28, 2016, docsouth.unc.edu/fpn//jacobs/jacobs.html.

21. Abdur-Rahman, "'Strangest Freaks of Despotism,'" 223–37.

22. Thomas A. Foster, "The Sexual Abuse of Black Men under American Slavery," *Journal of the History of Sexuality* 20, no. 3 (2011): 445–64; Christopher Morris, "The Articulation of Two Worlds: The Master-Slave Relationship Reconsidered," *Journal of American History* 85, no. 3 (1998): 982–1007.

23. Heinz L. Ansbacher, *The Individual Psychology of Alfred Adler: A Systematic Presentation in Selections from His Writings* (New York: Basic Books, 1956), 116–17.

24. M. Shawn Copeland, *Enfleshing Freedom: Body, Race, and Being* (Minneapolis: Fortress, 2010), 24.

25. Ibid.

26. James H. Sweet, *Recreating Africa: Culture, Kinship, and Religion in the African-Portuguese World, 1441–1770* (Chapel Hill: University of North Carolina Press, 2003), 74.

27. Abdur-Rahman, "Strangest Freaks of Despotism," 223.

28. Don Browning, *A Fundamental Practical Theology, Descriptive and Strategic Proposals* (Minneapolis: Fortress Press, 1991), 48.

29. Ibid., 39.

30. Hans-Georg Gadamer. *Truth and Method*, trans. Joel Weinsheimer (New York: Seabury Press, 1975), 330–31.

31. Ashton T. Crawley, "Circum-Religious Performance: Queer(ed) Black Bodies and the Black Church," *Theology and Sexuality* 14, no. 2 (January 2008): 208–14.

230 NOTES

32. R. Earl Riggins Jr., "Loving Our Black Bodies as God's Luminously Dark Temples: The Quest for Black Restoration," in *Loving the Body: Black Religious Studies and the Erotic*, ed. Anthony B. Pinn and Dwight N. Hopkins (New York: Palgrave, 2004), 249–69.
33. Paul Tillich, *Systematic Theology*, vol. 1 (Chicago: University of Chicago Press, 1973), 189. By framing the question as a form of survival, it helps to raise the desire of the Black Queer above the moral evaluation of what a right or wrong method is of preserving one's existence. Thereby we equate Black Queer survival with the basic human will to survive.
34. Copeland, *Enfleshing Freedom*, 74.
35. Peter J. Paris, *The Social Teaching of the Black Churches* (Philadelphia: Fortress Press, 1985), 11.
36. Ibid., 74.
37. Ibid.
38. Ibid., 78.
39. Ibid.
40. Robert E. Goss, *Queering Christ: Beyond Jesus Acted Up* (Cleveland, OH: Resource Publications, 2006), 213. "when queer churches, synagogues, and groups decenter heterosexual presumptions and readings that often suppress diversity, gender, race, class, ethnicity, and sexual alternatives" (213).
41. Paris, *The Social Teaching of the Black Churches*, 78.
42. Mark Vessey and Shelley Reid, *A Companion to Augustine* (Chichester, UK: Wiley-Blackwell, 2012), 358–60.
43. Ibid.
44. Hannah Arendt, Joanna Vecchiarelli Scott, and Judith Chelius Stark, *Love and Saint Augustine* (Chicago: University of Chicago Press, 1996), 93–97.
45. Horace L. Griffin, *Their Own Receive Them Not: African American Lesbians and Gays in Black Churches* (Cleveland, OH: Pilgrim Press, 2006), 32–33.
46. Ibid.
47. Ibid., 20.
48. Ibid., 2.
49. Patricia Hill Collins, *Black Sexual Politics: African Americans, Gender, and the New Racism* (New York: Routledge, 2005), 7.
50. Patricia Hill Collins, *Black Feminist Thought: Knowledge, Consciousness, and the Politics of Empowerment*, 2nd ed. (New York: Routledge, 2000), 299.
51. Ibid.
52. Ibid., Douglas, *Sexuality and the Black Church*, 20–25.
53. Ibid.
54. Griffin, *Their Own Receive Them Not*, 57.
55. Victor Anderson, "The Black Church and the Curious Body of the Black Homosexual," in *Loving the Black Body: Black Religious Studies and the Erotic*, ed. Anthony B. Pinn and Dwight N. Hopkins (New York: Palgrave, 2004), 297–312.
56. E. L. Kornegay Jr., *A Queering of Black Theology* (New York: Palgrave Macmillan, 2013). The concept of Protestant Puritanism is critical to understanding the evolution of African American homophobia and gender oppression. Puritanism engendered a

Du Boisian "double consciousness" in which persons of African descent experience the "quintessential social fury" of being Black and religious. According to Kornegay, "The metaphorical equation of [twoness] presupposes that Blackness cannot be compared equally to Whiteness and must therefore be likened to something that is less [than] and unequal to it. As such, the metaphorical equation makes Blackness the dumping ground for all that Puritanism deems unrighteous" (22). The Puritan ideal concealed a hermeneutic of "conquest and suppression" in which Enlightenment thinkers developed theories of race, color symbolism, and history to justify their conquest of foreign cultures. Kornegay asserts that the religious heritage of Protestant Puritanism limits the possibility for religion to offer a sense of "somebodiness" to Black people (25).

57. Ibid., 96.
58. Kornegay EL. 2013. *A Queering of Black Theology : James Baldwin's Blues Project and Gospel Prose* First ed. Basingstoke: Palgrave Macmillan, 48.
59. Kornegay, Queering of Black Theology, 25. Kornegay posits, "Baldwin's experience in the Black Christian church exposes the real issue, which persists beneath the surface of Black religion is its dependence on Protestant Puritanism, that makes it no more capable of offering human relief from danger than the Avenue", 25.
60. Adam Clayton Powell Sr., *Against the Tide: An Autobiography* (New York: R. R. Smith, 1938), 209–20; Gary David Comstock, *A Whosoever Church: Welcoming Lesbians and Gay Men into African American Congregations* (Louisville, KY: Westminster John Knox Press, 2001), 296; Griffin, *Their Own Receive Them Not*, 240.
61. Walter E. Fluker, *Ethical Leadership: The Quest for Character, Civility and Community* (Minneapolis: Fortress Press, 2009), 85.
62. Jeffrey C. Goldfarb, "Civility and Subversion Revisited: Twenty-First Century Media Intellectuals as Ideologists and Anti-Ideologists," *International Journal of Politics, Culture, and Society* 25, no. 4 (2012): 143–55.
63. Fluker, *Ethical Leadership*, 85.
64. Ibid., 99.
65. Orlando Patterson, *Slavery and Social Death: A Comparative Study* (Cambridge, MA: Harvard University Press, 1982), as quoted in ibid.
66. Fluker, *Ethical Leadership*, 92.
67. Ibid.
68. Harold Cruse, *The Crisis of the Negro Intellectual: From Its Origins to the Present* (New York: NYRB Classics, 2005), 451.
69. Fluker, *Ethical Leadership*, 86.
70. Thaddeus Russell, "The Color of Discipline: Civil Rights and Black Sexuality," *American Quarterly* 60, no. 1 (2008): 101–28, 104.
71. Martin Bauml Duberman, Martha Vicinus, and George Chauncey Jr., *Hidden from History: Reclaiming the Gay and Lesbian Past* (New York: Plume, 1990), 321.
72. Ibid.
73. Russell, "Color of Discipline," 104.
74. George Chauncey, *Gay New York: Gender, Urban Culture, and the Makings of the Gay Male World, 1890–1940* (New York: Basic Books, 1994).

232 NOTES

75. Russell, "Color of Discipline," 104.
76. Adam Clayton Powell Sr., *Against the Tide: An Autobiography* (New York: R. R. Smith, 1938), 209–20; Gary David Comstock, *A Whosoever Church: Welcoming Lesbians and Gay Men into African American Congregations* (Louisville, KY: Westminster John Knox Press, 2001), 296; Griffin, *Their Own Receive Them Not*, 240; G. Winston James and Lisa C. Moore, eds., *Spirited: Affirming the Soul and Black Gay/Lesbian Identity* (Washington, DC: Redbone Press, 2006), 91.
77. Powell, *Against the Tide*, 216.
78. Griffin, *Their Own Received Them Not*, 2.
79. Ibid., 20.
80. Patricia H. Collins, "Gender, Black Feminism and Black Political Economy," *Annals of the American Academy of Political and Social Science* 568 (March 2000): 41–53; Patricia H. Collins, "Learning from the Outsider Within: The Sociological Significance of Black Feminist Thought," *Social Problems* 33, no. 6 (1986): S14–S32.
81. Dawne Moon, *God, Sex, and Politics: Homosexuality and Everyday Theologies* (Chicago: University of Chicago Press, 2004), 5.
82. Jay E. Johnson, "Looking from the Outside In: Social Science and Sexual Identity in Today's Churches," *Anglican Theological Review* 90, no. 3 (2008): 631–47. Canon Kearon "added that the *Windsor Report*, issued by the Lambeth Commission created by Archbishop Rowan Williams to seek ways of healing the rift within the Communion over human sexuality, had encouraged the Archbishop 'to exercise very considerable caution in inviting him to the councils of the church.'" "In a statement, Bishop Gene Robinson called the refusal to include him 'among all other duly elected and consecrated bishops of the church an affront to the entire Episcopal Church.' He added, 'At a time when the Anglican Communion is calling for a "listening process" on the issue of homosexuality, how does it make sense to exclude gay and lesbian people from the discussion? Isn't it time that the bishops of the church stop talking about us and start talking with us?'" Sison, Marites N, and Marites De Santis, "Lambeth Invitations Exclude American Gay Bishop," *Anglican Journal* 133, no. 6 (May 22, 2007): 1.
83. Moon, *God, Sex, and Politics*, 58.
84. Ibid.
85. Ibid., 183.
86. Joy James, *Transcending the Talented Tenth: Black Leaders and American Intellectuals* (New York: Routledge, 1996), 19.
87. According to Kevin Gaines, *Uplifting the Race: Black Leadership, Politics and Culture in the Twentieth Century* (Chapel Hill: University of North Carolina Press, 1996), Anna Julia Cooper was a Black female intellectual who contributed to African American thought as a national social commentator who addressed American gender inequality, racial controversy, organized labor, and African American and American cultural identity (129). Cooper's cultural analysis on the previously stated national concerns was highly influenced by Western ethnocentrisms, staunch religious piety, and the Victorian standards of the bourgeois to which she subscribed (129). However, her evaluation of gender inequality was guilty of both contesting

and reflecting "the assumptions of the black intelligentsia and black middle-class ideology" (129). Despite the fact that Cooper recognized that the organic link between the Black elite and the Black majority had been scourged by the patriarchal trappings of the Black intelligentsia, she still believed that the writings of Black intellectuals would both defend and uplift the Black race (130). However, in light of her views on Black elites as "representative Negroes," it is important to highlight that Cooper's understanding of education and the organization of labor in the New South was very Booker T. Washington in nature (130). According to Gaines, Cooper's understanding of morality and power was tied into her belief that the American struggle between good and evil was nestled within the demands of organized labor. Cooper described organized labor as a contamination that was more threatening to the health of the American economic order than the white southern fear of Negro domination (147). She "located virtue and moral authority in power, as she preached a gospel of accommodation" (147). She empathized with the hearts of the Christian conscience of the South by creating a dichotomy between what she called the loyal Black American and the unassimilated immigrant worker who would "need an interpreter to communicate with their employer" (147). She argues that "the Negro was far more trustworthy by virtue of his instinct for law and order, his inborn respect for authority, his inaptitude for rioting and anarchy, his gentleness and cheerfulness as a laborer, and his deep-rooted faith in God" (148).
88. Russell, "Color of Discipline," 104.
89. Duberman, Vicinus, and Chauncey, *Hidden from History*, 313–32.
90. Griffin, *Their Own Receive Them Not*, 57.

Chapter 2

1. Jonathan L. Walton, "The Complicated Legacy of Bishop Eddie Long," Religion and Politics: A Project Publication of the John C. Danforth Center on Religion and Politics, Washington University in St. Louis, February 6, 2017, https://religionandpolitics.org/2017/02/06/the-complicated-legacy-of-bishop-eddie-long/; Jonathan L. Walton, "We Are Soldiers," in Walton, *Watch This: The Ethics and Aesthetics of Black Televangelism* (New York: NYU Press, 2009), 125.
2. This theological phrase denotes the symbolic interconnectedness between God and humanity and the ultimate indwelling and endowment of the Divine within humankind.
3. Judith Butler, *Bodies That Matter: On the Discourse Limits of "Sex,"* (New York: Routledge, 1990), 228.
4. Patrick E. Johnson, "'Quare' Studies or (Almost) Everything I Know about Queer Studies I Learned from My Grandmother," *Text and Performance Quarterly* 21, no. 1 (January 2001), 1–25.
5. The statement, resistance toward Womanism for the sake of gender demolition alone, is in reference to the Queer idea that gender should be abolished. Gender abolition is

234 NOTES

a violent form of Queer theorizing that erases Black womanhood and womanism as meaningful forms of meaning making.
6. Kornegay EL. 2013. A Queering of Black Theology : James Baldwin's Blues Project and Gospel Prose First ed. Basingstoke: Palgrave Macmillan, p. 5, 11, 101, 110, 171.
7. Kornegay EL. 2013. A Queering of Black Theology : James Baldwin's Blues Project and Gospel Prose First ed. Basingstoke: Palgrave Macmillan, p.110.
8. Kornegay EL. 2013. A Queering of Black Theology : James Baldwin's Blues Project and Gospel Prose First ed. Basingstoke: Palgrave Macmillan, p.101.
9. Patrick Cheng, *Radical Love: An Introduction to Queer Theology* (New York: Seabury Books, 2011), 6.
10. Ibid., 6, 10.
11. Ibid., 8.
12. Ibid., 10; Browning, *A Fundamental Practical Theology*, 5.
13. E. L. Kornegay, *A Queering of Black Theology: James Baldwin's Blues Project and Gospel Prose* (New York: Palgrave Macmillan, 2013), 35.
14. Horace L. Griffin, *Their Own Receive Them Not: African American Lesbians and Gays in Black Churches* (Cleveland, OH: Pilgrim Press, 2006), 54, 87–88, 121, 186, 206, 212; see also Ronald Enroth and Gerald Jamison, *The Gay Church* (Grand Rapids: Eerdmans, 1974), 29.
15. Anthony G. Reddie, *Working against the Grain: Re-Imaging Black Theology in the 21st Century* (London: Equinox, 2008), 3; see also Anne H. Pinn and Anthony B. Pinn, *Introduction to Black Church History* (Minneapolis: Fortress Press, 2002), 6–87; and Henry H. Mitchell's, *Black Church Beginnings: The Long-Hidden Realities of the First Years* (Valley Forge, PA: Judson Press, 2004), 8–45.
16. Griffin, *Their Own Receive Them Not*, 87–88.
17. Ibid.
18. Cheng, *Radical Love*, 11–13.
19. Kornegay, A *Queering of Black Theology*, 55..
20. Ibid., 10, 100.
21. Ibid., 100.
22. Ibid., 143–45.
23. Ibid., 54–56.
24. Dawne Moon, *God, Sex, and Politics* (Chicago: University of Chicago Press, 2004), 113, 159.
25. Kornegay, *Queering of Black Theology*.
26. See Michel Foucault, *The History of Sexuality*, Vol. 1: *An Introduction*, trans. Robert Hurley (New York: Vintage, 1980), 153.
27. See Michel Foucault, *Power/Knowledge: Selected Interviews and Other Writings 1972–1977*, ed. Colin Gordon (New York: Pantheon, 1980), 104, 158, 247.
28. In her book, *Sexuality and the Black Church,* Kelly Brown Douglas argues that the silence of Black churches on the topic of sexuality is due, in part, to its conscious and unconscious desire to maintain "White hegemonic, racist, sexist, classist, and heterosexist structures.", 142. She argues that the most critical discourse that is needed in Black communities is "a sexual discourse of resistance to help Black Christians

recognize how the White exploitation of Black sexuality has corrupted Black people," corrupted Black churches, and tainted the Black liberationist understanding of God, 142. Kelly B. Douglas, *Sexuality and the Black Church: A Womanist Perspective* (Maryknoll, NY: Orbis Books, 1999). For this reason, I argue that an ecclesiological investigation of how Black churches have amplified the unheard voices of their LGBTQIA congregants matters because it could significantly change how African American churches understand human nature, church missions, Christian practice, and ecclesiology. Patricia Hill Collins's understanding of Black sexual politics is used to examine the intersectionality of Black sexuality and the ideology of Black gender within Black churches. She defines Black sexual politics as "a set of ideals and social practices that are shaped by the intersection of gender, race, and sexuality", 6. Patricia Hill Collins, *Black Sexual Politics: African Americans, Gender, and the New Racism* (New York: Routledge, 2005).

29. Dale Andrews, *Practical Theology for Black Churches: Bridging Black Theology and African American Folk Religion* (Louisville, KY: Westminster John Knox Press, 2002), 1, 7, 51, 90, 107.
30. Ibid., 35.
31. In another work, the investigation of such social conditions will be necessary for assessing the types of protests that were indeed possible. The lack of fear that Dale Andrews speaks of should always be understood as dependent upon certain social conditions that were not afforded to all. The lack of such social conditions made it impossible to organize direct nonviolent protests against the established powers before 1955 because of the Supreme Court decisions in *Brown v. Board of Education*. Such protests would have been speaking into a moral vacuum, much like those in the Sharpeville massacre in South Africa in 1960. King and others could assume a spirit of goodwill among many in the body politic if it should become aware of the concealed evil on which the system of segregation was based. That was not the case prior to the 1954 decision.
32. Andrews, *Practical Theology for Black Churches*, 54.
33. Ibid., 36, 51, 52, 59, 102.
34. Ibid., 7, 10, 56, 98.
35. Ibid., 40.
36. Ibid.
37. Ibid., 5, 8, 9, 36, 42, 43, 47, 52, 58, 113.
38. See Cornel West, "The Prophetic Tradition in Afro-America," in *African American Religious Thought: An Anthology*, ed. Cornel West and Eddie S. Glaude Jr. (Louisville, KY: Westminster John Knox Press, 2003), 1044–45. Cornel West describes Dr. Martin Luther King Jr. as a "unique figure in Afro-American Christianity" because of his "heroic effort to reform and a suicidal effort to revolutionize American society and culture." After traveling to the urban neighborhoods of North America and surveying the American presence in the Dominican Republic, South Africa, and South Vietnam, Dr. King was convinced that a fundamental restructuring of American society and culture—a democratic socialist vision—was necessary to "provide Black freedom." This vision made Dr. King an outsider in mainstream Afro-American Christianity and American political discourse. King's campaigns to create a system that increased

the capabilities of Black citizens were attempts to Queer the political and social norms in America.
39. James H. Cone, *Black Theology and Black Power* (Maryknoll, NY: Orbis Books, 2008), 69.
40. Peter J. Paris, "The Social Teaching of the Black Churches: A Prolegomenon," in *Selected Papers from the Twenty-First Annual Meeting (Society of Christian Ethics)* (St. Cloud, MN: Society of Christian Ethics, 1980), 120.
41. Walton, "We Are Soldiers," 125; Walton, *Complicated Legacy of Bishop Eddie Long*
42. Griffin, Their Own Receive Them Not, 87–88; Stephen C. Rasor and Michael I. N. Dash. *The Mark of Zion: Congregational Life in the Black Churches* (Eugene, OR: Wipf and Stock, 2003), 53; Michael I. N. Dash, Stephen C. Rasor, and Jonathan Jackson Jr., *Hidden Wholeness: An African American Spirituality for Individuals and Communities* (Cleveland, OH: Pilgrim Press, 1997), 53. Rasor and Dash discuss key functions in Black congregational life that Black Queer bodies need. African American congregations were centers to prepare people for a life of faithful Christian witness. With small groups for religious education and doctrinal training, churches offer a "language-world" abounding with stories that empower people on their Christian journeys. Congregations also participate in large-scale social outreach, an outward expression of closely held beliefs. Black Queer ecclesiology requires language, religious support groups, and rituals that affirm religious heritage to provide a brave space for Black Queer bodies to be spiritually fed.
43. W. E. B. Du Bois, The Souls of Black Folks (1903; repr. San Diego, CA: Icon Group International, 2008); Melva Wilson Costen, African American Christian Worship, 2nd ed. (Nashville: Abingdon Press, 2007). Du Bois claims that the preacher, the music, and the frenzy are three things that characterize slave religion. The third characteristic, the frenzy, was the one "more devoutly believed in than all the rest." The frenzy ranged from personal, inconsequential moans and groans to emphatic, physical expressions. Within the frenzy was the belief that this visible manifestation was necessary for a transformative encounter with the invisible. Melva Costen describes the music of the Black church as a catalyst, which engendered the frenzy of ring shouts with wild chants. She notes that music, movement, and songs are the foundations of Black Christian worship.
44. Ibid.
45. Jane Bennett, The Enchantment of Modern Life (Princeton, NJ: Princeton University Press, 2001), 5.
46. Ibid.
47. Peter J. Paris, The Social Teaching of the Black Churches (Philadelphia: Fortress Press, 1985), 11.
48. Ibid., 6.
49. Ibid., 16.
50. Ibid., 15.
51. Ibid., 15–16. Although they use different descriptors, this entire paragraph reveals that both E. L. Kornegay and Peter Paris discuss the puritanical nature of white

oppression that engenders Blackness. See Kornegay, Queering of Black Theology, 138–39; Douglas, Sexuality and the Black Church, 127. Douglas judges heteronormativity and homophobia as sin. She writes, "[Homophobia] and concomitant heterosexist structures and systems are sin. In other words, it is not homosexuality but homophobia that is sinful. Furthermore, as the Black church and community espouse sexual rhetoric that castigates Queer persons for experiencing the fullness of their sexuality, this church and community have again participated in and abetted sin. Even more significantly, if God's revelation in Jesus draws us to hear the voices of those who are most marginalized in our society, then the Black church is certainly drawn to hear the voice of Black gay and lesbian persons as they struggle against the complexity of homophobia/ heterosexism" (127).

52. Anthony B. Pinn, "Working to Connect Religion, Black Bodies, and Sexuality: What Black Churches Should Know, Part One," *The African American Lectionary: A Project of the African American Pulpit Inc.*, accessed March 28, 2019, http://www.theafricanamericanlectionary.org/pdf/dialogue/WorkingToConnect_AnthonyPinn.pdf.

53. Lee Butler, "The Spirit Is Willing and the Flesh Is Too: Living Whole and Holy Lives through Integrating Spirituality and Sexuality," in *Loving the Body: Black Religious Studies and the Erotic*, ed. Anthony B. Pinn and Dwight N. Hopkins (New York: Palgrave Macmillan, 2004), 119.

54. Ibid.

55. Keri Day, *Unfinished Business: Black Women, the Black Church, and the Struggle to Thrive in America* (Maryknoll, NY: Orbis Books, 2012), 12–36.

56. Ibid., 31.

57. Ibid., 33.

58. Ibid., 37.

59. Ibid., 36.

60. Ibid., 30.

61. Ibid., 41.

62. John J. McNeill, *The Church and the Homosexual* (Kansas City, MO: Sheed Andrews and McMeel, 1976), 192.

63. Ibid.

64. Ibid., 193.

65. Ibid., 194.

66. Ibid., 190.

67. Robert E. Shore-Goss, Thomas Bohache, Patrick S. Cheng, and Ramona F. West, *Queering Christianity: Finding a Place at the Table for LGBTQI Christians* (Santa Barbara, CA: Praeger, 2013), 6. Because the Catholic Church has excluded Black Queer persons at the community table, Goss attempts to queer dominant white Christianity. He argues, "Queering the table refers to the process of exploding the cultural, theological, and ecclesial boundaries around the politics of the community table. Marcella Althaus-Reid's work has concentrated in unmasking the fascist regimes of heteronormative theology with transgressive, indecent sexualities and gender fluidities to create a Queeruption, creating space for theologies from Queer outsiders" (6).

238 NOTES

68. Albert J. Raboteau, *Slave Religion: The "Invisible Institution" in the Antebellum South* (New York: Oxford University Press, 1978); Reddie, *Working against the Grain*, 3; see also Pinn and Pinn, *Introduction to Black Church History*
69. The terms "brush arbor" and "hush harbor" are used in this book to describe "a secluded informal structure, often built with tree branches, set in places away from masters so that slaves could meet to worship in private." Paul Harvey, *Through the Storm, through the Night: A History of African American Christianity* (Lanham, MD: Rowman & Littlefield Publishers, 2011), 192.
70. Lawrence H. Mamiya and C. Eric Lincoln, *The Black Church in the African American Experience* (Durham, NC: Duke University Press, 1990), 2.
71. Ibid.
72. Reddie, "Black Ecclesiologies," 444.
73. Ibid.
74. Ibid., 445.
75. Cornel West, *Democracy Matters* (New York: Penguin Books, 2004), 147–72, 215. Cornel West distinguishes between two kinds of Christianity: prophetic Christianity and Constantinian Christianity. He defines Constantinian Christianity as a right-wing Christianity of the empire that often ends up on the wrong side of history. For him, Constantinian Christianity is synonymous with "America free-market fundamentalism, aggressive militarism, and escalating authoritarianism—[and] are often justified by the religious rhetoric of this Christian fundamentalism." He states, "And perhaps most ironically—and sadly—this fundamentalism is subverting the most profound, seminal teachings of Christianity, those being that we should live with humility, love our neighbors, and do unto others as we would have them do unto us" (147). He defines American prophetic Christianity as an offspring of the prophetic Black church tradition of Rauschenbuschian thought; it aims to expose the idolatry of Constantinian Christianity by bearing witness to Jesus's social gospel that was rooted in love and peace (147–50). West would argue that Black homophobia is an example of how Constantinian Christianity plays itself out in American life. He argues that "this terrible merger of the church and state has been behind so many of the church's worst violations of Christian love and justice—from barbaric crusades against the Jews and Muslims, to horrors of the Inquisitions and the ugly bigotry against women, people of color, and gays and lesbians" (149).
76. Albert Raboteau wrote Slave Religion: The "Invisible Institution" in the Antebellum South* (Oxford University Press, 1978; rev. ed., 2004 p. 59, 89–92; 213; 305).
77. James Cone, *God of the Oppressed* (New York: Orbis Books, 1975), 29.
78. Paris, *Social Teaching of the Black Churches*, 112.
79. Raboteau, *Slave Religion*, 291–92.
80. Lincoln and Mamiya, *Black Church in the African American Experience*, 12, 272.
81. Andrews, *Practical Theology for Black Churches*, 34.
82. Lawrence H. Mamiya and C. Eric Lincoln, *The Black Church in the African American Experience* (Durham: Duke University Press, 1990), 11–12.
83. Ibid.

84. Jessica Chasmar, "Joe Biden: Gay Marriage Ruling 'as Consequential as Brown v. Board,'" *Washington Times*, July 10, 2015, https://www.washingtontimes.com/news/2015/jul/10/joe-biden-gay-marriage-ruling-as-consequential-as-/.
85. Kornegay, *Queering of Black Theology*, 1.
86. Angelique C. Harris, "Homosexuality and the Black Church, Vol. 93 (2), 262–270." *Journal of African American History* 93, no. 2 (2008): 262–70. Harris writes, "For years, Powell Sr., and later his son and successor, Rev. Adam Clayton Powell, Jr., condemned homosexuality as a sin and used biblical passages to support their views. In fact, in an attempt to get Dr. Martin Luther King, Jr. to call off a civil rights protest planned for the Democratic National Convention in Los Angeles in August 1960, Powell Jr., who was also the Democratic congressman from Harlem, threatened to spread the rumor that Dr. King and Bayard Rustin, who was an essential advisor for King's Southern Christian Leadership Conference (SCLC), were lovers. The charge was untrue, but Rustin, who was homosexual, was forced to resign his SCLC position" (265).
87. Bayard Rustin, *Time on Two Crosses: The Collected Writings of Bayard Rustin*, ed. Devon W. Carbado and Donald Weise (New York: Cleis Press, 2015), excerpted by permission of Cleis Press. This 1987 essay by Bayard Rustin reveals a personal account of MLK's feelings toward gay people.
88. Michael G. Long, *Martin Luther King Jr., Homosexuality, and the Early Gay Rights Movement: Keeping the Dream Straight?* (New York: Palgrave Macmillan, 2012).
89. Ibid.
90. See Phoebe C. Godfrey, "Law and the Regulation of the Obscene," in *Introducing the New Sexuality Studies*, 2nd ed., ed. Steven Seidman, Nancy Fisher, and Chet Meeks (London: Routledge, 2011), 448.
91. Bayard Rustin, *I Must Resist: Bayard Rustin's Life in Letters* (San Francisco: City Lights, 2012), 120. Bayard Rustin was an openly gay activist who infused Gandhian nonviolence into the civil rights movement. As a trusted adviser of King, Rustin was the architect of the 1963 March on Washington for Jobs and Freedom. While he was a pivotal strategist and organizer for the movement, Rustin was alienated and disenfranchised by American politicians and civil rights leaders because of his sexual orientation and ties to the Communist Party. Rustin was also accused of draft dodging after filing for conscientious-objector status during the draft of World War II. Rustin's expertise in marshaling liberal funders and organizing nonviolent direct-action campaigns led to the creation of the Southern Christian Leadership Conference.
92. David L. Chappell, *A Stone of Hope: Prophetic Religion and the Death of Jim Crow* (Chapel Hill: University of North Carolina Press, 2004), 56.
93. Jared E. Leighton, "Freedom Indivisible: Gays and Lesbians in the African American Civil Rights Movement" (PhD diss., University of Nebraska-Lincoln, 2013).
94. Ibid., 56.
95. Chappell, *Stone of Hope*, 56. By Queer behavior, I refer to Rustin's statement in his 1952 "Easter Greeting" when he said, "Everyone saw Jesus as a lot of trouble." Rustin sought to connect with this Christological premise and shape the movement around prophetic and Christological equality. Thus, Rustin sought to queer white American laws and culture with civil disobedience and the civil rights movement. This is another example of Black queering in normative spaces. The civil rights movement sought to queer white America and turned it on its head to the point of retiring Jim Crow laws.

96. Lincoln and Mamiya, *Black Church in the African American Experience*, 212.
97. James J. Ferrell, *The Spirit of the Sixties: The Making of Postwar Radicalism* (New York: Routledge, 1997), 84–86. Dr. King used the personalist politics practiced in the Black church and taught at Boston University to queer American conceptions of Blackness and create alternative theologies and spaces essential to actualize Black freedom. King's mission was to infuse the personalist theology of liberation of African American religion into mainstream American political discourse. Black churches used a personalist lens to make sense of slavery and segregation. Personalism was used to decode the meaning of Genesis, revealing God's creation of the person in the image of God, and the exodus narrative, revealing God's desire for the freedom of a people. King's personalist politics translated into the assertion of "somebodyness," affirming the image of God in a person and rejecting negative projections that American culture places on a person. Heaven was used to imagine the possibility of Black "somebodyness" in a culture that negated it. Black churches would "combine the salvation of heaven and earth" and developed a theology of the cross that affirmed heaven could be won through unmerited suffering.
98. Cone, *Black Theology and Black Power*, 69.
99. Ibid., 69.
100. Ibid.
101. Ibid.

Chapter 3

1. Dale P. Andrews, *Practical Theology for Black Churches: Bridging Black Theology and African American Folk Religion* (Louisville, KY: Westminster John Knox Press, 2002). Dale Andrews died in 2017.
2. Patricia Hill Collins, *Black Sexual Politics: African Americans, Gender, and the New Racism* (New York; London: Routledge. press, 2004), 87–88.
3. Chernoh M. Sesay, "The Revolutionary Black Roots of Slavery's Abolition in Massachusetts," *New England Quarterly* 87, no. 1 (2014): 99–131.
4. D. Butler, "The Daughters of Myrtle Baptist Church: Womanist Consciousness in Motion," *Journal of the Motherhood Initiative for Research and Community Involvement* 9 (2007): n.p.; Susan Abele, "Building Newton in the Twentieth Century," Summer 2000, Newton Historical Society at the Jackson Homestead.
5. Evelyn B. Higginbotham, *Righteous Discontent: The Women's Movement in the Black Baptist Church, 1880–1920* (Cambridge, MA: Harvard University Press, 1994). According to Higginbotham, the diversity among African American churches in 1990 grew out of congregations' considerations of what type of role that the church should have in race advancement. In his 1983 history of Black churches in Boston, Robert Hayden suggests that even the African Meeting House went through an

NOTES 241

internal dispute in 1840 over the Black church's role in the abolition movement. See Robert C. Hayden, *Faith, Culture, and Leadership: A History of the Black Church in Boston* (Boston: Boston Branch of the National Association for the Advancement of Colored People, 1983). According to Omar McRoberts, Black churches in Boston in the early 1900s rarely resolved political differences internally by vote or the right of the majority but rather were prone to split over political issues as opposed to finding common ground. See Omar M. McRoberts, *Streets of Glory: Church and Community in a Black Urban Neighborhood* (Chicago: University of Chicago Press, 2003), 29–30.

6. McRoberts, *Streets of Glory*, 29–30.
7. George A. Levesque, "Inherent Reformers—Inherited Orthodoxy: Black Baptists in Boston, 1800–1873," *Journal of Negro History* 60, no. 4 (1975): 491–525.
8. George A. Levesque, *Black Boston: African American Life and Culture in Urban America, 1750–1860* (New York: Garland Publishing, 1994).
9. Hayden, *Faith, Culture, and Leadership*, 3–17.
10. Kathryn Grover and Janine V. da Silva, *Historic Resource Study Boston African American National Historic Site* (Boston: National Park Service, 2015), accessed March 28, 2019, https://npgallery.nps.gov/AssetDetail/0a7483f1-1396-4790-8ab0-f537dbb648d5; Leo W. Collins, *This Is Our Church: The Seven Societies of the First Church in Boston, 1630–2005* (Boston: Society of the First Church in Boston, 2005); Donald M. Jacobs, ed., *Courage and Conscience: Black and White Abolitionists in Boston* (Bloomington: Indiana University Press for the Boston Athenaeum, 1993).
11. McRoberts, *Streets of Glory*, 29.
12. Ibid.
13. Ibid.
14. Ibid., 32.
15. Ibid.
16. Ibid.
17. Hayden, *Faith, Culture, and Leadership*, 31.
18. McRoberts, *Streets of Glory*, 33.
19. Ibid., 17.
20. Ibid.
21. Ibid., 20.
22. Ibid.
23. Ibid., 43.
24. Tara L. Atluri, "When the Closet Is a Region: Homophobia, Heterosexism and Nationalism in the Commonwealth Caribbean," *Caribbean Review of Gender Studies*, no. 9 (March 2001): 287–326. According to Atluri, "Homophobia and heterosexism are reinforced by Caribbean nation states, based on a discriminatory nationalism that uses both religious conformity and conformity to capitalist patriarchy as a basis for inclusion." See also Violet Showers Johnson, *The Other Black Bostonians: West Indians in Boston, 1900–1950* (Bloomington: Indiana University Press, 2006).
25. Goodridge v. Department of Public Health, 798 N.E.2d 941 (Mass. 2003).
26. Ibid.

242 NOTES

27. Ibid.
28. Essdras M. Suarez, "Looking Back at the Legalization of Gay Marriage in Mass.," *Boston Globe*, June 26, 2015, https://www.bostonglobe.com/metro/2015/06/26/looking-back-legalization-gay-marriage-mass/uhCeyrSeJtWty9tSUde1PI/story.html; Frank Phillips, "Majority in Mass. Poll Oppose Gay Marriage," *Boston Globe*, February 22, 2004, http://archive.Boston.com/news/local/articles/2004/02/22/majority_in_mass_poll_oppose_gay_marriage.
29. Phillips, "Majority in Mass. Poll Oppose Gay Marriage."
30. Ibid.
31. Ibid.
32. Ibid.
33. McRoberts, *Streets of Glory*, 29–33.
34. Suarez, "Looking Back at the Legalization of Gay Marriage in Mass."
35. Nathan Cobb, "Bridge Builder Can You Help Heal a City's Violence from a Lofty Perch? Pastor Turner Thinks So," *Boston Globe*, January 23, 2005, http://archive.Boston.com/news/globe/magazine/articles/2005/01/23/bridge_builder/.
36. Ibid.
37. Yvonne Abraham, "On This Issue, Allies Are on Opposite Sides," *Boston Globe*, September 16, 2003, http://archive.Boston.com/news/local/articles/2003/09/16/on_this_issue_allies_are_on_opposite_sides/.
38. McRoberts, *Streets of Glory*, 29–33.
39. "The 10-Year Anniversary of Same-Sex Marriage in Massachusetts," *Boston Globe*, May 8, 2014, http://www.bostonglobe.com/magazine/2014/05/08/the-year-anniversary-same-sex-marriage-massachusetts/aidRTyvR72NkxgV8K6eg8J/story.html.
40. Patricia J. Thompson, *New England Conference Commission on Archives and History* (Boston: United Methodist Church, 2003); Peter P. Hinks, *To Awaken My Afflicted Brethren: David Walker and the Problem of American Slave Resistance* (University Park: Pennsylvania State University Press, 1997), 76–79.
41. Hinks, *To Awaken My Afflicted Brethren*, 76, 78–79.
42. Thomas H. O'Connor, *Civil War Boston: Home Front and Battlefield* (Boston: Northeastern University Press, 1997), 20; Hinks, *To Awaken My Afflicted Brethren*, 76, 78–79.
43. Union Church, "Our Story," accessed March 28, 2019, https://Unionboston.org/our-story/.
44. Thompson, *New England Conference Commission*.
45. Ibid.
46. Matthew J. Mimiaga et al., "Sex Parties among Urban MSM: An Emerging Culture and HIV Risk Environment," *AIDS and Behavior* 15, no. 2 (2011): 305–18. These data come from an "in-depth qualitative report of interviews with 40 men who have sex with men who attended and/or hosted private sex parties in Massachusetts 12 months prior to study enrollment. In 2009, 103 participants who reported attending at least one sex party in Massachusetts in the prior 12 months completed an in-depth, interviewer-administered quantitative assessment." S. L. Reisner et al., "Predictors of Identifying as a Barebacker among High-Risk New England HIV Seronegative Men

Who Have Sex with Men," *Journal of Urban Health: Bulletin of the New York Academy of Medicine* 86, no. 2 (2009): 250–62, https://doi.org/10.1007/s11524-008-9333-4; and M. J. Mimiaga et al., "Sexual Mixing Patterns and Partner Characteristics of Black MSM in Massachusetts at Increased Risk for HIV Infection and Transmission," *Journal of Urban Health: Bulletin of the New York Academy of Medicine* 86, no. 4 (2009): 602–23, https://doi.org/10.1007/s11524-009-9363-6.

47. Lauren Prescott, *Boston's South End* (Charleston, SC: Arcadia Publishing, 2018); Anthony M. Sammarco and James Z. Kyprianos, *Boston's South End* (Charleston, SC: Arcadia Publishing, 2005); Lynne Potts, *A Block in Time: A History of Boston's South End from a Window on Holyoke Street* (New York: Local History Publishers, 2012).
48. Boston, Parks, and Recreation Commission, Open Space and Recreation Plan, February 7, 2015, 347, https://www.cityofboston.gov/images_documents/Section-7.2.15_tcm3-53005.pdf.
49. Ibid.
50. Prescott, *Boston's South End*.
51. When railroad companies could no longer find lenders and had more bonds on hand than they could sell, this led to the financial crisis known as the Panic of 1873.
52. Bostonian Society and Philip Bergen, *Old Boston in Early Photographs, 1850–1918: 174 Prints from the Collection of the Bostonian Society* (New York: Dover Publications, 1990), 87.
53. Jon Chesto, "Concord Baptist Church Settles in at New Milton Home," *Patriot Ledger*, October 28, 2011, http://www.patriotledger.com/article/20111028/NEWS/310289187.
54. Union Church, "Our Story."
55. O'Connor, *Civil War Boston*, 20; Hinks, *To Awaken My Afflicted Brethren*, 76, 78–79.
56. Senior Pastor (removed), church #101, interview, February 23, 2018. (All interviews conducted by author unless otherwise indicated.)
57. Stephanie Y. Mitchem and Emilie M. Townes, *Faith, Health, and Healing in African American Life* (Westport, CT: Praeger, 2008), 140.
58. Member #374 of church #101, interview, August 17, 2017.
59. Member #237 of church #101, interview, 2016.
60. Senior Pastor Emeritus of church #101, interview, September 2018.
61. Ted Roberts, *A Confession and Historical Note on Union's Decision to Be a Welcoming Church*, September 12, 2018.
62. Ruby of church about Hilda because Hilda is deceased #101, interview, March 23, 2017.
63. Ruby of church #101, interview, March 23, 2017.
64. Roberts, *Confession and Historical Note*.
65. Ibid.
66. Cynthia of church #101, interview, August 23, 2018.
67. See chapter 1 for a recap on biblical literalism in Black churches.
68. Dorothy Williams, *The Church Studies Homosexuality: A Study for United Methodist Groups Using the Report of the Committee to Study Homosexuality* (Nashville: Cokesbury, 1994).

69. The Reconciling Congregation Program, now known as the Reconciling Ministries Network, was founded in 1983 as an affiliation of and support system for United Methodist congregations championing for lesbian/gay concerns and rights within the national church.
70. Williams, *The Church Studies Homosexuality*, 14. Lockhart interview, September 2018.
71. Lockhart interview, September 2018.
72. Williams, *The Church Studies Homosexuality*, 14.
73. Ibid., 15.
74. W. Stephen Gunter, *Wesley and the Quadrilateral: Renewing the Conversation* (Nashville: Abingdon Press, 1997).

    John Wesley and Albert Cook Outler, *A Library of Protestant Thought* (New York: Oxford University Press, 1964).
75. Williams, *The Church Studies Homosexuality*, 19.
76. Ibid.
77. Steven T. Kimbrough, ed., *Orthodox and Wesleyan Ecclesiology* (Crestwood, NY: St. Vladimir's Seminary Press, 2007), 149; *The Book of Discipline of the United Methodist Church* (Nashville: United Methodist Publishing House, 1968); *The United Methodist Book of Worship* (Nashville: United Methodist Publishing House).
78. "Understandings of Ecclesiology in United Methodism," in Kimbrough, *Orthodox and Wesleyan Ecclesiology*, 149. See also Russell E. Richey, Dennis M. Campbell, and William B. Lawrence, *Marks of Methodism: Practices of Ecclesiology*, vol. 5. United Methodism and American Culture (Nashville: Abingdon Press, 2005); Russell E. Richey, Kenneth E. Rowe, and Jean M. Schmidt, *The Methodist Experience in America: A Sourcebook*, vol. 2 (Nashville: Abingdon Press, 2000), 1784a, 72; Scott J. Jones, *United Methodist Doctrine: The Extreme Center* (Nashville: Abingdon Press, 2002); Walter Klaiber and Manfred Marquardt, *Living Grace: An Outline of United Methodist Theology*, trans. J. Steven O'Malley and Ulrike R. M. Guthrie (Nashville: Abingdon Press, 2001), 17–92; Scott J. Jones, *John Wesley's Conception and Use of Scripture* (Nashville: Kingswood Books / Abingdon, 1995); Gunter et al., *Wesley and the Quadrilateral*; Thomas A. Langford, ed., *Doctrine and Theology in the United Methodist Church* (Nashville: Kingswood Books / Abingdon, 1991), 154–61, 75–88.
79. Present senior pastor of church #101, interview, February 16, 2017.
80. Patrick Cheng, *Radical Love: An Introduction to Queer Theology* (New York: Seabury Books, 2011).
81. See Phyllis Bird, "The Bible in Christian Ethical Deliberation Concerning Homosexuality: Old Testament Contributions," in *Homosexuality, Science and the "Plain Sense" of Scripture*, ed. David Balch (Grand Rapids: Eerdmans, 2000), 142–76; Michael Carden, "Homophobia and Rape in Sodom and Gibeah: A Response to Ken Stone," *Journal for the Study of the Old Testament* 82 (1999): 83–96; William Countryman, *Dirt, Greed, and Sex: Sexual Ethics in the New Testament and Their Implications for Today* (Philadelphia: Fortress Press, 1988); James De Young, *Homosexuality: Contemporary Claims Examined in Light of the Bible and Other Ancient Literature and Law* (Grand Rapids: Kregel, 2000); Hans Debel, "An Admonition on Sexual Affairs: A Reconsideration of Rom 1:26–27," *Louvain Studies*

34 (2009): 39–64; John Elliott, "No Kingdom of God for Softies? Or What Was Paul Really Saying? Corinthians 6:9–10 in Context," *Biblical Theology Bulletin* 34 (2004): 17–40; Brad Embry, "The 'Naked Narrative' from Noah to Leviticus: Reassessing Voyeurism in the Account of Noah's Nakedness in Genesis 9:22–24," *Journal for the Study of the Old Testament* 35 (2011): 417–33.

82. Mitchem and Townes, *Faith, Health, and Healing*, 179; Anthony Stanford, *Homophobia in the Black Church: How Faith, Politics, and Fear Divide the Black Community* (Santa Barbara, CA: Praeger, 2013), 157; Kelly B. Douglas, *Black Bodies and the Black Church: A Blues Slant* (New York: Palgrave Macmillan, 2012); Suzanne McLaren, "The Interrelations between Internalized Homophobia, Depressive Symptoms, and Suicidal Ideation among Australian Gay Men, Lesbians, and Bisexual Women," *Journal of Homosexuality* 63 (2016): 156–68; R. Haile et al., "An Empirical Test of Racial/Ethnic Differences in Perceived Racism and Affiliation with the Gay Community: Implications for HIV Risk," *Journal of Social Issues* 70 (2014): 342–59; M. L. Hatzenbuehler et al., "The Impact of Institutional Discrimination on Psychiatric Disorders in Lesbian, Gay, and Bisexual Populations: A Prospective Study," *American Journal of Public Health* 100 (2010): 452–59; Olivier Ferlatte et al., "Suicide Attempts across Multiple Social Identities among Gay and Bisexual Men: An Intersectionality Analysis," *Journal of Homosexuality* 65, no. 11 (September 2017): 1507–26; Ilan H. Meyer, "Minority Stress and Mental Health in Gay Men," *Journal of Health and Social Behavior* 36 (1995): 38–56; D. Frost, J. T. Parsons, and J. E. Nanin, "Stigma, Concealment and Symptoms of Depression as Explanations for Sexually Transmitted Infections among Gay Men," *Journal of Health Psychology* 12 (2007): 636–40; Anne P. Haas et al., "Suicide and Suicide Risk in Lesbian, Gay, Bisexual, and Transgender Populations: Review and Recommendations," *Journal of Homosexuality* 58 (2011): 10–51; Ilan H. Meyer, "Prejudice, Social Stress, and Mental Health in Lesbian, Gay, and Bisexual Populations: Conceptual Issues and Research Evidence," *Psychological Bulletin* 129 (2003): 674–97.
83. Williams, *The Church Studies Homosexuality*, 20.
84. Ibid., 22.
85. Ibid., 26.
86. Ibid., 28.
87. Ibid.
88. Ibid., 31–37.
89. Ibid., 41–42.
90. Ibid., 48–52.
91. Ibid., 53.
92. Ibid., 54.
93. Ibid., 35.
94. Committee on Lesbian and Gay Concerns, "Avoiding Heterosexual Bias in Language," *American Psychologist* 46, no. 9 (1991): 973–74.
95. Jeremy W. Peters, "The Decline and Fall of the 'H' Word," *New York Times*, March 23, 2014, https://www.nytimes.com/2014/03/23/fashion/gays-lesbians-the-term-homosexual.html.
96. Williams, *The Church Studies Homosexuality*, 35.

97. Ibid., 40.
98. Ibid., 53.
99. The above discussion rules were used by the Union United Methodist task force, but they were adapted from ibid., 5. Lockhart interview, September 2018.
100. Member #746 of church #101, interview, August 23, 2018.
101. Anne Maclean, "Right and Good: False Dichotomy?," *Philosophy* 60, no. 231 (1985): 129–32.
102. This statement simply seeks to delineate between Black UMC churches like Union and the various strains of Black American Methodism—namely the African Methodist Episcopal, Christian (Colored) Methodist Episcopal, or African Methodist Episcopal Zion traditions.
103. Senior Pastor Emeritus of church #101, interview, July 2018. The number is not quantifiable due to the nature of African American homophobia at the time. Many could have very well been out in the gay community and in their professional lives but more discreet in Black religious spaces.
104. It is also important to note that the plurality of the many dynamics of Queer life are detrimental to the success of Black ecclesial queering. Essentially, there is no such thing as a homogeneous Queer univocality.
105. The PrideLights Foundation is a collaborative organization that works to eliminate homophobia and to bring straight and gay communities together.
106. Member #844 of church #101, interview, August 23, 2018.
107. Theodore Roberts, "Remembrances from a Former Itinerant Elder Stationed at Union United Methodist Church" (paper presented at the New England Annual Conference of the United Methodist Church, January 28, 2002).
108. Ibid.
109. Member #844 of church #101, interview, August 23, 2018.
110. Member #745 of church #101, interview, August 23, 2018.
111. Member #746 of church #101, interview, August 23, 2018.
112. Union Church, accessed March 29, 2019, https://Unionboston.org.
113. Present senior pastor of church #101, interview, February 16, 2017.
114. United Methodist Church, *The Book of Discipline of the United Methodist Church* (Nashville: United Methodist Publishing House, 2000), 87.
115. Present senior pastor of church #101, interview, February 16, 2017.
116. Ibid.
117. Ibid.
118. United Methodist Church, *Book of Discipline*, 701.
119. Senior Pastor Emeritus of church #101, interviews, July–October 2018; senior pastor (removed) of church #101, interviews, July 2017–January 2018; Reverend Lockhart, Ruby, June, and Cynthia, interviews, January 2018.

Chapter 4

1. Karen Yeary, "Religious Authority in African American Churches: A Study of Six Churches," *Religions* 2, no. 4 (2011): 628–48.

2. Peter Paris, *Virtues and Values: The African and African American Experience* (Minneapolis: Fortress Press, 2004), 67.
3. Ibid.
4. Ibid.
5. To honor the wishes of the current pastor and members of this church, the name of the church, its location, and any names used have been fictionalized. The listed ministries of the church have not been fictionalized.
6. Lisa Krissoff Boehm, *Making a Way out of No Way: African American Women and the Second Great Migration* (Jackson: University Press of Mississippi, 2009).
7. It is also important to note that Trenton has a large Caribbean and immigrant population that is not addressed or included in this particular project. US Census Bureau, American Community Survey 1-year estimates are as follows, "The population of Trenton is 39.6% White, 39.5% Black, and 10.1% Hispanic. 40.2% of the people in Trenton speak a non-English language, and 88.5% are U.S. citizens."
8. Laurie Maffly-Kipp, "African American Religion, Pt. II: From the Civil War to the Great Migration," National Humanities Center, accessed March 29, 2019, http://natio nalhumanitiescenter.org/tserve/nineteen/nkeyinfo/aarcwgm.htm.
9. C. Sernett Milton, "Bound for the Promised Land: African American Religion and the Great Migration," *Journal of the American Academy of Religion* 67, no. 3 (September 1999): 709–11.
10. E. Franklin Frazier and C. Eric Lincoln, *The Negro Church in America*, Sourcebooks in Negro History (New York: Schocken Books, 1974), 101–10.
11. "Class Interview Project on the Great Migration in Advanced Newswriting and Reporting" (Details of students' names and institution removed for purposes of maintaining anonymity), accessed March 29, 2019, http://Trentonsgreatmigration. blogspot.com/p/historical-6.html.
12. Senior Pastor Emeritus of church #202, interviews, June 1–August 24, 2016.
13. Members #937, #589, #837, and #563 of church #202, interview, Church Leadership restaurant dinner, May 2016.
14. Ibid.
15. Ibid.
16. Senior Pastor Emeritus of church #202, interview, August 10, 17, and 24, 2016; members #1284, #2374, #3274 of church #202, interviews, August 2016 and June 12, 2018.
17. Gerard Loughlin, ed., *Queer Theology: Rethinking the Western Body* (Malden, MA: Blackwell, 2007), 31; see also Robert E. Goss, *Queering Christ: Beyond Jesus Acted Up* (Cleveland: Pilgrim, 2002); Robert E. Goss and M. West, eds., *Take Back the Word: A Queer Reading of the Bible* (Cleveland: Pilgrim Press, 2000); D. Boyarin, D. Itzkovits, and A. Pellegrini, eds., *Queer Theory and the Jewish Question* (New York: Columbia University Press, 2003); Marcella Althaus-Reid, *Indecent Theology: Theological Perversions in Sex, Gender and Politics* (Abingdon, UK: Routledge, 2000); M. Althaus-Reid, *The Queer God* (New York: Routledge, 2003).
18. Loughlin, *Queer Theology*, 31.

248 NOTES

19. Senior Pastor Emeritus of church #202, interviews, August 10, 17, and 24, 2016; Ecclesiastes 10:19: "Feasts are made for laughter; wine gladdens life, and money meets every need."
20. Senior Pastor Emeritus of church #202, interview, August 24, 2016.
21. See John Roach, "Friday the 13th Phobia Rooted in Ancient History," *National Geographic News*, August 12, 2004, http://www.freerepublic.com/focus/f-news/1718807/posts; Kevin R. Foster and Hanna Kokko, "The Evolution of Superstitious and Superstition-Like Behavior," *Proceedings of the Royal Society B* 276 (2009): 31–37; Brian M. Lucey, "Friday the 13th: International Evidence," *Applied Economics Letters* 8, no. 9 (2001): 577–79; David A. Hirshleifer, Ming Jian, and Huai Zhang, "Superstition and Financial Decision Making," *Management Science* 64 (2018): 235–52; B. M. Lo et al., "Answering the Myth: Use of Emergency Services on Friday the 13th," *American Journal of Emergency Medicine* 30, no. 6 (July 2012): 886–89; T. Kramer and L. Block, "Conscious and Nonconscious Components of Superstitious Beliefs in Judgment and Decision Making," *Journal of Consumer Research* 34, no. 6 (2008): 783–93.
22. Member #2374 of church #202, interview, August 2016.
23. Member #1284 of church #202, interview, August 2016; member #2374 of church #202, interview, August 2016; member #5937 of church #202, interview, May 17, 2017; member #6589 of church #202, interview, May 17, 2017; member #3274, interview, June 12, 2018; interview #061217-102 with Sister Sally Madden, June 12, 2018, member; interview #060618-102 with Deacon George Moore, March 27, 2017; interview #061617-102 with Trustee Chair, March 3, 2017; interview #031718-102 with Rachel Adams, March 10, 2017, director of Christian Education; interview #041018-102 with Deacon Cynthia Moore, March 12, 2017; interview #061217-102 March 2, 2017. (Names omitted because they pulled out of the process after the third interview. They have a gay son who was the first gay male to be married by a pastor who was a church official. Everyone was shocked that they withdrew their names. However, they did give permission for the notes from the group interview to be included in this research.)
24. Associate pastor, interview, May 17, 2017.
25. Member #6589, interview, May 17, 2017.
26. Newly elected senior pastor of church #202, interview, December 13, 2017.
27. Senior Pastor Emeritus of church #202, interview, August 24, 2016.
28. Reverend Franklin hand-selected his successor and presented him to the church for them to accept. This is yet another example of his autonomous authority.
29. Quote from church website.
30. There are several ways of interpreting this phrase. I am choosing to define "historical revisionism" after the manner of Dennis A. Gioia, Kevin G. Corley, and Tommaso Fabbri, "Revising the Past (While Thinking in the Future Perfect Tense)," *Journal of Organizational Change Management* 15, no. 6 (2002): 622–34. In the article, they define "revisionist history" as a method that enlarges the discussion about the role that history plays in the identity of an organization. Subtle revisions to history allow for the maintenance of a valued sense of continuity with the past, while still preparing the organization for a different future. It is a type of leadership model in which the future informs the past as opposed to vice versa. However, this type of historical change also tampers with the foundations of an organization's identity. It is a reinterpretation of

history that benefits a particular corporate or organizational aim that has been put in place by a new board or a leader seeking to alter the trajectory of the company. See also H. Schuman, B. Schwartz, and H. D'Arcy, "Elite Revisionists and Popular Beliefs: Christopher Columbus, Hero or Villain?," *Public Opinion Quarterly* 69, no. 1 (January 2005): 2–29.

31. My usage of the phrase "actual history" in this sentence references the fact that I located the original history of the church in documents like church anniversary programs from the 1970s, church records at the local library, and documents and records from members.
32. Member #1284 of church #202, interview, 2016; member #2374 of church #202, interview, 2016.
33. Member #231 of church #202, interview, May 2018.
34. Bible study for January 18, 2018. See the Appendix for Bible study handouts that the pastor was going to use. Prior to the Bible study, I had the chance over dinner to discuss how the new pastor understood his parish.
35. Former pastor #3274, interview, May 11, 2018.
36. Member #3274, interview, June 12, 2018.
37. Ibid.
38. Letty M. Russell, *Church in the Round: Feminist Interpretation of the Church* (Louisville, KY: Westminster/John Knox Press, 1993).
39. Senior Pastor Emeritus of church #202, interview, August 17, 2016.
40. Ibid.
41. Present senior pastor of church #202, interview, March 19, 2018.
42. Ibid.
43. It should be noted that many of these congregations were not pastorally queered in the sense of Mount Nebo. By this I mean that often the pastors were affirming while not pressing the matter congregationally. These pastors queered their pastorates, not their churches. Nevertheless, I include them in these numbers because of the compatible element of the pastor in both equations.
44. Preston King, Fisk University graduate, chair of the Political Philosophy Research Committee of the International Political Science Association (IPSA), and founder/coeditor of the *Critical Review of International Social and Political Philosophy* (CRISPP).
45. Preston King, "The Problem of Tolerance," *Government and Opposition* 6, no. 2 (1971): 172–207.
46. Member #3274 of church #202, interview, June 12, 2018; *Brandon*: "Do you remember any backlash?" *Member*: "Yes, we actually had this couple that actually left the church because he used to mention the words a lot: LGBT, and, you know, everybody had the same rights. He actually married a gay couple one time and they definitely left after that."
47. Nancy T. Ammerman, *Studying Congregations: A New Handbook* (Nashville: Abingdon Press, 2006). Ammerman argues that congregations have cultures and that the culture of a congregation is essentially its identity. The collective's activity, habits, rituals, symbols, stories, experiences, artifacts, history, and beliefs constitute the congregation's culture.

48. Robert Bellah, "Civil Religion in America," *Daedalus* 96, no. 1 (January 1967): 40–55. Bellah argues that American "civil religion is a transcendent religious reality as seen in or, one could almost say, as revealed through the experience of the American people" (49). For Bellah, American civil religion is "a genuine vehicle of national religious self-understanding" (46); Robert E. Stauffer, "Bellah's Civil Religion," *Journal for the Scientific Study of Religion* 14, no. 4 (1975): 390–95, https://doi.org/10.2307/1384412. The present volume is essentially saying that Black civil religion is a queered version of what Bellah calls "civil religion." Likewise, for the African American community (or Black community or Black America), a Black civil religion serves as a vehicle for African American self-understanding and identity. Black civil religion is rooted in religiously framed and intentionally theologized experiences of African American people. This religious and spiritual purview is one of the significant pillars of Black identity because Black civil religion was, for many years, the central sustaining force behind the survival and construction of Black identity. Throughout slavery, segregation, Jim Crow laws, racism, and oppression, Black civil religion's relevance and power were not limited but rather most widely present in Black churches. However, Black churches were only one of the many physical manifestations of Black civil religion. Black churches were the spaces that taught, created, shaped, reformed, theologized, and interpreted Black civil religion. For many years, Black churches were the shrines of Black civil religion in that they were spaces of liberation for battered othered bodies.
49. Eric Woodrum and Arnold Bell, "Race, Politics, and Religion in Civil Religion among Blacks," *Sociological Analysis* 49, no. 4 (Winter 1989): 353–67; and see Frazier and Lincoln, *The Negro Church in America*, 101–10.
50. Peter J. Paris, *The Social Teaching of the Black Churches* (Philadelphia: Fortress Press, 1985), 11.

Chapter 5

1. AME pastor, church leader #107, interview, June 15, 2018.
2. Evana D. Upshaw, AME Church Maintains Same-Sex Marriage Stance But Wants to Hear Black LGBTQ Christians' Testimonies, Faithfully Magazine, July 12, 2021. Date accessed: October 2021. https://faithfullymagazine.com/ame-church-marriage-lgbtq-christians/
3. Brandon Crowley, "The Demonization of Honesty: How the Black Church Subconsciously Deifies the Closet" (MDiv thesis, Harvard Divinity School, 2011), 30.
4. Gary David Comstock, *A Whosoever Church: Welcoming Lesbians and Gay Men into African American Congregations* (Louisville, KY: Westminster John Knox Press, 2001), 34–46.
5. Ibid.
6. Horace L. Griffin, *Their Own Receive Them Not: African American Lesbians and Gays in Black Churches* (Cleveland, OH: Pilgrim Press, 2006), 20.
7. Comstock, *Whosoever Church*, 36.
8. Ibid.

9. Ibid.
10. Ibid.
11. Roger A. Sneed, *Representations of Homosexuality: Black Liberation Theology and Cultural Criticism* (New York: Palgrave Macmillan, 2010), 48.
12. Jeremiah A. Wright Jr., *Good News! Sermons of Hope for Today's Families* (Valley Forge, PA: Judson Press, 1995).
13. Comstock, *Whosoever Church*, 9–21.
14. Ibid.
15. Ibid.
16. Ibid., 75–85.
17. Ibid.
18. Cassandra Chaney and Le'Brian Patrick, "The Invisibility of LGBT Individuals in Black Mega Churches: Political and Social Implications," *Journal of African American Studies* 15, no. 2 (2012): 199–217; R. N. Pitt, "Killing the Messenger: Religious Black Gay Men's Neutralization of Anti-Gay Religious Messages," *Journal for the Scientific Study of Religion* 49, no. 1 (2010): 56–72.
19. J. L. Woodyard, J. L. Peterson, and J. P. Stokes, "'Let Us Go into the House of the Lord': Participation in African American Churches among Young African American Men Who Have Sex with Men," *Journal of Pastoral Care* 54 (2000): 451–60.
20. Ibid.
21. "Don't ask, don't tell" church parishioner #273, interview, October 12, 2018.
22. Peter J. Paris, *The Social Teaching of the Black Churches* (Philadelphia: Fortress Press, 1985), 11.
23. Patrick Cheng, *Radical Love: An Introduction to Queer Theology* (New York: Seabury Books, 2011), 13n25. See Cheng's 25th footnote for an overview of the biblical texts the Christian church has traditionally used to terrorize LGBTQIAP+ persons.
24. Linn Marie Tonstad, *Queer Theology: Beyond Apologetics* (Eugene, OR: Cascade Books, 2018).
25. Mark D. Jordan, "In Review: Waiting for Queer Theology", *Harvard Divinity Bulletin,* Autumn/Winter 2020, https://bulletin.hds.harvard.edu/waiting-for-queer-theology/.
26. Scripture is written and socially spoken within congregations with a particular type of language that can often manifest itself using complex metrical structures.
27. Joan M. Martin, "The Notion of Difference for Emerging Womanist Ethics," *Journal of Feminist Studies in Religion* 9, no. 1–2 (1993): 39; Jacquelyn Grant, *White Women's Christ and Black Women's Jesus: Feminist Christology and Womanist Response* (Atlanta: Scholars Press, 1989); Jacquelyn Grant, "Black Theology and the Black Women," in *Black Theology: A Documentary History,* Vol. 1: *1996–1979,* ed. James H. Cone and Gayraud S. Wilmore (Maryknoll, NY: Orbis Books, 1993), 326.
28. Frank Furedi, "Fake Holocaust Memoirs: History as Therapy," July 7, 2009, fronkfuredi.com; "An Emotional Striptease." *The Spiked Review of Books*, 17 May 2007. Web. 08 June 2009; Miller, Alyson. "The Pornography of Trauma: Faking Identity in 'Misery Memoirs'. [Paper in Special Issue: Life Writing...Performing Lives. Graham, Pamela and Hocking, Melanie (Eds).]." LiNQ 39, no. Dec 2012 (2012): 90–103.

29. Austin Hartke, *Transforming: The Bible and the Lives of Transgender Christians* (Louisville: Westminster John Knox Press, 2018).
30. *Building an Inclusive Church: A Welcoming Toolkit 3.0* by Reconciling Works, 2021, accessed June 24, 2019, p. 21 https://www.reconcilingworks.org/trainings/bic/. This toolkit explains the concept of core teams in more detail. Several of the churches I studied used this resource. The language from this document showed up regularly in the data.
31. Ibid., 23.
32. Ibid., 28.
33. Ibid., 27.
34. Ibid., 21.
35. E. Gilbert Patterson, "Marriage: A Proclamation to the Church of God in Christ Worldwide," October 12, 2004, www.cogic.org/marriageproclamation.htm, 20, accessed June 4, 2006.
36. Human Rights Campaign, "Stances of Faiths on LGBTQ Issues: The African Methodist Episcopal Church," https://www.hrc.org/resources/stances-of-faiths-on-lgbt-issues-african-methodist-episcopal-church.
37. S. Donald Fortson and Rollin G. Grams, *Unchanging Witness: The Consistent Christian Teaching on Homosexuality in Scripture and Tradition* (Nashville: B&H Publishing Group, 2016).
38. Human Rights Campaign, "Stances of Faiths."
39. Christian Methodist Episcopal Church, *The Doctrines and Discipline of the Christian Methodist Episcopal Church* (Memphis, TN: General Board of Publication Services, CME Church, 2010), 38.
40. C. James Clements, "Church Conflict in the Atlanta-Rome District: Developing a Systematic Approach to Conflict and Membership Attrition" (MA thesis, Liberty University, 2018), 20; Committee on Compilation, *The Book of Discipline of the Christian Methodist Church* (Memphis, TN: CME Publishing, 2014); Norman Geisler and Frank Turek, *Legislating Morality* (Eugene, OR: Wipf and Stock, 1998); Roderick Lewis, *The Book of Discipline of the Christian Methodist Episcopal Church* (Memphis, TN: CME Publishing, 2014).
41. College of Bishops from the Christian Methodist Episcopal Church Statement on Supreme Court marriage decision, July 15, 2015.
42. Dennis Vernon Proctor and William Darin Moore, "Quadrennial Episcopal Address to the Fiftieth Session of the General Conference of the African Methodist Episcopal Zion Church," 2016, http://connectionallaycouncil.org/wp-content/uploads/2017/03/Quadrennial-Address-2016.pdf, 28.
43. Cheng, *Radical Love*, 124.
44. Emily Lenning, Sara Brightman, and Carrie L. Buist, "The Trifecta of Violence: A Socio-Historical Comparison of Lynching and Violence against Transgender Women," *Critical Criminology* (Richmond, BC) 29, no. 1 (2020): 151–72.
45. Hartke, *Transforming*.
46. Beloved Arise, accessed March 10, 2021 https://www.belovedarise.org/youthpastors.
47. The Trevor Project, "National Survey on LGBTQ Youth Mental Health 2021," accessed April 5, 2023, https://www.thetrevorproject.org/survey-2021/?section=Introduction.

48. Pamela R. Lightsey, *Our Lives Matter: A Womanist Queer Theology* (Eugene, OR: Pickwick Publications, 2015), 33.
49. Trevor Project, "National Survey on LGBTQ Youth Mental Health 2021."
50. Not all nonbinary people, for example, appear or desire to appear androgynous.

Conclusion

1. Horace L. Griffin, *Their Own Receive Them Not: African American Lesbians and Gays in Black Churches* (Cleveland, OH: Pilgrim Press, 2006), 54, 186, 206, 212.
2. Kevin Mumford, *Not Straight, Not White: Black Gay Men from the March on Washington to the AIDS Crisis* (Chapel Hill: University of North Carolina Press, 2016), 100–102, 105–23.
3. Moultrie Monique Nicole. 2023. Hidden Histories: Faith and Black Lesbian Leadership. Durham: Duke University Press, p. 136; Dolinsky Rebecca C. 2010. "Lesbian and Gay Dc: Identity Emotion and Experience in Washington Dc's Social and Activist Communities (1961-1986)." Dissertation University of California Santa Cruz. University of California Santa Cruz. p. 239).
4. James Tinney, "Why a Gay Church?," in *In the Life*, ed. Joseph Beam (Boston: Alyson Publications, 1986), 73–78.
5. Ibid.
6. Ellen Lewin, *Filled with the Spirit: Sexuality, Gender, and Radical Inclusivity in a Black Pentecostal Church Coalition* (Chicago: University of Chicago Press, 2018), 147.
7. Ibid.
8. Ibid.
9. Stanley Hauerwas, "A Story-Formed Community: Reflections on Watership Down (1981)," in Hauerwas, *The Hauerwas Reader*, ed. John Berkman and Michael G. Cartwright (Durham, NC: Duke University Press, 2001), 171–99; Hauerwas, *Hauerwas Reader*, 172–73.
10. Michael Lipka, "Millennials Increasingly Are Driving Growth of 'Nones,'" Pew Research Center, May 12, 2015, https://www.pewresearch.org/fact-tank/2015/05/12/millennials-increasingly-are-driving-growth-of-nones/; Michael Dimock, "Defining Generations: Where Millennials End and Generation Z Begins," Pew Research Center, January 17, 2019, https://www.pewresearch.org/fact-tank/2019/01/17/where-millennials-end-and-generation-z-begins/; Justin McCarthy, "U.S. Confidence in Organized Religion Remains Low," Gallup, July 8, 2019, https://news.gallup.com/poll/259964/confidence-organized-religion-remains-low.aspx; and Daniel A. Cox, "Emerging Trends and Enduring Patterns in American Family Life," AEI Survey Center on American Life, February 9, 2022.
11. Deborah Anapol, "When Is Sex a Spiritual Practice?," 2019, https://www.scienceandnonduality.com/article/when-is-sex-a-spiritual-practice; Audre Lorde, *Uses of the Erotic: The Erotic as Power* (Tucson, AZ: Kore Press, 2000); D. N. Hopkins, "The Construction of the Black Male Body: Eroticism and Religion," in *Loving the*

Body: Black Religion / Womanist Thought / Social Justice, ed. A. B. Pinn and D. N. Hopkins (New York: Palgrave Macmillan, 2004).

12. Michael Eric Dyson, "When You Divide Body and Soul, Problems Multiply: The Black Church and Sex," in *TRAPS: African American Men on Gender and Sexuality*, ed. Rudolph P. Byrd and Beverly Guy-Sheftall (Bloomington: Indiana University Press, 2001), 316–17; Miriam DeCosta-Willis, "Introduction," in *Erotique Norie: Black Erotica*, ed. Miriam DeCosta-Willis, Reginald Martin, and Roseann P. Bell (New York: Anchor Books, 1992), xxix.

13. Kelly Brown Douglas, *Sexuality and the Black Church: A Womanist Perspective* (Maryknoll, NY: Orbis Books, 1999), 123.

14. Hazel Glen Beh and Milton Diamond, "The Failure of Abstinence-Only Education: Minors Have a Right to Honest Talk about Sex," *Columbia Journal of Gender and Law* 15, no. 1 (2006): 12–62; Alice M. Miller and Rebecca A. Schleifer, "Through a Glass Darkly or through the Looking Glass? Abstinence-Only until Marriage Programs and Their Impact on Adolescent Human Rights," *Sexuality Research and Social Policy*, Journal of NSRC 5, no. 3 (2007):, 28–43; Hannah Brückner and Peter Bearman, "After the Promise: The STD Consequences of Adolescent Virginity Pledges," *Journal of Adolescent Health* 36 (2005): 271–78; S. I. McClelland and M. Fine, "Embedded Science: A Critical Analysis of Abstinence-Only Evaluation Research," *Cultural Studies, Critical Methodologies* 8, no. 2 (2008), 50–81:) Peter C. Van Dyck, MD, MPH, acting associate administrator for maternal and child health, Health Resources and Services Administration, US Department of Health and Human Services, Statement before Hearing on Abstinence Education before the Subcommittee on Oversight and Investigations of the House Committee on Commerce, 105th Congress (1998), https://www.govinfo.gov/content/pkg/CHRG-109shrg29758/pdf/CHRG-109shrg29758.pdf; Rebecca A. Maynard et al., "Mathematic Policy Research, First-Year Impacts of Four Title V, Section 510 Abstinence Education Programs" (2005), http://aspe.hhs.gov/hsp/05/abstinence/report.pdf.

15. Hameed S. Williams, *Herukhuti. Conjuring Black Funk: Notes on Culture, Sexuality, and Spirituality* (New York: Vintage Entity Press, 2007); Jonathan Mathias Lassiter, Russell Brewer, and Leo Wilton, "Toward a Culturally Specific Spirituality for Black Sexual Minority Men," *Journal of Black Psychology* 46, no. 6–7 (September 2020): 482–513; S. Maat, "Toward an African-Centered Sociological Approach to Africana Lesbian, Gay, Bisexual, Transgender, Queer, and Intersexed Identities and Performances: The Kemetic Model of the Cosmological Interactive Self," *Critical Sociology* 40, no. 2 (2014): 239–56; Donna Aza Weir-Soley, *Eroticism, Spirituality, and Resistance in Black Women's Writings* (Gainesville: University Press of Florida, 2017)..

16. Audre Lorde, "The Master's Tools Will Never Dismantle the Master's House" (1984), in Lorde, *Sister Outsider: Essays and Speeches* (Berkeley, CA: Crossing Press, 2007), 112.

17. W. E. B. Du Bois, *The Souls of Black Folk* (1903; repr. New York: Vintage Books, 1990), 50–59, 138.

18. bell hooks and Cornel West, *Breaking Bread: Insurgent Black Intellectual Life* (Toronto: Between the Lines, 1991), 35.

19. Lorde, "The Master's Tools Will Never Dismantle the Master's House."
20. Lorde, *Uses of the Erotic*, 89.
21. Ibid.
22. Ibid. "The erotic functions for me in several ways, and the first is in providing the power which comes from sharing deeply any pursuit with another person. The sharing of joy, whether physical, emotional, psychic, or intellectual, forms a bridge between the sharers which can be the basis for understanding much of what is not shared between them, and lessens the threat of their difference."
23. Ibid., 87.
24. Ibid., 89.
25. Pamela R. Lightsey, *Our Lives Matter: A Womanist Queer Theology* (Eugene, OR: Pickwick Publications, 2015), 22.
26. Ibid.
27. Ibid., 50.
28. Lorde, *Sister Outsider* (New York: Penguin Publishing Group, 2020), 49 (excerpt from an essay introduction to a paper presented at the Fourth Berkshire Conference on the History of Women, Mount Holyoke College, August 25, 1978); Nikki Young, "'Uses of the Erotic' for Teaching Queer Studies," *WSQ: Women's Studies Quarterly* 40, no. 3 (2013): 301–5.
29. Marlon M. Bailey, *Butch Queens up in Pumps: Gender, Performance, and Ballroom Culture in Detroit* (Ann Arbor: University of Michigan Press, 2013); Marlon M. Bailey, "Black Gay (Raw) Sex," in *No Tea, No Shade: New Writings in Black Queer Studies*, ed. E. Patrick Johnson (Durham, NC: Duke University Press, 2016), 239–61; Lisa Bowleg, "'Once You've Blended the Cake, You Can't Take the Parts Back to the Main Ingredients': Black Gay and Bisexual Men's Descriptions and Experiences of Intersectionality," *Sex Roles* 68 (2013): 754–67; Cathy J. Cohen, "Punks, Bulldaggers, and Welfare Queens: The Radical Potential of Queer Politics?," *GLQ: A Journal of Gay and Lesbian Studies* 3, no. 4 (1997): 437–65; Cathy J. Cohen, "Deviance as Resistance: A New Research Agenda for the Study of Black Politics," *Du Bois Review* 1, no. 1 (2004): 27–45; Brandon Andrew Robinson, "The Queer Potentiality of Barebacking: Charging, Whoring, and Breeding as Utopian Practices," in *A Critical Inquiry into Queer Utopias*, ed. Angela Jones (New York: Palgrave Macmillan, 2013), 101–28.
30. David Holmes, Patrick O'Byrne, and Denise Gastaldo, "Raw Sex as Limit Experience: A Foucauldian Analysis of Unsafe Anal Sex between Men," *Social Theory & Health* 4 (2006): 319–33.
31. Ibid.
32. Anthony P. Natale, "Sex and Culture: A Mixed Methods Study of Denver MSM (Men Who Have Sex with Men) in the Third Decade of AIDS" (Ph.D. diss., University of Denver, 2005).
33. Marlon M. Bailey, "Black Gay Sex, Homosex-Normativity, and Cathy Cohen's Queer of Color Theory of Cultural Politics," *GLQ: A Journal of Lesbian and Gay Studies* 25, no. 1 (2019): 162–68.
34. Holmes, O'Byrne, and Gastaldo, "Raw Sex as Limit Experience," 320.

35. Ibid., 321.
36. Eddie S. Glaude Jr., "The Black Church Is Dead," Huffington Post, https://www.huffpost.com/entry/the-Black-church-is-dead_b_473815.
37. Mary Shawn Copeland, *Enfleshing Freedom: Body, Race, and Being* (Minneapolis: Fortress Press, 2010).
38. Subir K. Kole, "Globalizing Queer? AIDS, Homophobia and the Politics of Sexual Identity in India," *Global Health* 3, no. 8 (2007), https://doi.org/10.1186/1744-8603-3-8.
39. For a more detailed discussion, see Adriaan van Klinken and Ezra Chitando, eds., *Public Religion and the Politics of Homosexuality in Africa* (New York: Routledge, 2016), https://sfonline.barnard.edu/queer-religion/queer-studies-and-religion-in-contemporary-africa-decolonizing-post-secular-moves/.
40. Kole, "Globalizing Queer?"
41. Leah Buckle, *African Sexuality and the Legacy of Imported Homophobia*, Black History Month x Stonewall Articles, October 1, 2020, https://www.stonewall.org.uk/about-us/news/african-sexuality-and-legacy-imported-homophobia; Marc Epprecht, Stephen O. Murray, and Will Roscoe, *Boy-Wives and Female Husbands: Studies in African Homosexualities* (Albany: State University of New York Press, 2021); Amar Wahab, "'Homosexuality/Homophobia Is Un-African'?: Un-Mapping Transnational Discourses in the Context of Uganda's Anti-Homosexuality Bill/Act," *Journal of Homosexuality* 63, no. 5 (2016): 685–718; Marc Epprecht and Lindsay Clowes, *Unspoken Facts: A History of Homosexualities in Africa* (Harare: Gays and Lesbians of Zimbabwe, 2008); Marc Epprecht, "Tracing the Roots of Common Sense about Sexuality in Africa," in *A Companion to African History* (Chichester, UK: John Wiley & Sons, 2018), 13–33; Marc Epprecht, "Transnationalism in Sexuality Studies," in *Understanding Global Sexualities* (Routledge, 2012), 186–202; Theo G. M. Sandfort and Vasu Reddy, "African Same-Sex Sexualities and Gender-Diversity: An Introduction," *Culture, Health & Sexuality* 15, supp. 1 (2013): 1–6; Marc Epprecht, "'Bisexuality' and the Politics of Normal in African Ethnography," *Anthropologica (Ottawa)* 48, no. 2 (2006): 187–201; Leila J. Rupp, *Sapphistries: A Global History of Love between Women* (New York: New York University Press, 2009).
42. Ekine Sokari and Hakima Abbas, eds., *Queer African Reader* (Dakar: Pambazuka Press, 2013); Stella Nyanzi, "When the State Produces Hate: Rethinking the Global Queer Movement through Silence in The Gambia," in *The Global Trajectories of Queerness: Re-thinking Same-Sex Politics in the Global South*, ed. Ashley Tellis and Sruti Bala (Boston: Brill, 2015), 179–94; Zethu Matebeni, ed., *Reclaiming Afrikan: Queer Perspectives on Sexual and Gender Identities* (Cape Town: Modjaji, 2014); Karen Martin and Makhosazana Xaba, eds., *Queer Africa: New and Collected Fiction* (Braamfontein: MaThoko's Books, 2013); Kevin Mwachiro, *Invisible: Stories from Kenya's Queer Community* (Nairobi: Goethe Institute 2013).
43. Adriaan van Klinken, "Changing the Narrative of Sexuality in African Christianity: Bishop Christopher Senyonjo's LGBT Advocacy," *Theology & Sexuality* 26, no. 1 (2020): 1–6, doi: 10.1080/13558358.2020.177004.

Index

For the benefit of digital users, indexed terms that span two pages (e.g., 52–53) may, on occasion, appear on only one of those pages.

Tables are indicated by *t* following the page number

Abdur-Rahman, Aliyyah I., 12, 18, 21
Abyssinian Baptist Church, 5–6, 10–11, 33–36, 54–55, 82
Adler, Alfred, 18–19
African American Ministers Leadership Council, 160
African Methodist Episcopal (AME) Church
  Book of Discipline of, 157
  community building at, 203–4
  denominational queering potential for, 156–58
  ordination of openly gay persons prohibited by, 182
  prophetic calling of, 203–4
  same-sex marriage stance of, 182–83
Allen, Richard, 50–52, 202
Althaus-Reid, Marcella, 51, 237n.67
Ammerman, Nancy, 249n.47
Anderson, John (formerly enslaved person), 70–71
Anderson, Victor, 6, 32
Andrews, Dale
  discovering call to queer and, 55–61
  folk religion as starting point for, 56, 81
  liberation and, 56–57
  otherworldliness and, 56–57, 59
  practical theology of, 3, 23, 56, 81–82
  Refuge-vs-Prophetic Dichotomy and, 55–61, 72–73
  remodeling of ecclesiologies and, 54–55
Anglican Communion, 232n.82
Asante, Molefi, 11, 15–16
Atluri, Tara, 241n.24

Bailey, Marlon M., 212, 214–15
Baldwin, James, 53–54, 73–74, 111–12

Bellah, Robert, 150–51, 250n.48
Bennett, Jane, 59
Bethune, Mary McLeod, 93
Bible. *See* scriptural references; Scripture
biblical literalism, 37–38, 39–40, 97–98, 215–16
Black Christian heteronormativity
  Abyssinian Baptist Church and, 33–36
  Augustinian influence on, 27–28
  Black ecclesial queering and, 1–2, 3, 4–5, 58
  Black family as protected by, 30–31, 33–34, 37–38, 41, 159–60
  Blackness violated by, 24, 29
  Black Sexual Politics and, 29–30
  civility and, 9–10, 31–32, 33–36, 68
  Civil Rights Movement and, 73–75
  cultural explanations for, 23–24, 28–31, 60
  definition of, 9
  female senior pastors lacking as sign of, 185
  Harlem in early twentieth century and, 36–39
  history of, 11–15
  intersectionality and, 29–30
  manhood Christianity and, 58
  nonracist orientation of Black church and, 63–64
  overview of, 9–15
  power's relation to, 4–5, 23
  practical theology and, 21–22
  precursors to, 15–16
  prophetic calling and, 168–69
  Puritanism and, 32–33

Black Christian heteronormativity (*cont.*)
  racism as explanation of, 25, 28–32, 60
  Scripture and, 9–10, 38, 39–43
  sexual trauma and, 9–10, 13, 14, 15–21
  silence and secrecy of Black homosexual activity and, 17–21
  slavery and, 15–21, 30–31, 58, 64
  sources of, 9–10, 21–22, 23–24, 25, 28–32, 60
  theological explanations for, 9–10, 21–22, 28–31
  theory-laden nature of, 21–23
  white Christian heteronormativity's relation to, 9, 15–16, 25, 30–33, 58
  white rape culture of buck breaking and, 15–16
Black church. *See also* Abyssinian Baptist Church; African Methodist Episcopal (AME) Church; Boston's Black Churches; Don't ask, don't tell churches; Harlem's Black churches; Mount Nebo Missionary Baptist Church; Union United Methodist Church
  "Black culture's" influence on, 40–41
  Blackness of, 24, 47, 69–70
  Black women and, 61–63, 184–85
  Civil Rights Movement role of, 77–78
  death of, 79–80, 215–17
  exodus narrative and, 69–70
  expanding and reimagining image of, 61–65
  meaning of queering of, 78–80
  nonracist orientation of, 38, 60–65, 150–51
  pre-Reconstruction period of, 47, 61–65, 71–72, 82, 203–4, 213–14, 215–16
  priestly aspects of, 71–73, 97, 168–69
  prophetic function of, 55–62, 71–73, 97, 168–69, 203–4
  refuge function of, 55–65, 142, 213–14
  role as listener and learner, 67
  slavery and, 68–72
  transcendent image of, 62–63
  as transgressive, 47
Black civil religion, 150–51

Black ecclesial queering. *See also* congregational queering; denominational queering; Don't ask, don't tell churches; pastoral queering
  African contexts and, 217–18, 219–20
  aims of, 54–55
  ancient and Indigenous precedents of, 219
  apologetics avoided by, 171, 174
  application of, 78–80
  as-if world of Black ecclesiology and, 59–60
  being "out" as not always an option and, 213
  biblical literalism and, 97–98
  Black Christian heteronormativity and, 1–2, 3, 4–5, 58
  Blackness and, 6, 82–83, 110–15, 171
  Black practical theology and, 2–5, 50
  Black sexuality and, 54, 60–61, 67–68
  Black women as essential to, 171–72
  challenges of conducting research on, 143–49
  civility and, 54–55, 68
  Civil Rights Movement and, 73–78
  commonalities across types of, 167–69
  commonalities of interviewed congregants and, 169–70
  current state of, 199
  definition of, 2, 49, 54–55, 67–68
  development of, 2, 23
  elements of, 170–74, 225
  experience of Black Queer persons centered in, 112, 202
  future of, 209–17
  global application of, 218–20
  hermeneutic of spiritual intimacy and affirmation of, 216
  historical precedents of, 51–53
  as instance of congregational queering, 170–71
  LGBTQIAP+ persons not to be misused for, 66–68, 147, 187, 189
  listening and engaging required in, 108–9
  methodology for, 2–5, 23, 47, 50, 58, 171

INDEX   259

motivation for volume on, 1–6, 23
narratology and, 108, 175–77
overview of, 1–5, 44–47, 54–55, 78–80, 200–10, 215–20
performative allyship contrasted with, 155, 200
preexisting conditions of Churches and, 150–51, 167–69
as purging of white ecclesial sin of oppression, 60
queerness and queering defined in, 44–51
as reclaiming and owning of Black churches by Black Queer persons, 53, 67–68
refuge and, 61–65
role of Black Queer men in, 212–15
role of Black women in, 167, 171–72, 211–12
role of transgender persons in, 211–12
sacred eroticism and, 209, 211–15
Scripture and, 97–98, 102, 174
stages of, 97, 112, 120–22, 177–80, 223–25
structure of volume on, 5–8
subversive nature of, 68, 168–69, 171, 179–80
transparency and openness required in, 110, 112–13, 199
white Christian heteronormativity and, 60, 68–72, 107–8
Black family, 30–31, 33–34, 37–38, 41, 159–60
Black intellectuals, 35, 207–8, 232–33n.87
Black liberation theology, 3–4
Blackness
    Black Christian heteronormativity as violating, 24–25, 29
    Black Church and, 24–25, 47, 69–70
    Black ecclesial queering and, 6, 82–83, 110–15, 171
    Black theology and, 29
    Civil Rights Movement and, 73
    Jesus and, 25–26, 70, 78–79
    Puritanism and, 33, 171
    queering as destabilizing negative judgments of, 159
Black pastors. *See* pastoral queering

Black practical theology
    application of, 23–26, 81
    Augustinian perspective and, 27–28
    Black ecclesial queering and, 2–5, 50
    definition of, 2–3, 21–23, 56
    experience of Black people as starting point of, 4, 24
    marriage and, 27–28
    methodology of, 3–4, 23–24, 81
    overview of, 23
    prophetic calling and, 3–4
    Queer forms of, 23–26
    sexuality associated with sin and, 27–28
    as spiritual gardening, 4–5, 23
    theory's relation to, 21–22
    understanding and, 21–22
    white practical theology's relation to, 3–4, 22–23
Black Queer identity
    artistic representation of, 12–13
    Black Queer bodies, 2, 11
    Black Queer Christians and, 23–26
    as byproduct of European influence, 11, 15–16
    challenge of tracing history of, 11–12
    closetedness and, 23–24
    history of, 9–15
    internalized guilt and, 23–25
    mass incarceration and, 11, 15–16
    moral evaluation and, 24–25
    precolonial precedents of, 12–13
    scholarship on, 11, 12–13, 15–16
    self-acceptance and, 23–24
    sexual trauma and, 12–14, 15–16
    slavery and, 12–14, 15–16
    survival techniques of, 25
Black Queer sexuality, 11, 32, 205–7, 208–9
Black Queer theology, 174, 201–2
Black Queer Womanism (Lightsey), 185
Black Sexual Politics (BSP), 29–30, 54
Black theology. *See also* Black liberation theology; Black practical theology
    Black ecclesial queering's relation to, 201
    Blackness and, 29
    folk religion and, 56
    liberation and, 56–57

Black theology (*cont.*)
  primary challenge of, 56
  Puritanism as moral flaw of, 33
  Refuge-vs-Prophetic Dichotomy and, 55–61
  whiteness and, 3–4
Black Theology and Black Power (Cone), 57–58
Black women
  Black church and, 61–63, 184–85
  Black ecclesial queering and, 167, 171–72, 211–12
  as center, 202
  lesbianism and, 210–11
  refuge and, 61–62
  sacred eroticism and, 210–11
  sexuality of, 29–30
  slavery and, 13–14
  Womanism and, 58, 171–72, 180–81, 190, 201, 210–12
Bonauto, Mary, 87
Book of Discipline (AME), 157
Book of Discipline (CME), 183
Book of Discipline (UMC), 117, 119
Boroughs, Nannie Helen, 61–62
Boston's Black Churches. *See also* Myrtle Baptist Church; Union United Methodist Church
  communities and culture of, 83–87
  historic south end and, 90–93
  northern and southern forms of worship and, 84–85
  overview of, 81–83
  Panic of 1873 and, 91
  queer rights and, responses to, 87–106
  same-sex marriage and, 87–89
Brooks, Douglas, 112
Brown, Amos, Rev. Dr., 159–60
Brown, Theresa Fry, Rev. Dr., 157–58
Browning, Don, 3, 21–23, 50
Brown v. Board of Education (1954-55), 93, 151, 235n.31
buck breaking, 15–16, 82
Butler, Judith, 46
Butler, Lee, 60–61

Catholic Church queering, 65–68, 202
Chaney, Cassandra, 162
Charles Street AME Church, 84–85
Chauncey, George, 105–6
Cheng, Patrick, 49–50, 101–2, 183–84
Chevrisky, Gerry, 87–88
Christian heteronormativity. *See* Black Christian heteronormativity; white Christian heteronormativity
Christian Methodist Episcopal (CME), 182–83
Christian queering, 45–46, 49–54
churches. *See* Abyssinian Baptist Church; African Methodist Episcopal (AME) Church; Black church; Boston's Black Churches; Don't ask, don't tell churches; Harlem's Black churches; Mount Nebo Missionary Baptist Church; Myrtle Baptist Church; Union United Methodist Church
Church of God in Christ, 181–82, 202–3
Church Studies Homosexuality, The (Williams), 98, 99–106, 107–9
civility
  Black Christian heteronormativity and, 9–10, 31–32, 33–36, 68
  Black ecclesial queering and, 54–55, 68
  Black family and, 159–60
  definition of, 34
  dysfunctional civility, 34–35
  Harlem and, 36, 37, 41–42
  pastoral queering and, 35, 159–60
  problematic nature of quest for, 208–9
  recognition and, 34–35
  sacred eroticism and, 208–9
  subversive civility, 34–35
  transformative civility, 34–35
  types of, 34
civil religion, 150–51, 169
Civil Rights Movement
  Black Christian heteronormativity and, 73–75
  Black church's role in, 77–78
  Black ecclesial queering and, 73–78
  Blackness and, 73
  as form of legal queering, 73–78
  gay rights as new, 73
  sexuality and Black gay bodies and, 73–76

Collins, Patricia Hill, 26, 29–31, 39, 54, 82, 110–11
Committee of Fourteen, 36–37, 41
Cone, James
  Blackness and Jesus and, 78–79
  Black power and theology merged by, 57–58
  controversial nature of sexuality in Black church and, 1
  God of the oppressed and, 52, 202
  prophetic calling and, 57–58
  slave religion and, 70
  white Church and, 57–58
Confessions (Augustine), 28
congregational queering. *See also* Union United Methodist Church
  backlash to, 113–14
  Black ecclesial queering as, 170–71
  church history and mission and, 178
  commonalities with other forms of queering and, 167–69
  core teams and, 166–67, 170, 172, 173–74, 177–80
  definition of, 82–83
  divine impartation and, 177–78
  ecclesial scapegoating potential for, 107
  elements of, 170–74
  essential things for clergy and lay leaders to remember, 196
  examples of, 165–67
  fluid and ever-evolving methodology of, 170–71
  foreknowledge required for, 166–67
  global application of, 218
  as intentional journey of reeducation, 155, 170–73
  Jesus and, 179–80
  lamentation and repentance during, 181, 183–84
  LGBTQIAP+ persons in, 180–81, 187
  narratology and, 175
  pastoral queering as preceding, 166–67
  percentage of Black churches queered through, 170–71
  potential of a church for, 155–56
  prayer and discernment as central to, 165–66
  process of dismantling hegemonic heteronormativity in, 170–73
  pronouns and, 194–96
  Scripture and, 173–74
  stages of, 177–80, 181
  standing committees in, 178
  strengthening of, 180–84
  subversive nature of, 173, 179–81
  success or failure as dependent on context of, 155–56
  transgender persons and, 184–86
  youth ministries and, 191–94
Constantinian Christianity, 69–70
Cooper, Anna Julia, 42
Copeland, M. Shawn, 19–20, 24, 216–17
core teams, 166–67, 170, 172, 173–74, 177–80, 189–90, 192–93
Costen, Melva, 236n.43
Covenant Baptist Church (CBUCC), 167–68, 221–22
Crawley, Ashton, 23–24
Cruse, Harold, 35

Dash, Stephen, 236n.42
Day, Keri, 61–63
Deborah (Union member), 93–94, 95, 113–14
Delectable Negro, The (Woodard), 13–14
denominational queering
  AME as potential case for, 156–58
  commonalities with other forms of queering and, 167–69
  methodology of, 157–58
  overview of, 156–58
  power of, 157–58
  as theoretical, 156, 170–71
  toxic apologetics and, 157–58
Dill, Augustus Granville, 14
Don't ask, don't tell churches
  Black ecclesial queering most possible at, 151, 166–67
  Black Queer leadership of, 163
  as continuation of history of sexual silence, 162, 163–65
  critiques of, 163
  definition of, 162
  detachment of Queer parishioners as result of, 162–63

Don't ask, don't tell churches (*cont.*)
   identity politics and, 162
   liminal space of, 164–65
   overview of, 162–66
   as safety zones, 163
   spiritual hypocrisy of, 163
Douglas, Kelly Brown, 26, 30–31, 32, 54, 236n.51
Drew, Simon P. W., Rev., 85–86
Drexler-Dreis, J., 3–4
Du Bois, W. E. B.
   Black church and, 61–62
   Black Queer identity and, 15
   Dill's work with, 14–15
   double consciousness and, 230–31n.56
   frenzy and, 58–59, 206–7
   Protestant Puritanism and, 230–31n.56
   slave religion and, 236n.43
Durnell, Josephine (Mount Nebo member), 125–26

Earl, Riggins, Jr., 23–24
elements of Black ecclesial queering, 170–74, 225
Enfleshing Freedom (Copeland), 25
eroticism. *See* sacred eroticism
Estey, Alexander R., 91–93

Faith Temple, 202–3
Farley, Edward, 227n.5
Finneran, Tom, 87–88
First Iconium Baptist Church, 160
Fitzgerald, Grant-Michael, 202
Florence, Matthew, 112
Floyd, George, 184–85
Fluker, Walter, 34
Foster, Thomas, 18
Foucault, Michel, 54, 207–8
Franklin, Robert Williams, Rev.
   autonomy of, 132, 133–34
   Blackness and, 142
   challenges of conducting research and, 143–49
   congregational trust in, 139–41, 143–45
   conscious preaching and teaching and, 141–43
   divine call and mandate and, 138–39
   early pastorate experiences of, 136
   economic inequality efforts of, 151
   inclusivity as public performance for, 149, 152
   lack of pushback to queering by, 143
   legacy of, 126
   liberation for all as motivation for, 168–69
   methodology of, 133–38
   overview of, 125–28, 129–33
   pastoral authority of, 127, 139–41
   personality of, 126, 129–30
   as practitioner of gospel foolishness, 129–30
   prophetic preaching and teaching and, 125–26, 129, 141–43
   prophetic refuge traditions and, 142
   Queer shaming dismantled by, 136–37
   relational meetings model of, 133–38
   retirement of, 145–47, 152–53
   social capital of, 131–32
   three phases of pastoral queering of, 138–44
Fundamental Practical Theology, A (Browning), 21–22
Furedi, Frank, 175–76

Gadamer, Hans-Georg, 21–22
Gaines, Kevin, 232–33n.87
Ganzevoort, R. Ruard, 4–5, 23
Garrison, William Lloyd, 89–90
Gay and Lesbian Associate Defenders (GLAD), 87
Glaude, Eddie S., Jr., 215–17, 235–36n.38
God, Sex, and Politics (Moon), 40
Godfrey, Phoebe, 75–76
Goldfarb, Jeffrey, 34–35
Goodridge, Hillary, 87
Goodridge, Julie, 87
Goodridge v. The Massachusetts Department of Public Health (2004), 87
Goss, Robert, 25–26, 67–68
Great Awakening, 69, 83–84
Great Migration, 36, 86, 124–26, 151–52, 169
Griffin, Horace
   Augustinian perspective and, 28
   Black Christian heteronormativity and, 25, 28–29, 30–32, 38–39, 41, 43, 58–59

Blackness and, 159
lesbians and gays leaving Black church
    and, 202
reinvention of Christian Methodism
    and, 51–52
white Christian heteronormativity and,
    25, 28–29, 30–32, 41, 43

Harlem's Black churches. *See also*
    Abyssinian Baptist Church
Black Christian heteronormativity and,
    36–39
Black family and, 37–38
civility and, 36, 37, 41–42
drag balls in, 36–37, 41
early twentieth century history of,
    36–39
rent parties and, 36–37
Hartke, Austen, 176, 185–86
Hayden, Robert C., 84–85, 240–41n.5
hermeneutics, 26, 32–34, 58, 70–71,
    100–1, 113, 173–74, 201–2,
    204–5, 216
heteronormativity and homophobia. *See*
    Black Christian heteronormativity;
    white Christian heteronormativity
Higginbotham, Evelyn, 240–41n.5
history of Black congregations. *See* Black
    Christian heteronormativity; Black
    church
History of Sexuality (Foucault), 207–8
Hodges, Obergefell v. (2015), 1
homophobic valley of dry bones, 45, 58
hooks, bell, 207–8
hypermasculinity, 58

identity. *See* Black Queer identity
imago Dei, 1, 45, 189
Incidents of a Slave Girl (Jacobs), 17
inclusive language, 104, 106, 107, 145–46
intersectionality, 22, 26, 29–30, 46, 63–64,
    142, 166, 168–69, 184–85, 190, 204

Jacobs, Harriet, 17
Jesus Christ
    Blackness and, 25–26, 70, 78–79
    congregational queering and, 179–80
    prophetic symbolism of, 77
    Queer Christology and, 25–26
    queerness of works of, 25–26, 45–46, 77
    slave religion and, 70
    subversive nature of teachings of, 51–52,
        179–80
Johnson, Emerson, 40, 46
Johnson, Rosa Lee, 94–96
Jordan, Mark, 172–73
Justice, the Church and the Homosexual
    (McNeill), 65

Kilgore, Thomas, 75
King, Martin Luther, Jr.
    concerns about Black gay equality for
        civil rights, 75
    injustice anywhere is a threat to justice
        everywhere saying of, 142
    personalist politics of, 240n.97
    queerness of teachings by, 50–51,
        73–75, 159
    Rustin's work with, 73–75
    Vietnam War opposed by, 169
King, Preston, 147–48
Klinken, Adriaan van, 219–20
Kole, Subir K., 218
Kornegay, E. L., Jr.
    Black Christian heteronormativity and,
        32–33
    Black church's mission and, 52–53
    Puritanism and, 230–31n.56,
        236n.51
    queering and, 49, 50–51, 52–53
    queer theory's contribution to theology
        and, 53–54

Lambeth Commission, 232n.82
Langi people, 12–13, 219
language, inclusive, 104, 106, 107, 145–46.
    See also pronouns
legal queering, 73–78
Lewin, Ellen, 203–4
Lewis, G., Rev. Dr., Sr., 88
Lightsey, Pamela, 1, 185, 191, 210–11
Lincoln, Eric, 72–73, 77
Lockhart, Theodore L., Rev.
    biblical literalism and, 113
    Blackness and, 110–11
    discussion rules and, 107–10

Lockhart, Theodore L., Rev. (*cont.*)
  inclusive language and, 107
  personal interest not motivation for, 96–97
  prophetic power of dialogue and, 97
  Scripture and, 98, 113
  whiteness and, 110–11
Long, Eddie Lee, 58
Long, Michael, 75
Lorde, Audre, 73–74, 111–12, 206–11, 212
Luke (enslaved person), 17–20

Mamiya, Lawrence, 72–73, 77
manhood Christianity, 58
Martin, Trayvon, 184–85
Martin Luther King Jr., Homosexuality, and the Early Gay Rights Movement (Long), 75
Massachusetts Department of Public Health, Goodridge v. The (2004), 87
Matebeni, Zethu, 219–20
McClain, Ed, 112
McDonald III, Timothy, Rev., 160
McNeill, John J., Father
  obligations of Catholic homosexuals and, 66–68
  overview of, 65–68
  queering in the Catholic Church and, 65–68
  right to organize and, 66–67
  structured social injustices and, 65–66
McRoberts, Omar, 83–86
Meth-Union Manor, 93–94, 151
Metropolitan Community Church (MCC), 51–52
Mitulski, Jim, 159–60
Moon, Dawne, 40–41, 53
Moore, William Darin, 183
Mother Bethel, 51–52
Mount Nebo Missionary Baptist Church
  analysis of research on, 149–50
  challenges of conducting research at, 143–49
  demographics of, 123–25, 124t
  divine call and mandate at, 138–39
  history of, 123–26
  interpersonal challenges at, 142–43
  lack of pushback to queering at, 143
  overview of, 123–28
  pastoral authority and congregational trust at, 123, 139–41, 149–50
  political complexity of, 142–43
  preexisting conditions prior to queering at, 150–51
  prophetic and conscious preaching and teaching at, 141–43
  retirement of Rev. Franklin and, 145–47
  risk of backsliding from Queered state and, 145–47
  theology of inclusivity difficult to understand, 143–45
  three phases of pastoral queering at, 138–44
  toleration rather than acceptance at, 147–49
  Trenton Black communities and, 123–26
  Union compared to, 150–53
Mumford, Kevin, 202
Myrtle Baptist Church
  challenges during queering of, 189
  conditions for success at, 188–89
  as Don't ask, don't tell church initially, 189–90
  homophobia and racism and, connection between, 189
  lessons from queering of, 190
  overview of, 187–91
  Philip baptizing Ethiopian eunuch stained-glass at, 178
  Queer persons not required to lead queering process, 189
  questioning necessity of queering for, 189
  transgender persons and, 187–88, 189
  youth ministries and, 187–88

narratology, 175–77
National Association for the Advancement of Colored People (NAACP), 37, 84, 151
National Baptist Convention, 182–83
nonracist orientation of Black church, 60, 62–65, 150–51
Northup, Solomon, 16
Not Straight, Not White (Mumford), 202
Nyanzi, Stella, 219–20

INDEX 265

Obergefell v. Hodges (2015), 1
otherworldliness, 59, 206-7
Our Lives Matter (Lightsey), 191, 210-11
Outler, Albert C., 99
overviews
    Black Christian heteronormativity, 9-15
    Black ecclesial queering, 1-5, 44-47, 54-55, 78-80, 200-10, 215-20
    Black practical theology, 23
    denominational queering, 156-58
    Don't ask, don't tell churches, 162-65
    Mount Nebo Missionary Baptist Church, 123-28
    Myrtle Baptist Church, 187-91
    Union and, 81-83

Parents, Families, and Friends of Lesbians and Gays (PFLAG), 192
Paris, Peter
    affirmation of the Black person, 168-69
    authority of Black pastors and, 123
    Black Christian normativity and, 58
    Black church and, 24, 60
    civil religion and, 150
    enslaved queering and, 70-71
    manhood Christianity and, 58
    prophetic calling of Black ecclesiologies, 150
    Protestant Puritanism and, 236n.51
    refuge and, 60, 62
    slave religion and, 70
    white Christian tradition and, 60-61, 70
pastoral queering. *See also* Mount Nebo Missionary Baptist Church
    authority of pastors and, 123-27, 139-41, 149-50
    Black family and, 159-60
    civility and, 35, 159-60
    commonalities with other forms of queering and, 167-69
    congregational queering preceded by, 166-67
    congregational trust and, 139-41, 149-50, 158-59, 160-61
    conscious preaching and teaching and, 141-43
    context required for, 159-161
    divine call and mandate and, 138-39
    examples of, 158-61
    as most common form of queering, 158-59
    other pastorally queered congregations, 158-61
    phases of, 138-44
    prophetic preaching and teaching and, 141-43
Patrick, Le'Brian, 162
performative allyship, 155, 200
Perry, Terry, Rev., 88-89
Perry, Troy, 51-52, 202
Peterson, J. L., 162-63
phases of Black ecclesial queering, 138-44, 223-25
Pinn, Anthony, 60-61
Powell, Adam Clayton, Rev., Sr.
    anti-homosexuality campaign of, 33-36, 37, 41, 239n.86
    biblical literalism and, 37-38
    Black family and, 37-38
    civility and, 34-36, 37-38, 41, 42-43
    Civil Rights Movement and, 73-75
    Committee of Fourteen and, 41
    drag balls and, 37
    social uplift ideology and, 42
    white Christian heteronormativity and, 33-36
practical theology. *See* Black practical theology
Practical Theology for Black Churches (Andrews), 55
pre-Reconstruction Black church, 47, 61-65, 71-72, 82, 203-4, 213-14, 215-16
Proctor, Dennis Vernon, 183
Progressive National Baptist Convention, 183
pronouns, 108-9, 185-86, 187, 193-98
prophetic calling, 3-4, 54, 55-62, 67, 71-73, 77, 97, 141-43, 150, 168-69, 184-85, 203-4, 238n.75
Puritanism, 32-33, 171

Quare theory, 2, 46-47
Queer Christology, 25-26

Queer identity. *See* Black Queer identity
Queering of Black Theology, A (Kornegay), 50–51, 53–54
queerness and queering overview, 44–51. *See also* Black ecclesial queering; congregational queering; denominational queering; Don't ask, don't tell churches; pastoral queering
Queer theory, 3–4, 5, 7–8, 46–47, 53–54, 171–72, 174, 219–20

Raboteau, Albert, 68–69, 70
Radical Love (Cheng), 49, 183–84
Rasor, Stephen, 236n.42
Recreating Africa (Sweet), 20–21
Reddie, Anthony, 68–70
refuge function of Black church, 55–65, 142, 213–14
relational meetings model, 133–38
Report of the Committee to Study Homosexuality, 98, 111
Richey, Russell E., 100–1
Roberts, Rev., 135–36
Roeland, Johan, 4–5, 23
Romney, Mitt, 87–88
Rustin, Bayard, 73–75, 76–77, 239n.91

sacred eroticism
 Black ecclesial queering and, 209, 211–15
 Black lesbianism and, 210–11
 Black Queer men and, 212–15
 Black women and, 210–11
 civility and, 208–9
 definition of, 208, 209–10
 demonization of sex contrasted with, 208
 integrative completion and, 209–10
 other Black Queer spaces and, 212–15
 oversexualization of Queer bodies and, 208–9
 reclaiming of Black Queer sexuality and, 11, 32, 205–6, 208–9
 transgender persons and, 208–9, 211–12
St. George's Methodist Church, 51
Samuel, Kenneth L., 158–59, 167

scriptural references
 I Corinthians
  1:18, 129
  6:9-11, 9–10
  6:17-20, 112–13
  7:9, 27
 II Corinthians 3:6, 101–2
 Ecclesiastes 10:19, 130–31
 Genesis 19:1-38, 9–10
 Hebrews 13, 112–13
 Leviticus
  11:7, 39–40
  11:10, 39–40
  18:22, 9–10, 112–13
  19:19, 39–40
  20:13, 9–10, 112–13
 Matthew 25:40, 202
 Numbers 13, 179
 Romans 1, 112–13
  18-32, 28
  25-27, 9–10
 I Timothy 1:9-10, 9–10
Scripture
 biblical literalism and, 37–38, 39–40, 97–98, 215–16
 Black Christian heteronormativity and, 9–10, 38, 39–43
 Black ecclesial queering and, 97–98, 102, 174
 congregational queering and, 173–74
self-acceptance, 23–24, 181, 216
Sension, Nicholas, 16
sexuality, 11, 32, 205–7, 208–9. *See also* sacred eroticism
Sexuality and the Black Church (Douglas), 30–31
sexual trauma, 9–10, 13, 14, 15–21
Shore-Goss, Robert E., 67–68
Sims, Claude, 160
Slave Religion (Raboteau), 70
slavery
 Black Christian heteronormativity and, 15–21, 30–31, 58–59, 64
 Black church and, 68–72
 Black Queer identity and, 12–14, 15–16
 Black women and, 13–14
 buck breaking during, 15–16, 82
 enslaved queering, 70–71

mental resistance to, 19–20
slave religion and, 68–72, 115–16, 236n.43
as structured social injustice, 66
white rape culture during, 15–16
Smith, James L. (enslaved person), 229n.19
Snowden, Samuel, Rev., 89–90, 93
Spirit (Tinney), 202–3
stages of Black ecclesial queering, 97, 112, 120–22, 177–80, 223–25
Stoke, J. P., 162–63
Streets of Glory (McRoberts), 83–84
Swann, William Dorsey, 12–13

Their Own Received Them Not (Griffin), 54
Thelma (Union member), 95–96, 113–14
theology. *See* Black liberation theology; Black practical theology; Black theology
Third Baptist Church, 159–60
Till, Emmitt, 184–85
Tillich, Paul, 24, 52
Tinney, James, 202–3
Tonstad, Linn Marie, 172
Transforming (Hartke), 176, 185–86
transgender persons
affirmation of, 184–86
Black cisgender male bodies valued over, 184–85
Black ecclesial queering and, 181, 211–12
congregational queering and, 184–86
gender fluidity and, 186
Myrtle Baptist Church and, 187–88, 189
name use and, 185–86
as overlooked by Black church, 184–85
oversexualization of, 208–9
practical example for engaging with, 187–91
pronouns and, 108–9, 185–86, 187, 193–98
recommendations for engaging with, 185–86
sacred eroticism and, 208–9, 211–12
transgender theology and, 185–86
violence faced by, 184
youth ministries and, 189–90, 193

Turner, Samuel L., Rev. Dr., 88–89
Tutu, Desmond, 188

Underground Railroad, 58, 89–90
Unfinished Business (Day), 61–62
Union United Methodist Church
affirmation of the Black person and, 168–69
architecture of, 91–93
Bible study groups at, 94, 97, 98, 117
biblical literalism and, 97–98, 113
Blackness of queering of, 110–15
Civil Rights Movement and, 150
communal worship tradition at, 98, 115–17, 118, 126
context of, 90–93
demographics of, 92*t*, 93
discussion rules and, 106–7
experience with justice of, 100–6
group study overview for, 99–100
historic south end and, 90–93
inclusive language and, 106
Mount Nebo compared to, 150–53
NAACP and, 151
overview of, 81–83, 120–22
preexisting conditions at, 150–51
present queered ecclesiology of, 115–20
profile of, 89–90
prophetic calling and, 97, 150
pushback to queering of, 113–14
quadrilateral queering and, 93–99
queering rules of engagement and, 106–10
reason and, 100–6
reimagining of, 93–99
report on homosexuality and, 98–99
Scripture and, 100–6
sources of theological reflection for, 99–100
steps of queering at, 120–22
tradition and, 100–6
transparency and openness practiced by, 112–13, 114
Wesleyan Quadrilateral used in, 100–6
whiteness's relation to queering of, 110–15
UnionWorships, UnionDisciples, UnionServes, and UnionLeads (project), 115

United Methodist Church's Committee Report on Homosexuality (1997), 98–99
Uses of the Erotic (Lorde), 208, 211

Victorian sexual code, 14, 28–29, 31, 42
Victory for the World Church, 158–59
Vivian (Union member), 94, 95–96, 97, 113–14

Walker, Alice, 201, 217
Walker, David, 86, 89–90
Walton, Jonathan, 45, 58
Wesley, H. Wiley, Rev., 167–68
Wesley, John, 99
Wesleyan Quadrilateral, 99, 100–6
West, Cornel, 207, 235–36n.38, 238n.75
white Christian heteronormativity, 9, 15–16, 25, 30–32, 60, 68–72, 107–8
whiteness, 3–4, 47, 70–71, 85–86, 110–11, 201
white practical theology, 3–4, 22–23
white rape culture of buck breaking, 15–16
Wilde, Oscar, 14
Wiley, Christine, 167–68, 177–78
Wiley, Dennis, Rev. Dr., 167–68, 177–78

Williams, Albert Cecil, 161
Williams, Dorothy, 99, 103–4, 105–6
Williams, Gerald Jay, Rev. Dr., Jr., 115, 117, 118–19, 161, 217–18
Williams, Rowan, 232n.82
Williams, Wesley, Rev., 110–11
Womanism, 58, 171–72, 180–81, 190, 201, 210–12
women, Black. *See* Black women
Woodard, Vincent, 13–14, 229n.19
Woodyard, J. L., 162–63
Wooten, Todd, 15–16
Wright, Jeremiah, Rev., 159–60

youth ministries
    background checks and, 193
    congregational queering and, 191–94
    discussion and support groups for, 191–93
    need for open and affirming forms of, 191–94
    parent involvement in, 192
    recommendations for, 191–93
    reporting mandates and, 193–94
    transgender persons and, 189–90, 193

Zimmerman, George, 184–85

Printed in the USA/Agawam, MA
August 30, 2024

871898.042